50 More Hikes
In Ohio

First Edition

RALPH RAMEY

BACK COUNTRY

Backcountry Guides

Woodstock, Vermont

AN INVITATION TO THE READER

With time, access points may change, and trails, signs, and landmarks referred to in this book may be altered. If you find that such changes have occurred, please let the authors and publisher know so that corrections may be made in future editions. Other comments and suggestions are also welcome. Address all correspondence to:

Editor
50 Hikes™ Series
Backcountry Guides
P.O. Box 748
Woodstock, Vermont 05091

917
.7104
44
Rame

LIBRARY OF CONGRESS CATALOGING-IN-PUBLICATION DATA

Ramey, Ralph
  Fifty more hikes in Ohio / Ralph Ramey.—1st ed.
    p. cm.—(50 hikes series)
  Includes index
  ISBN 0-88150-447-5
  1. Hiking—Ohio—Guidebooks. 2. Backpacking—Ohio—Guidebooks. 3. Ohio—Guidebooks. I. Title. II. Fifty hikes series.
GV199.42.O3 R365 2002
917.7104'44—dc21   2001056649
                        CIP

Maps by Mapping Specialists Ltd., Madison, WI
Interior photographs by the author unless otherwise noted.
Cover photograph © Frank Moegling, The Image Finders

Copyright © 2002 by Ralph Ramey
First Edition

Published by Backcountry Guides, a division of The Countryman Press, P.O. Box 748 Woodstock, Vermont 05091

Distributed by W. W. Norton & Company, Inc. 500 Fifth Avenue New York, NY 10110

Printed in the United States of America

10 9 8 7 6 5 4 3 2 1

DEDICATION

To my Alaskan grandchildren, Kalen, Tristan, and Tanner Ramey, that they will come to love time spent on the trail as much as their father and grandfather.

50 Hikes at a Glance

HIKE	REGION
1. Barkcamp State Park	Unglaciated Allegheny Plateau
2. Blue Rock State Park	Unglaciated Allegheny Plateau
3. Forked Run State Park	Unglaciated Allegheny Plateau
4. Gifford State Forest	Unglaciated Allegheny Plateau
5. Lake Alma State Park	Unglaciated Allegheny Plateau
6. Rockbridge State Nature Preserve	Unglaciated Allegheny Plateau
7. Salt Fork State Park	Unglaciated Allegheny Plateau
8. Seneca Lake Park	Unglaciated Allegheny Plateau
9. Shawnee State Forest	Unglaciated Allegheny Plateau
10. Edge of Appalachia Preserve–The Wilderness	Interior Low Plateau
11. Mount Airy Forest	Interior Low Plateau
12. Blendon Wood Metro Park	Till Plains
13. Deer Creek State Park	Till Plains
14. Fowler Woods State Nature Preserve	Till Plains
15. Gahanna Woods Park and State Nature Preserve	Till Plains
16. Green Lawn Cemetery and Arboretum	Till Plains
17. Highbanks Metro Park	Till Plains
18. Indian Lake State Park	Till Plains
19. Kendrick Woods Metropark	Till Plains
20. Kiser Lake State Park & Wetlands State Nature Preserve	Till Plains
21. Lake La Su An State Wildlife Area	Till Plains
22. Lake Loramie State Park	Till Plains
23. Lawrence Woods State Nature Preserve	Till Plains
24. Morris Woods State Nature Preserve	Till Plains
25. Mount Gilead State Park	Till Plains

50 More Hikes in Ohio

DISTANCE (miles)	VIEWS	GOOD FOR KIDS	CAMPING	X-C SKIING	NOTES
2	★		★	★	Belmont Lake; campground; beach
3	★		★		19th-century Muskingum waterway lock and dam
2.6	★	★	★	★	Spring wildflowers; Forked Run Lake
3	★			★	Open for hunting in fall
2.25		★	★		Quiet; good for canoeing
2	★	★	★		Site of Ohio's largest natural arch
1.9	★	★	★		Ohio's largest state park; many recreational facilities
2	★	★	★		Nature center; swimming; campground; marina
6.5	★		★		Strenuous; for the seasoned hiker
2.5	★			★	Many rare plant and animal species
3.5					City park; Mount Airy Reservoir
1.9–4.2	★	★		★	Good site for birdwatching
3.5		★	★	★	Many prairie plants; a naturalist's paradise
1.3					Popular for viewing spring wildflowers
1					Well-developed trail system
3.75					Houses more than 200 species of birds
4.75	★	★		★	Shale bluffs; ancient earthworks
2		★	★	★	Paved hike/bike trails
3					Features wheelchair-accessible boardwalk
2.5					Trails traverse rich wetlands
5	★			★	Fishing and canoeing opportunities
4		★	★	★	Lake views
1.1					Old-growth forest; several species of rare plants
1.5					Bird sanctuary
2.52		★	★		Popular for family excursions

50 Hikes at a Glance

HIKE	REGION
26. Paint Creek State Park	Till Plains
27. Sandusky State Scenic River—Howard Collier Area	Till Plains
28. Sears Woods State Nature Preserve	Till Plains
29. Seymour Woods State Nature Preserve	Till Plains
30. Slate Run Metro Park	Till Plains
31. Stonelick State Park	Till Plains
32. Sycamore State Park	Till Plains
33. Augusta-Anne Olsen State Nature Preserve	Huron-Erie Lake Plains
34. French Creek Reservation	Huron-Erie Lake Plains
35. Magee Marsh State Wildlife Area	Huron-Erie Lake Plains
36. Secor Metropark	Huron-Erie Lake Plains
37. White Star Park	Huron-Erie Lake Plains
38. Charles F. Alley Park	Glaciated Allegheny Plateau
39. Charles Mill Park	Glaciated Allegheny Plateau
40. Cuyahoga Valley National Park—Virginia Kendall Unit	Glaciated Allegheny Plateau
41. Deep Lock Quarry Metro Park	Glaciated Allegheny Plateau
42. Girdled Road Reservation	Glaciated Allegheny Plateau
43. Great Seal State Park	Glaciated Allegheny Plateau
44. Johnson Woods State Nature Preserve	Glaciated Allegheny Plateau
45. Punderson State Park	Glaciated Allegheny Plateau
46. Pymatuning State Park	Glaciated Allegheny Plateau
47. Ramser Arboretum	Glaciated Allegheny Plateau
48. Shallenberger State Nature Preserve	Glaciated Allegheny Plateau
49. Silver Creek Metro Park	Glaciated Allegheny Plateau
50. Tinkers Creek State Nature Preserve	Glaciated Allegheny Plateau

DISTANCE (miles)	VIEWS	GOOD FOR KIDS	CAMPING	X-C SKIING	NOTES
4.75	★	★	★	★	Large lake; fishing opportunities
1.5	★			★	Home to resident and neotropical bird species
1.5				★	Spring wildflowers brilliant in May
1.5				★	Abandoned cottages provide glimpse of history
3.5		★		★	Lake; Slate Run Living Historical Park
2		★	★	★	Picnic area; beach; popular vacation destination
7				★	Tree-lined trails; creek
2.5	★			★	Trails through deep woods; views of the Vermilion River
2.5		★		★	Nature center; wildflowers
2					Great spot for birdwatching
2		★		★	Nature Discovery Center; rich with wildlife
2.25		★		★	Prairie-like vegetation
2.5	★			★	Nature education center
2			★		Views of rivers from bluffs
2.5	★	★			Ritchie Ledges; cave; sandstone cliff
1.5					Lock 28 on Ohio & Erie Canal
3.75–6.25					Spectacular spring wildflowers
4.75	★		★	★	Views of Ohio's Great Seal skyline
1.5					Magnificent old trees; boardwalk
3.25		★	★	★	Hike around Stump Lake
1		★	★	★	Woodland trail; variety of trees and wildlife
3.25	★			★	Ramser Arboretum
1.5	★				Knobs capped with Black Hand sandstone
2–3.25		★		★	Remains of family farmstead
2.5				★	Wetlands; blue heron and bald eagle sightings

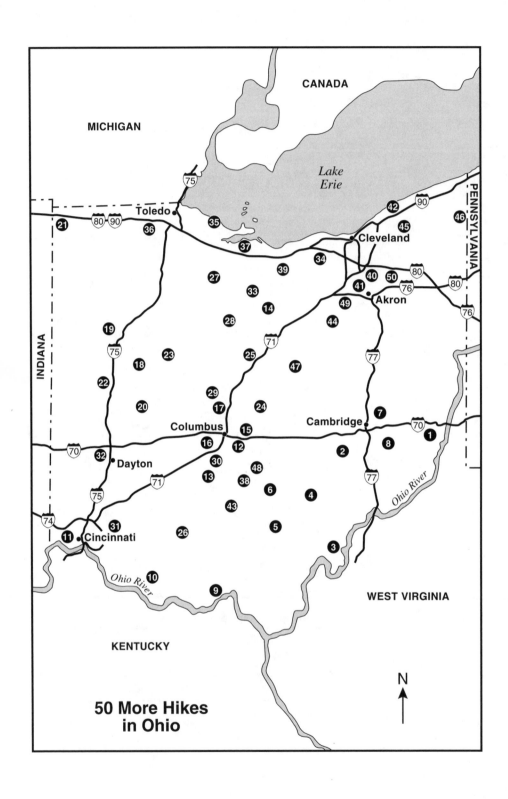

50 More Hikes
in Ohio

CONTENTS

Acknowledgments 13
Introduction 15

I. Unglaciated Allegheny Plateau
1. Barkcamp State Park 23
2. Blue Rock State Park 27
3. Forked Run State Park 30
4. Gifford State Forest... 34
5. Lake Alma State Park 38
6. Rockbridge State Nature Preserve 43
7. Salt Fork State Park... 47
8. Seneca Lake Park 51
9. Shawnee State Forest 55

II. Interior Low Plateau–Bluegrass Section
10. Edge of Appalachia Preserve–The Wilderness 60
11. Mount Airy Forest... 65

III. Till Plains
12. Blendon Woods Metro Park 72
13. Deer Creek State Park 78
14. Fowler Woods State Nature Preserve 84
15. Gahanna Woods Park and State Nature Preserve...... 88
16. Green Lawn Cemetery and Arboretum........................ 92
17. Highbanks Metro Park 101
18. Indian Lake State Park 105
19. Kendrick Woods Metropark 110
20. Kiser Lake State Park and
     Kiser Lake Wetlands State Nature Preserve 115
21. Lake La Su An State Wildlife Area 120
22. Lake Loramie State Park 125
23. Lawrence Woods State Nature Preserve 130
24. Morris Woods State Nature Preserve 134
25. Mount Gilead State Park... 138
26. Paint Creek State Park... 143
27. Sandusky State Scenic River–Howard Collier Area .. 148
28. Sears Woods State Nature Preserve........................ 153
29. Seymour Woods State Nature Preserve 157
30. Slate Run Metro Park 162
31. Stonelick State Park 167
32. Sycamore State Park 171

IV. Huron-Erie Lake Plains

33. Augusta-Anne Olsen State Nature Preserve 178
34. French Creek Reservation 181
35. Magee Marsh State Wildlife Area 185
36. Secor Metropark 189
37. White Star Park 193

V. Glaciated Allegheny Plateau

38. Charles F. Alley Park 200
39. Charles Mill Park 204
40. Cuyahoga Valley National Park—Virginia Kendall Unit .. 207
41. Deep Lock Quarry Metro Park 212
42. Girdled Road Reservation 217
43. Great Seal State Park 222
44. Johnson Woods State Nature Preserve.................... 228
45. Punderson State Park 233
46. Pymatuning State Park.. 238
47. Ramser Arboretum 244
48. Shallenberger State Nature Preserve........................ 249
49. Silver Creek Metro Park.. 254
50. Tinkers Creek State Nature Preserve 257

Index 263

Acknowledgments

No book that includes as many outdoor areas in all parts of the state as this one does could possibly be pulled together without the help of many of my fellow Ohioans.

I am especially indebted to C. Scott Brockman of the Ohio Geological Survey for his suggestion to base the arrangement of the book on physiographic regions of the state. Scott provided me with annotated maps and reports and patiently answered my questions when I was uncertain about map and data interpretation. Scott's colleagues in the Publication Center filled my requests for additional geological maps and reports to help increase my knowledge of the land beneath my feet in all corners of the state.

At the Division of Natural Areas and Preserves, my last place of employment before retirement, Jennifer Windus and Stephen Goodwin returned my calls and provided answers to my queries with their usual congeniality. I thank them for that. I also owe thanks to Chief Stu Lewis, for arranging for providing copies of the management plans for state nature preserves included in the book and for providing me with any permits required for my continuing exploration of Ohio's special places. Area managers replied promptly with material I sought when I called or e-mailed them about areas they oversee.

Emmett Conway, the "Olde Forester" from Chillicothe, has long been an inspiration. The knowledge he has passed in my direction regarding Indian trails, salt mining, iron furnaces, and so many other things is a treasury into which I dip often. I have enjoyed his companionship on the trail for more than 30 years and nowadays via occasional e-mail messages.

The personnel at each of the several park districts whose facilities are featured in *50 More Hikes in Ohio* have been generous with their time and resources in providing maps and historical information about their areas. Longtime friend and former student Stephen Madewell, now with the Lake County Park District, and his colleagues there have once again gone beyond the call of duty in providing me with maps and background material on their superb facilities. Burt Szabo, retired chief naturalist with the Akron Metropolitan Park District, graciously searched both his brain and the written records for answers to my queries about the history of the Deep Lock Quarry and Virginia Kendall areas.

Personnel in the central office and parks offices, from managers to clerks, all made suggestions and provided answers when I called or stopped to visit. They weren't always able to control the weather on days when I was hiking a trail or overnighting in some of the campgrounds, but it's difficult to pin the blame on them. I was treated with kindness and courtesy in every state park I visited.

The ultimate indebtedness is to my companion of 50 years, my wife Jean, who provided me with encouragement and support through the months of walking and writing. She has grown use to my late return from the field, knowing that I will stay on the trail as late as I can when the weather is right and I have a mission to accomplish. I love her dearly for the comfort and nourishment she has provided my body, mind, and soul during our lifetime together. She has certainly earned the title of "long-suffering spouse" because of my peregrinations, though!

My son John of Anchorage and my brother-in-law Stanley Harshfield of Atlanta have been my computer "gurus" throughout this book and several other projects, helping me with all sorts of cyberproblems at all sorts of hours of the day and night. Without them, I might still be scribbling away on a yellow pad.

When I had a technical problem or special need with camping or hiking gear, my younger son Jim of the Seattle area and his wife Karyn, both in the outdoor equipment business, bailed me out. Karyn can make a tent zipper work when I have long ago given up on ever hoping to get it operating again. I thank them for that, and for many words and deeds that helped make the book project easier.

Lastly, I carry with me on every hike the memory of my late daughter, Carolyn, who, along with her brothers and father, loved the out-of-doors but because of the handicaps with which she was born was unable to fulfill all her ambitions and goals. She spent most of her life with braces on her legs and much of it in a wheelchair. As age and infirmities take their toll on my walking ability, I more deeply appreciate the difficulties she had in moving about. Even with her problems, she set an example of determination that I have difficulty keeping up with. Cut short by cancer at 42, her life was an exemplary one of will and determination. I miss her very much.

Introduction

Exploring the woods and fields of my native state has been my passion for more than 60 years. I have been walking the trails of the Buckeye State since before the American fleet was attacked at Pearl Harbor. In the fall of 1941, as a second-class scout working hard to advance, I was faced with Requirement 5 that said, "Make a round trip alone (or with another Scout) to a point at least seven miles away (fourteen miles in all) going on foot, or rowing a boat, and write a satisfactory account of the trip and the things observed." By 1948 the infamous "14-mile hike" had been reduced to 5 in the scout manual, but that did not help me. I spent 5 cents on streetcar fare and rode to the corner of the OSU campus where, at the Varsity Supply Store for 25 cents, I purchased the USGS 15' East Columbus quadrangle. With a map in hand and a trusted combination hand lens and compass in my pocket (I still have both), I made my way from my home in Bexley by back road and field and US 40, the old National Road, to Reynoldsburg and back. Two weeks after World War II began, I received my first-class rank in a solemn ceremony at St. Alban's Episcopal Church where Troop 3 met.

Life was never the same after that fall. The war turned the world upside down. Our scoutmaster, Mac Lee Henney, went off to serve in the Military Air Transport Command. In his place came a wonderful new scoutmaster, Bill Cohen, a transplanted engineer from Buffalo. He had moved to Columbus to help build war birds, Hell-divers and Seagulls, at the Curtis-Wright plant that had been rushed to completion alongside the long east–west runway at Port Columbus. Rationing was upon us. Outings squeezed parents' gasoline allotments—and the cars of the day never did boast great fuel efficiency. Civil defense messenger service became a part of a scout's duty to country, so when a blackout drill occurred, we reported to a designated station to carry messages in the dark on our old one-speed bicycles. And former members of the troop and older boys from the neighborhood went off to war. Most came back but some did not, paying the price of freedom for us all with their lives.

My first outing with the new scoutmaster was to "Henney's Hole," a cabin in Hocking County near a community on the Laurelville quadrangle called Apple that was owned by Mr. Henney. We carpooled using carefully hoarded rationed gasoline. I and five other scouts who were about to become a new patrol were sent cross-country, 15' USGS map in hand, to Tar Hollow State Forest, a round-trip distance of about 6 miles. When we returned, with fresh road tar on our shoes and a "tarred-out" feeling in our bodies, we decided to become the Tar Patrol. We used that name for several years, I daresay probably a patrol name unique to our troop. I loved both treks. I have been hiking Ohio, still with a topographic map in hand (albeit one of the newer 7½' quads), ever since.

In 1935 I began spending part of my summer weeks at the Columbus YMCA's

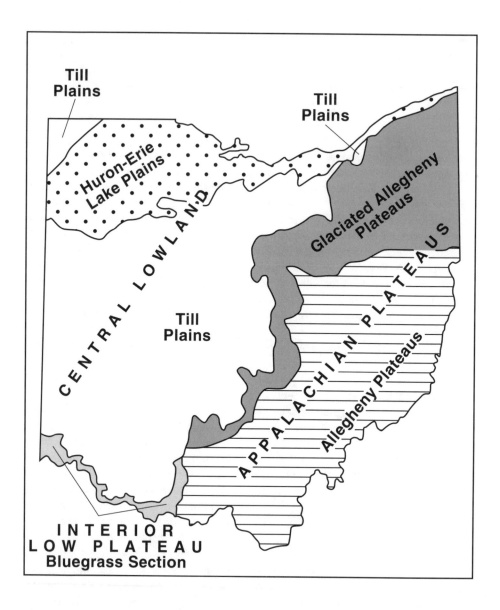

Till Plains

Till Plains

Huron-Erie Lake Plains

Glaciated Allegheny Plateaus

CENTRAL LOWLAND

Till Plains

APPALACHIAN PLATEAUS

Allegheny Plateaus

INTERIOR LOW PLATEAU
Bluegrass Section

Camp Alfred L. Willson at Bellefontaine, traveling there that year on the Cincinnati & Lake Erie traction. It wasn't long until I was spending the entire summer there, loving the outdoor life. In 1946 I switched to Big Brothers Camps in Hocking County as a camp counselor and nature resource person. I had no car so on my days off, I

hiked and took pictures. On a day off in 1948, I walked cross-country, with map in hand, to Camp Wyandott where my sister was working, had lunch with her, and returned to Big Brothers before sundown—a distance of 20 miles as the crow flies.

Upon graduation from college, I put $12 in my jeans and a pack on my back

16

and, with camera in hand, hitchhiked to Gatlinburg, Tennessee, to hike in the Great Smoky Mountain National Park. The hard reality of global politics came to me with full force when, after a day hike to Gregory's Bald, I returned to Gatlinburg to find that the North Koreans had invaded South Korea—and we would soon be involved. I was classified 1A by the Selective Service Administration. By year's end I was off to the army. Through a series of circumstances, I ended up as an instructor in a chemical defense school in Texas. The commissioned officers soon learned that I liked to hike, so every three weeks they happily let me lead students on a 3-mile trek under the hot Texas sun during which gas masks were occasionally called for by someone lugging a tear gas grenade upwind of our route of travel.

Return to civilian life found me on the road in southeastern Ohio as a pharmaceutical salesman, staying for weeks at a time in country hotels and motels. After doctors' offices shut down for the day, I looked for old iron furnaces, coal tipples, rare plants, covered bridges, gristmills, and the like, hiking along abandoned township roads.

The early 1960s found me with an all-Columbus "territory," and it was payback time: time to help the boys of my church and neighborhood find the joy of the "outing" that to my way of thinking was the heart of scouting. Troop 417 at Upper Arlington Lutheran Church was born, and not a month went by for more than a decade that I was not camping or hiking at least one weekend a month. The memories of those trips are among my most cherished.

The 1970 holidays found me back on the Appalachian Trail (AT) in the Smoky Mountains hiking, this time with my 16- and 11-year-old sons. It was their first

taste of long-distance backpacking and since then they have spent many miles on the trail in all parts of the world, especially Alaska. In the meantime, I have returned to the Smoky Mountains alone half a dozen times over the years.

Seventeen years as director of Antioch College's Glen Helen Nature Preserve at Yellow Springs provided many experiences exploring the prairies, forests, and wetlands of Ohio and the Midwest and my first opportunities to travel to such faraway places as Kenya, Botswana, Costa Rica, and the Galapagos Islands.

After a year as director of the Miami County Park District, I returned to Columbus as chief of the Division of Natural Areas and Preserves, heading the state's 20-year-old nature preserve system. Years before, I had helped pass the law that created the system, and I had served on the Natural Areas Council for 11 years, so it was like coming home. And what an opportunity to see more of Ohio on foot or in a canoe. I took every advantage to do so until retirement in 1994.

In 1989, by asking me to write *50 Hikes in Ohio,* Carl Taylor and The Countryman Press gave me the unexpected opportunity to step back to the first scout requirements of 1941 by "taking a hike alone and writing an account of the trip and what I observed." I walked every mile that I wrote about in that book and in *Walks and Rambles in Southwestern Ohio,* which followed in 1994. Since then, I have just kept on hiking.

Though I dutifully tell people that for safety's sake, they should hike with one or more other people, I confess to preferring to hike alone. For 10 years I have been artfully putting off all the people who have said, "If you are ever heading out on a hike and need a companion, call me." Until recently I felt a little guilty about it. Then I read a book by David Petersen titled *Nature Writing: A Down-to-Earth Guide to Nature Writing.* In the preface, before he even gets into the meat of the writing skill drill, the author says, "You must spend every minute you can manage out there, in the most natural (wildest) possible environs within ready reach and occasionally beyond. And *often as not, alone* [emphasis mine]. And while you're out there, you must strive to be an uncommonly keen observer." Finally, right there in type is the excuse I have been seeking for saying, "Honey, I'm going hiking today"—and maybe even for that recent two-week trip without my wife to Siberia and Lake Baikal.

At seventy-three, with braces on both legs and too many joints that ache, I still hit the trail alone on a regular basis. As I advise others to do, I carry a fanny pack with a couple of half-liter water bottles attached, a compass (mine is a Brunton, but there are many good brands), an extra-loud whistle, two small flares, a small first-aid kit with extra prescription medicine including pain medication, a poncho, head net, sunscreen, insect repellent, watertight container of strike-anywhere matches (a good Ohio product), an agency map of the area I will be traveling plus a computer-printed USGS map of the area, a Mylar "space blanket," a small trowel, toilet paper, a small weather alert radio when bad weather is threatening, a hand lens, a small flashlight, a tick removal kit, a magnifier/splinter removal tweezers, clean undershorts, dry socks, and at least one trash bag to haul out my own trash and litter left by others. I carry two pairs of prescription glasses, plain and UV blocking, packing whichever pair I am not wearing in a crushproof container. There is usually a bag or two of commercially prepared "trail mix"—nuts and raisins—handy. I often carry a pair of lightweight binoculars and am never without a camera. Nowadays it's a Rollei Prego 140 point-and-shoot camera for black-and-white film and an older Rollei 35SE for color slides. Sometimes I still carry a small spiral-bound notebook and a pencil in my shirt pocket, but most often that is replaced by a microcassette tape recorder on which I record my observations.

I carry a Leki hiking staff and a Swiss army–type knife, and I wear a broad-brimmed hat (mine is an Ultimate) that has been certified to block ultraviolet rays. The shoes on my feet are the only ones I own—very expensive custom-made orthopedic boots that have built-in braces—but Ohio-built leather, Gore-Tex-lined Rocky Boots served me well for hundreds of miles. Depending upon the weather, I may carry a lightweight nylon anorak. In summer my cotton/poly cargo pants will have been treated ahead of time with Permanone spray to repel ticks.

When I have reason to believe that there is a telephone cell within reach, I carry a cell phone. I call home just before heading out on a trail, telling my wife where I am parked, what my hiking plans are, when I expect to be off the trail (allowing a good 33 percent more time than I hope for), and who to call at what number if she doesn't hear from me. As soon as I can after coming off the trail, I check in at home again. In some parts of the state, this means driving to the top of the nearest high hill first. My basic philosophy is one of being well prepared and exercising the greatest caution but believing that if I have an accident on the trail and end up food for the vultures, it's better than a nursing home. Rest in peace.

The hiking opportunities in Ohio are splendid and plentiful. They range from large state wildlife areas with no designated trails where you can bushwhack your way cross-country to small private nature centers where designated trails offer great opportunities to enjoy the splendors of the natural world close up. State forests, wildlife areas, parks, and nature preserves have hundreds of miles of good foot trails. The metro park systems of the state provide some of the best hiking opportunities around, and private nature centers offer good trails that often lead past special environments. In southeastern Ohio, the Wayne National Forest has developed fine foot trail systems within its units; in the Cleveland area, the Cuyahoga National Park continues to increase the number of the hiking trails available. The various national corridor projects, especially the one in Cuyahoga Valley, are constantly working on expanding their multiuse trails, and various state and local agencies throughout the state have seized upon opportunities to convert abandoned railroad rights-of-way into hiking/biking trails. The absence of the latter from this volume is not a commentary on their quality; it is because most feature nonmotorized vehicles mixed with foot traffic, and they are not easily adapted to loop routes.

Ohio has a wide network of locally controlled convention and visitors bureaus with toll-free numbers that can and will provide copious amounts of printed material and assist in other ways if you are going to an unfamiliar area. And a toll-free call to the Ohio Travel and Tourism office (1-800-BUCKEYE) will almost always get you all the information you need.

The world wide web has made planning a trek much easier than in the past: Most of the state and local natural resource agencies have web sites where you can obtain information and from which you can often download park and preserve maps. I have listed those I know about; I am certain there are others coming online all the time.

What kind of weather I choose to go abroad in depends upon my mission. If I am looking for picture-postcard scenic shots, I try for a day with nice drifting cumulus clouds, then try to take pictures when the sun is behind one of the clouds, thus softening the shadow. The most spectacular landscapes are often taken an hour after sunrise and an hour before sunset. If I am out for flower photos, a sunny bright day is what I look for. Butterflies generally don't fly when it's cloudy and when it gets below about 55 degrees, so choose your day carefully if it's lepidoptera you're looking for. And every hiker knows that there are times when there is a special kind of magic in the air. Walking in a lightly falling warm rain is always one of these times.

The arrangement of hikes in this volume is different from my original *50 Hikes in Ohio:* Rather than being arranged in five geographic regions of the state, the hikes are arranged in five ecological regions defined by the common characteristics of the land. These regions are the till plain of western Ohio, the Huron-Erie Lake Plains of northwestern Ohio and the Lake Erie shoreline to the east, the Glaciated Allegheny Plateau and the Unglaciated Allegheny Plateau regions of Ohio Appalachian Plateau, and the Outer Bluegrass Region of Adams County and the southern edge of southwestern Ohio. Each of these areas has unique characteristics, and it seemed logical to group them in this manner as a way of helping hikers better undertand the land they are exploring.

I hope that you enjoy these hikes as much as I did when I walked them. Some were completely new to me; others, like the trail to Rockbridge State Nature Preserve, are old haunts that I have returned to many times through the years. In any case, plan to be on the trail often. And if you see a gray-haired guy who looks like the picture on the back of this book, be sure to give him a hearty "Hi Ralph" and stop for a chat.

——	main trail
• • •	side trail
℗	parking area
⊼	shelter

I

Unglaciated Allegheny Plateau

1

Barkcamp State Park

Total distance: 2 miles (3.2 km)

Hiking time: 1½ hours

Maximum elevation: 1,210 feet

Vertical rise: 110 feet

*Map: USGS 7½' Series Bethesda;
ODNR Barkcamp State Park map*

At the heart of Barkcamp State Park lies Belmont Lake, a 117-acre impoundment completed in 1963 to provide fishing opportunities in this part of the state. Located in the heart of Ohio's number one coal-producing county, Belmont, Barkcamp is about a mile south of busy Interstate 70 and US Route 40, the historic National Road, off State Route 149. Ohio's youngest rock—the sandstones, shales, and coal measures of the Dunkard series of the Permian age—is found in the higher elevations here, with similar strata of the Monongahela of Pennsylvanian age found in the valleys. This is the highly dissected country of the Little Switzerland Plateau region of Ohio, where the streams east of the Flushing Escarpment flow east to the Ohio River.

Belmont County is one of Ohio's oldest. It was formed in 1801, two years before statehood, as the ninth county of the Northwest Territory. Before that, in the days leading up to the Treaty of Greeneville, the area had been the scene of several skirmishes with Native Americans. During the explorative years of the 18th century, timber and coal production were king in the backcountry area near the park. While today's surface mining leaves healing scars on the land, the deep mining of early years left permanent scars on the miners who spent 14 to 16 hours a day deep within the earth. Several enterprising entrepreneurs built rail lines into the interior to haul away the bounty. A narrow-gauge line ran to the south of where Barkcamp is today; this was the Bellaire, Zanesville & Cincinnati, also

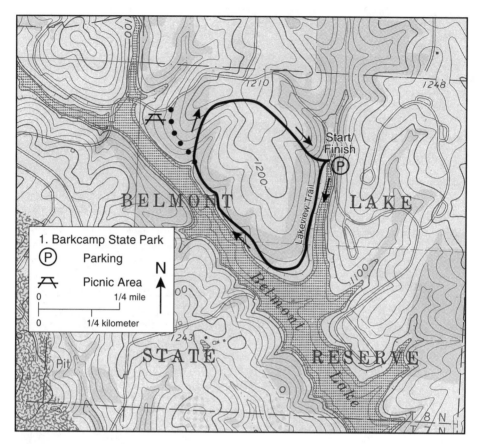

known as the Poor Man's Railroad. Asked what the "B, Z & C" stood for, locals would answer, "Badly zigzagged and crooked." When traveling the byroads of the area by modern auto today, it is easy to understand the derivation of that nickname.

Shortly after the completion of Belmont Lake, the 1,232-acre area then known as the Belmont Lake State Reserve was assigned to the Division of Parks and Recreation for the establishment of a state park. The name for the park is derived from the name of the creek impounded to create the lake. The creek, in turn, got its name because of the early existence in the area of a logging camp where bark was stripped from oak and chestnut logs; then its tannin was

extracted to be used in the conversion of animal hides to leather. Today the park offers a full range of facilities that include a campground, beach, bridle trail, and 4 miles of hiking trails. It was October when I explored Barkcamp's trails, and the maples and oaks were in their full glory; a perfect day for a hike. There were others on the trail enjoying the crisp fall weather that afternoon, even thoughit it was in the middle of the week.

How to Get There

To travel to Barkcamp State Park, drive east from central Ohio on I-70 to exit 208. Go south about a mile on SR 149, then turn left (east) onto Township Road 92. The park

This short bridge is the access to the trails at Barkcamp State Park.

entrance is on the left less than a mile from the intersection.

The Trail

The 2-mile-long Lakeview Trail originates from a small parking lot on the east side of the loop road a little over a mile from the park entrance. Upon entering the park, follow the main road down the hill and across the upper arms of the lake, past a rest room and parking area, and up and over a hill to the upper end of the valley of another arm of the lake. The small parking lot is on the left side of the road, nearly opposite a trailhead sign and a bridge that provides access to the trail.

A set of steps leads to a split in the trail offering the choice of clockwise or counterclockwise travel. I usually make my choice based on the time of day and which direction the sun will be falling in relation to pictures that I may want to take. Traveling clockwise, the trail begins at a level of about 20 feet above the not-yet-visible lake but soon drops slowly as the lake comes into view. Ignore a trail to the right that is the beginning of a 0.5-mile loop called the Woodchuck Trail. Continuing straight ahead, the Lakeview Trail eventually goes nearly to the water's edge at several points, providing opportunities for taking photographs or scanning the lake with binoculars for the presence of waterfowl. The trail is in young mixed-oak forest or planted evergreen grove for almost its entire length.

After the trail leaves the lake and begins climbing, you will reach an unsigned fork. Directly ahead is a service access trail leading to the rest room area along the road at the upper end of the lake. Do not take this trail. To return to the trailhead on the Lakeview Trail, turn right and climb gently through a small pine planting. In some places you can see the park road through

---

Barkcamp State Park

the trees. The trail passes through a thicket area, soon reaching another spot where a side trail enters from the right. This is the other end of the Woodchuck Trail. Bear left downhill, and the steps and bridge to the road soon come into view.

In past years this area has been open to hunting. A sign indicating that it is a hunting area should be posted at the trailhead if that is the case. The park office can also provide information on hunting season and areas.

There are two other short hiking trails in the park. Both originate within the camping area on the southwest side of the lake The Hawthorn Trail originating near the equestrian camp is 0.6 mile in length; the Hawk Trail, which starts from the road near the antique barn in the campground, is less than 0.25 mile long.

An especially good hike can be found in nearby Dysart Woods Preserve, located off SR 147 south of the community of Belmont. Many of the trees are over 300 years old, more than 4 feet in diameter, and more than 140 feet tall. A description of the trail can be found in *50 Hikes in Ohio.*

2

Blue Rock State Park

Total distance: 3 miles (4.8 km)

Hiking time: 2 hours

Maximum elevation: 940 feet

Vertical rise: 105 feet

*Map: USGS 7½' Series Ruraldale; ODNR
Blue Rock State Park map*

Blue Rock State Park is a 335-acre recreation area located within a larger state forest, in this case the 4,579-acre Blue Rock State Forest. The rugged hill country just east of the Muskingum River was home to a succession of tribes of Native Americans before being settled by whites of European descent at the beginning of the 19th century. In fact, a Shawnee village known as Old Town once stood in the vicinity of the nearby present-day village of Duncan Falls on the banks of the Muskingum River.

Commercial exploitation of the natural resources of the area began shortly after settlement. The Muskingum River offered waterpower for mills and a transportation route for the coal, gravel, and timber of the area; by the middle of the 19th century the region hummed with activity. In 1856 the area was shaken by one of the most remarkable mine disasters in history. At 11 AM on Friday, April 26, the ceiling of a mine collapsed, leaving four people unaccounted for inside the mine. A dangerous round-the-clock rescue effort was mounted, combining speed and caution. As work went on, an immense crowd of folks from the surrounding countryside and village gathered outside the mine entrance offering help, encouragement, and prayers. At 1 PM on Friday, May 9, after having been entombed in the mine for 14 days, the men were reached and brought to safety—alive. Any mining in the area today is surface mining; the hills that were at one time stripped of their trees for timber for mine props, railroad ties, and tanbark are once again forested. The Blue Rock name comes

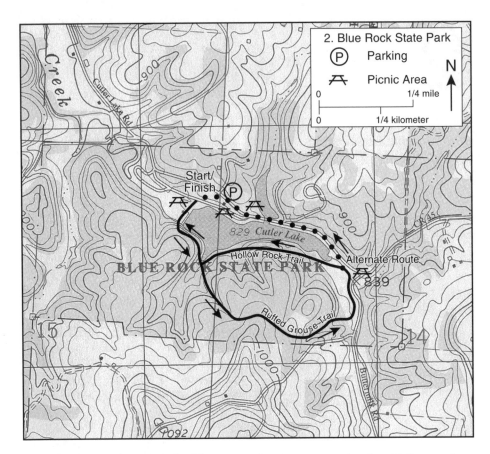

from the Pennsylvanian-age shale of the area, which has a blue hue, particularly when wet.

In the dark days of the Great Depression, the federal Resettlement Administration began purchasing the land that now comprises Blue Rock State Park and State Forest. In 1936 ownership was transferred to the state of Ohio, with the federal government retaining three-fourths interest in the oil and gas rights. Cutler Lake was built by the Works Progress Administration in 1938, and when the Department of Natural Resources was established in 1949, the area around the lake was transferred to the new Division of Parks and Recreation. Meanwhile, the Division of Forestry has reforested the worn-out marginal farms of the pre-Depression days and applied

forest management and protection practices that have transformed the area to a beautiful and productive region of mostly oak–hickory forest.

Blue Rock is a compact park tucked in the valley and slopes alongside Salt Creek where it was dammed to make Cutler Lake. A good place to begin hiking is the parking lot across the road from the bathhouse. After locking your vehicle, with all possessions stowed safely out of sight, cross the road and head downhill to the bridge across the lake's emergency spillway. The trailhead for the Hollow Rock Nature Trail is located there. Canada geese use the picnic area here for grazing when few people are around, so watch your step.

Unglaciated Allegheny Plateau

How to Get There

To reach the Blue Rock area by car, travel 56 miles east from Columbus on I-70 to Zanesville. There take SR 60 for 10 miles south to the village of Duncan Falls. Turn left onto County Road 45 (Cutler Lake Road), which winds its way to the center of the park.

The Trail

Begin your hike by crossing the bridge; then use the dam to reach the far side of the lake. One of the park's two camping areas is located to the right and downstream of the dam. Once off the dam, follow the trail to the left around the shore of the lake. It was a late-October day when I scouted the trail, and the reflections of the fall-colored hardwoods on the glassy still lake were spectacular. Ignore the trail to the right; it connects with the camping area. After paralleling the shore of a small embayment, the trail makes a junction with two other trails. The 0.2-mile Deer Trail to the right leads uphill to a campground. The Hollow Rock Trail turns left to continue around the lake on a fairly level course. Directly ahead, the 0.5-mile Ruffed Grouse Trail begins climbing up a wooded draw to take you through the woods past the walk-in camping area and downhill to a grassy area along Buttermilk Road. Here a turn to the right leads to the other end of the Hollow Rock Trail and the upper end of Cutler Lake.

I chose the Ruffed Grouse Trail, which provided me with the option of returning to my vehicle on the Hollow Rock Trail or, at quiet off-season times or weekdays, walking the shoreline and Cutler Lake Road on the opposite side of the lake. I've done both; the time and distance are about the same.

An additional mile of hiking is offered on the Turtle and Beechnut Trails. The trailhead for the Turtle Trail is roughly opposite the boat-launch area on the north side of Cutler Lake. The trail follows the edge of another lake embayment before climbing to a

In August the tiger swallowtail butterflies of the season's second brood find this Joe-pye weed a good source of food in the form of sweet nectar.

picnic area where there is a small shelter house. Beyond there, the Beechnut Trail makes a 0.3-mile loop back to the Turtle Trail. There a short trail connects with a picnic area parking lot.

In addition to hiking, Blue Rock State Park offers camping, fishing, swimming, and boating (canoes and small boats with nothing bigger than electric trolling motors). I put in my canoe and explored the shoreline for a couple of hours. Depending upon the state of the Division of Parks and Recreation's budget, there may be a naturalist posted at the park during the summer offering a variety of interpretive programs.

Blue Rock State Forest has no hiking trails but it does have many miles of bridle trails for folks who want to pull in their own horses. These are accessed from parking lots near the forest headquarters about 2 miles north of the park and from several other lots within the forest. A map is available from the Division of Forestry.

While in the area, you may want to visit the 19th-century Muskingum waterway lock and dam system. The Wilds, well known for its African animal breeding programs and, to birders, for its wintertime populations of birds of prey, is located about 7 miles northeast of the park near the town of Cumberland. It's an attraction you won't want to miss while you're in the area.

3

Forked Run State Park

Total distance: 2.6 miles (4.2 km)

Hiking time: 2 hours

Maximum elevation: 850 feet

Vertical rise: 230 feet

Maps: USGS 7½' Series Portland; ODNR Forked Run State Park map; Shade River State Forest map

On the early-November day when I walked the trails at Forked Run State Park, I and a lone fisherman on the lake were the only people in the park. Meigs County, where the park and Shade River State Forest are located, is a long way from any population centers. At the last count, only about 25,000 folks resided in the county. Forked Run State Park, named for the stream that in 1952 was dammed to make 102-acre Forked Run Lake, is certainly among Ohio's least known and most underutilized recreation areas.

The state forest lands are rugged and several blocks are separated from one another, so you won't find a trail system like those in other state forests. White and the non-native red and loblolly pines were planted in blocks on abandoned farmland in the 1950s; native pitch, shortleaf, and Virginia pine are found in the area. Most of the forest, however, consists of the stands of mixed oak so common in this part of Ohio. The spring wildflowers are typical of the acidic soils derived from the Permian-age sandstones and shales of the area. The greenbrier on the narrow ridges of this deeply dissected part of unglaciated Ohio will chew away at your shins. The sandstone you'll see exposed on hillsides within the park and forest is among Ohio's youngest bedrock.

How to Get There

Meigs County, named for Return Jonathan Meigs, Ohio's governor from 1810 to 1814, is located about 85 miles southeast of

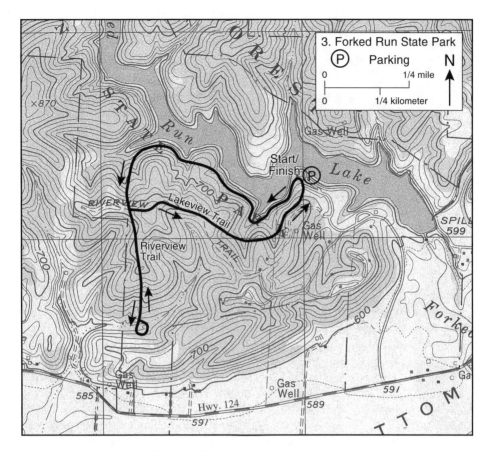

Columbus in the rolling Allegheny Plateau. To reach Forked Run, travel US 33 to Athens and US 50 to SR 7. Turn south through Tuppers Plains to SR 681. Turn right and go to Reedsville, then right onto SR 124 to the park entrance.

The Trail

Four miles of trails in the park include hiking trails and a self-guided nature trail. The 2.6-mile Lakeview Trail begins at the beach parking lot. Follow the signs directing you to the beach, park and lock, and look for the trail entrance—it's labeled with a small sign—at the far end of the lot. Since I am always looking for photographs with good fall color reflections, I began by walking along the

shoreline, going counterclockwise on the loop trail. The very nature of shoreline trails makes them difficult at times, with streams entering the lake from side valleys. This one is no exception, but you will have no trouble passing.

After about a mile of following close to the lake, the trail makes an abrupt left turn and begins climbing a ravine toward the area known as Riverview at the end of the campground road. You'll find a latrine there as well as a picnic area and playground equipment. The 0.75-mile Riverview Trail leaves the picnic area to the right of the swing set. Head due south toward a spot where you can look out over the Ohio River Valley. Forest and park trails intermingle and

Forked Run Lake is visible from the ridge through the woods of Forked Run State Park.

are not well defined in this area, so be sure you retrace your steps if you add this out-and-back trail with its end loop to your day's adventure.

To return to your vehicle, head a very short distance back the trail you traveled, gaining the summit. You will soon see the trail entrance to the right; this is the continuation of the Lakeview Trail Loop. It stays on the high ground just out of the camping area for several hundred yards before gently, then more steeply dropping to the lake and the beach parking lot.

For a good introduction to the tree species of the woods in this part of the state, consider walking the self-guided Honey Suckle Trail that starts near the park office. Among the less common native trees identified along the trail are persimmon and the yellow buckeye, a cousin of the more familiar Ohio buckeye.

Marie J. Desonier State Nature Preserve, described in *50 Hikes in Ohio,* is located

about 15 miles from Forked Run along CR 56, a short way north of US 50 in the southeast corner of Athens County. It offers a 2-mile woodland walk with a maximum 220-foot vertical rise that includes a high hillside meadow. Here butterflies often nectar on the native butterfly weed on warm, sunny midsummer afternoons.

Downriver from the park on SR 124, in the boot-shaped part of Ohio, you will want to visit the site of the skirmish on July 19, 1863, between the Ohio home guard and federal troops and the Confederate raiders led by the notorious John Hunt Morgan. A small park with a shelter house, prehistoric Indian mound, and historical markers denotes the vicinity of Ohio's only Civil War battle. Nearby, a roadside monument commemorates the death of U.S. Army paymaster Major Daniel McCook as a result of wounds received in that attempt to trap Morgan and his men. McCook of Carollton, Ohio—who enlisted in the army at the age of

63–was the father of two generals and five other sons fighting with the Union forces. He was the brother of U.S. Army surgeon John McCook of Steubenville, who was himself the father of one general and four other sons under arms for the North. Together the "Tribe of Dan" and the "Tribe of John" were known as the "Fighting McCooks."

4

Gifford State Forest

Total distance: 3 miles (4.8 km)

Hiking time: 2 hours

Maximum elevation: 915 feet

Vertical rise: 220 feet

Map: USGS 7½' Series Amesville; ODNR Gifford State Forest brochure

In 1959 William Gifford Selby donated a 320-acre tract of second-growth hardwood forest and pastureland in Athens County to the Ohio Division of Forestry on the condition that it be used for experimentation and research. It was named after Selby's mother, Virginia Gifford, and her family. In fulfillment of the conditions of the gift, the Division of Forestry has established a number of single-species stands of trees for the production of seeds. Among those grown are the much-admired white pine, the stalwart red and white oaks, sweet gum, and black walnut. The area brochure shows the locations of these and other plantings.

Gifford is the smallest of Ohio's state forests, but it offers some very pleasant hiking opportunities in the Marietta Plateau district of Unglaciated Allegheny Plateau in southeastern Ohio. Located just north of the Athens County crossroads community of Sharpsburg, it is on a southeast-facing slope above Opossum Run, a small tributary of the Hocking River. This is an area of generally high relief with mostly fine-grained rocks. Red shales and red soils are relatively common in the area. Landslides are common. It is thought that prior to settlement, beech–maple–tuliptree forests grew in the valleys, and mixed-oak forests covered the hills. Like other state forests, Gifford is open to public hunting during the fall; hikers should take the necessary precautions.

Visitor parking is provided at a lot uphill a couple of hundred feet to the west of SR 377. The gated entrance drive is just north of the area office and service buildings.

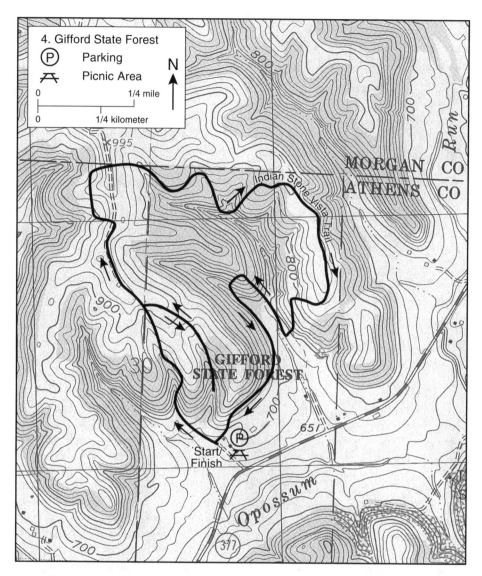

There you will find a bulletin board with a map and a picnic table. There is a small pond alongside the driveway. On the blue-sky day in late October when I was scouting this area, a single monarch butterfly was nectaring on an aster alongside the pond, perhaps taking on fuel for the next day's 50 to 90 miles of flying toward central Mexico, where millions of its kind overwinter in the

oyamel fir trees at 10,000 feet, awaiting the coming of spring.

How to Get There

Take US 33 southeast from Columbus, traveling about 75 miles. Before reaching Athens, turn east onto SR 550 and go 15 miles to the community of Sharpsburg. This is a winding road, and there will sometimes

---

The single-brooded Aphrodite butterfly is one of many species that use thistle flowers as a source of energy-producing nectar.

be valley fog. At Sharpsburg, SR 550 makes a hard right turn. Instead of turning, using caution, go straight ahead on SR 377. The entrance to Gifford State Forest is on the left side of the road less than 0.5 mile north of the intersection.

The Trail

To begin hiking, follow the entrance drive to a track that goes to the right in front of the pond dam. Though they are not given names on the Division of Forestry's map, the trails of the area do have names; it is on the Indian Stone Trail that you head up the hill. The trail looks like an old road, but in some places the currently mowed trail veers away from, then returns to, the old track. The Pennsylvanian-age sandstone bedrock of this part of unglaciated Ohio protrudes from the trail or is evident in the banks of the road cut. Most trees are young, filling areas that the topographic map shows as treeless. But there are some lovely old sugar maple trees beside the long-abandoned road.

After a 200-foot gain in elevation from the parking lot, just beyond a huge white oak tree, you will find a sign identifying a side trail to the right that follows a ridge covered with scrubby vegetation for about 0.3 mile to a vista overlooking the valley of Opossum Creek. Before being acquired by the state, this was likely a hilltop pasture. Now the regenerating forest is gradually closing in, obscuring the view.

Back on the Indian Stone Trail you continue paralleling the boundary of the forest, following the old road. It is quite obvious when the trail passes from young woodlands into an area that, though probably second growth, has been uncut for many years. Look for sandstone outcrops. After crossing the head of one ravine, the trail climbs steeply for a distance of about 100 feet to a junction where a sign indicates that the Vista Trail is to the right and the Indian Stone Trail to the left. The Indian Stone Trail climbs through an area that looks to have had some earth removed for one purpose or another, perhaps to remove coal. It then follows the west boundary fence line for a short distance before dropping to cross a culvert at the head of the major valley of the forest. Now turning east, the trail winds at about the 815-foot level above the steep slope to the valley bottom. The area is in a period of regrowth from a timber harvest. Not surprisingly, when I was hiking I saw my first deer of the day here. The area map indicates that the "Indian Stone" is close by, but I failed to locate anything matching that description. I suspect that it is a sandstone outcrop or block located downslope from the trail, well hidden while foliage is on the trees. Not finding it gives me an excuse to return in another season, perhaps when spring wildflowers are in bloom but the tree leaves have not come out.

Next the trail begins to swing to the right to head south through another area shown on the topographic map as unforested. Here you will find several seed orchard plantings, including one of white pine along the left side of the trail. Where the trail drops toward the valley floor there are sweet gum trees, with their star-shaped leaves, on both sides. The floor of the forest is covered with club moss. For a short way, the trail travels on the surface of the sandstone bedrock.

A trail sign indicates a turn right and, though your instinct may say otherwise, it is correct. About 600 feet upstream, the trail passes a sign pointing to the trailhead, turns left across a new culvert, climbs the hillside for short distance, then heads down the valley, hugging the right hillside.

As the trail follows the contour of the land, you can look left to see black walnut plantings. When the leaves are off the walnuts, the white plantings are visible. With the parking lot in view, you can cross the field to your vehicle or follow the trail to the pond, where it closes the loop.

If you enjoy traveling the lesser-trod trail, this is a hike you will not want to miss.

5

Lake Alma State Park

Total distance: 2.25 miles (3.6 km)

Hiking time: 2 hours

Maximum elevation: 820 feet

Vertical rise: 175 feet

Maps: USGS 7½' Series Hamden

I have always liked Lake Alma State Park. It's a quiet, lesser-used park with a not-so-fancy campground. You can pitch a tent toward the back of the camping area and not feel out of place between giant motor homes with generators, TV satellite dishes, and strings of "Japanese" lanterns. In summer the beach has always been a good place for young children to wade in safety while parents watch. In spring bluegills fan nest in the sandy-bottom lake near the swimming area, making it a perfect place for a little fly-rod action. With an electric-trolling-motors-only policy for boats, it is a good place for lake canoeing. Most of all, Lake Alma's location in Ohio's 19th-century industrial heartland makes it a perfect home base for a week of exploring old iron furnaces, covered bridges, brick factories, and charcoal ovens—a veritable mecca for an amateur industrial archaeologist. To that, add a nice easy-to-walk trail system that can be accessed directly from the campground or from a parking lot.

Lake Alma is one of several Ohio state parks that include an early-20th-century amusement park in their history. But really, this park's roots go further back than that. In 1837 Ohio's first geological survey identified the mineral riches of the Jackson and Vinton County area: Coal, iron ore, a flinty limestone suitable for millstones, and the timber of the region attracted investors, and industrial development took off. By the middle of the century the area was a leading producer of iron for industrial uses and weapons, of ties for the growing railroad

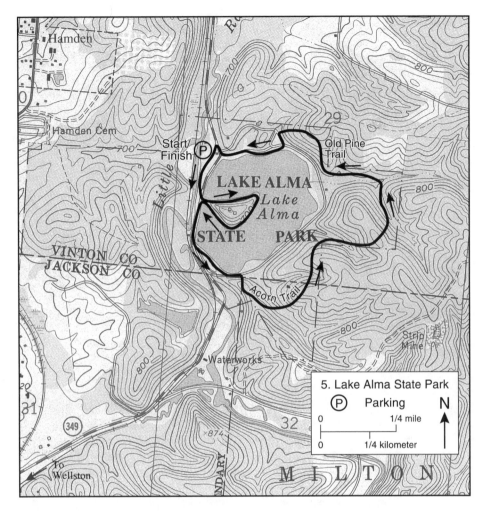

5. Lake Alma State Park

P Parking N

0 ——————— 1/4 mile
0 ——————— 1/4 kilometer

systems of the country, and of millstones for the water-powered gristmills that lined the nation's rivers and streams. But by the end of the century, much of the bubble had burst.

In 1901–02 local businessman C. K. Davis dammed Little Raccoon Creek to create a picturesque lake that he named after his wife, Alma. He planned to build an amusement park, a popular recreational diversion of the era, on an island in the lake. In June 1903, with much fanfare, he opened the park. Folks began coming from far and wide, at first on horse or by horse and buggy and later by electric railroad and Model T Ford. But in 1910 mounting personal problems caused Davis to close Lake Alma Park. In 1926 the city of Wellston, in nearby Jackson County, purchased the lake for a water supply. In 1931 the Ohio Division of Conservation, predecessor of the Department of Natural Resources, took a 99-year lease on the land. When the new department with its Division of Parks and Recreation was created in 1949, the area became Lake Alma State Park.

This pedestrian bridge at Lake Alma leads to restrooms, a group camping area, and a shoreline trail around a wooded island.

How to Get There

To get to Lake Alma State Park, travel 75 miles southeast from Columbus on US 33 to Logan, then 30 miles south on SR 93 to its intersection with SR 349 on the north edge of Wellston. The park is about a mile north on both sides of SR 349. Motels and restaurants can be found at the intersection of SR 32 and SR 93 on the south edge of Jackson.

The Trail

Unless you are camped in the park and want to start walking the trail where it crosses the campground, a good place to begin is from the parking lot below the levee on the west side of SR 349, where there are rest rooms and picnic facilities. Walk out the driveway at the south end of the lot, then carefully cross the road to walk south on the left side. Turn left onto the bridge

leading to the island that a century ago was home to an amusement park but is now the park's group camping area. Though the park map does not show it, there is a shoreline path completely around the island. It's an easy 0.5-mile hike. It makes no difference which direction you travel. I've always heard better with my left ear, so in springtime when the land birds are active in the woods, I walk counterclockwise. At other times, when I am listening for the call of a passage loon on the lake or a pileated woodpecker on the mainland, I go the other way. It was mid-October when I last walked this trail. The sun had just burned off the fog, leaving an azure blue sky, and the lake was as calm as glass. I probably used too much film on reflections of gorgeous fall foliage, but I could not resist. There are some massive sandstone outcrops along the trail on the south shore, but passage is not difficult. In

Unglaciated Allegheny Plateau

winter, if you look carefully, you can spot part of the hoist for the Ferris wheel still hanging in a tree. Anytime of year, by using your imagination, you can hear the noise of the crowd and the music of the merry-go-round that nearly five generations back made this the place to be on a summer day.

After coming off the island, head south along the left side of the road. After a couple of hundred yards, at the end of the guardrail, turn left onto the shoreline path leading to the interior park road. A number of times I have seen a great blue heron or two spear-fishing in these shallows, and from early spring to late fall there are usually mallard ducks paddling about. There is also a beaver house along the shore; you can see trees that have been chewed on by these aquatic engineers.

When you climb to the road, be aware that all traffic will be coming from your left, as this is a one-way drive. Walking east along the road, you will very soon come to a sign indicating that the Acorn Trail—which leads to the campground—exits right. The trail angles up the right side of a valley in which there is a picnic area. Numbered signposts indicate that there is a self-guided nature trail on this path. If you are interested in the interpretive information that has been prepared for these stations, ask for a folder at the park office. They were out of print when I asked, but I did obtain a copy of the text.

Large tuliptree and sugar maple trees line this trail. As you reach the head of the valley, the trail dips to cross the streambed. At post 4 you can see two large rocks. The shiny black rock with moss is Zaleski flint, a rock the Native Americans used for arrow points, knives, and scrapers. This is a different formation than the flint found at Flint Ridge in Licking County and is not as well known by the public. The second large rock

is a dark limestone (notice the large fossil at the bottom and to the right). Formed from dead animal and plant material deposited in water, after millions of years of pressure the organic material has been replaced by minerals. Only an imprint of the fossil is left.

As the trail climbs to the ridge, scarlet, chestnut, red, and white oaks begin to dominate the forest. The large pits on either side of the trail were created when a windstorm toppled the trees of the area many years ago. The wind-throws turned up large balls of earth with the root system, leaving a hole that remained long after the downed tree decayed and returned to the soil. The Acorn Trail descends steeply among beech and maple trees on this north-facing slope, then crosses the creek and tracks down the valley on the side of the hill. It soon swings right and follows at a fairly even level. The lake is clearly visible to the north. Following very close to the park boundary, the trail drops steeply into a ravine before turning downstream past an Acorn Trail sign. Red blazes mark the trail as it winds its way along the park boundary to the upper end of the campground.

This is a good place to refill water bottles and use a rest room. Either pick up the trail behind campsite 47 and work your way toward the lake or walk out the campground road to the amphitheater, where a bridge leads to the trail. In either case, just west of the corner of the park property a wide trail heads nearly due north uphill, gaining 100 feet in elevation before it swings to the west to follow the fence line to a trailhead across the road from the beach parking lot.

Cross the beach parking lot and turn left to follow the shoreline past the beach concession and boat dock. Skirt around or cross the west beach and return to the parking lot and your vehicle via the park roads.

While in the area, you may want to visit the reconstructed iron-making complex at Buckeye Furnace State Memorial off SR 124 southeast of Wellston. In *50 Hikes in Ohio* I have described two hikes in the nearby Jackson area that are interesting because of their cultural and natural history. They are Lake Katharine State Nature Preserve west of Jackson and Cooper Hollow Wildlife Area southeast of Jackson.

6

Rockbridge State Nature Preserve

Total distance: 2 miles (3.2 km)

Hiking time: 1½ hours

Maximum elevation: 960 feet

Vertical rise: 220 feet

Maps: USGS 7½' Series Rockbridge; ODNR Rockbridge State Nature Preserve brochure

One of the most spectacular rock formations of the Hocking Hills region of southeastern Ohio is not a part of the Hocking Hills State Park complex and thus gets little attention from folks headed to the area for a day of hiking. Rockbridge State Nature Preserve is the site of Ohio's largest natural arch or bridge, a 100-foot-long bridge varying from 10 to 20 feet in width that gracefully arches over a rock-rubble- and sand-filled ravine a little over 100 feet back from the west bank of the Hocking River. Located about 1.5 miles from the small Hocking County town that bears its name, Rockbridge has a long history as an attraction to travelers.

The bridge is comprised of Mississippian-age Black Hand sandstone, the same rock formation as the cliffs, gorges, and rock shelters of Hocking Hills State Park, the cliffs of Lancaster's Rising Park, the cliffs of Clear Creek Metro Park, and the cliffs of Blackhand Gorge State Nature Preserve. The scenic features of all these areas have resulted from the destructive power of wind and water and below-freezing temperatures on the different layers of this 100-foot-plus-thick rock. Various layers of this massive formation are affected differently by these erosive forces, depending upon how well the sand grains are cemented. In the upper zone the sand grains are well cemented by iron and silica, making the caprock very resistant to erosion. Sand grains in soft lower zones are weakly cemented, allowing more rapid erosion and resulting in the development of shallow recesses undercutting the caprock.

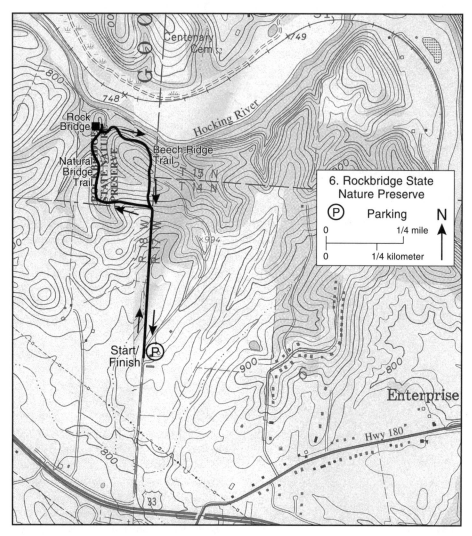

The spectacular overhangs, canyon rims, and rock shelters of the Hocking Hills area have thus been formed. Rockbridge is thought to have started out as a deep rock shelter created by such differential weathering. In time, the stream coming down the valley above the shelter began cutting through bedding-plane cracks behind the rock shelter's lip. The cement along the bedding planes and cracks began to dissolve, causing zones of weakness. Over

millennia, the forces of erosion and gravitational pull won. A portion of roof of the shelter collapsed, leaving the front part of the caprock standing alone as an arch.

Rockbridge probably provided shelter to Native Americans living or hunting in the area long before settlement by white Europeans. But in the mid–19th century, it became a popular picnic spot for folks traveling on the nearby Hocking Canal. This waterway connected the Ohio & Erie Canal at

The trail to Ohio's largest natural bridge begins at this kiosk and entrance sign.

Carroll with the Hocking River at Athens, allowing farm products and mineral resources to be moved to other parts of the nation. Traffic passed by Rockbridge from 1840 until 1891, after which those portions of the towpath that were necessary for roadbed were leased to the Columbus, Hocking Valley & Athens Railroad. Though people scrambled up the slope from the Hocking to picnic under the impressive natural bridge, it was never operated as a commercial venture. As late as the mid-1960s, I joined dozens of canoe enthusiasts for a bean soup lunch under the shelter as we made an annual Christmas season trip down the Hocking River. It gave splendid shelter from wind, rain, and snow.

In late 1973 the Division of Natural Areas and Preserves purchased the tract that included the rock bridge. Over the next 16 years it bought additional land to provide buffer and access to bring the size to just under 100 acres.

How to Get There

To reach Rockbridge State Nature Preserve, follow US 33 south from Columbus to 1.5 miles south of the community of Rockbridge. Turn northeast from US 33 onto TR 35, between the roadside rest and Rockbridge. Continue southeast past the first roadway, turning off on the second—Dalton Road (TR 503). Dalton Road dead-ends at the Rockbridge Preserve parking lot and trailhead.

The Trail

Begin hiking by following the 2,800-foot access lane due north. I find that through most of the summer and early fall, the lane is frequented by a variety of species of butterflies. A bridge and some boardwalk have been provided to traverse a wet area on the early part of the trail. As you climb to higher ground, the view of the surrounding Allegheny Plateau countryside is splendid. About three-fourths of the way up the hill and at the top, seats are provided for weary hikers or those who simply want to contemplate the beauty of the landscape. I often hear a red-tailed hawk calling as I walk this lane. The woods to the right of this trail offer good examples of the many species of hardwoods that are a part of the mixed-mesophytic forest of this part of the state.

Rockbridge State Nature Preserve

One hundred feet beyond the hilltop, the trail enters the woods. This is at least second-growth forest, as nearly all the timber in this part of Ohio was cut in the middle of the 19th century to be used for the making of charcoal to fire iron furnaces. Such a furnace operated not many miles to the southeast at Logan.

Twenty-five feet into the woods, a sign reads NATURAL BRIDGE TRAIL and points in two directions. I suggest going to the right, heading downslope toward the bridge. Here the trees are quite young, probably growing as the result of release from pasturing when the property was acquired 25 years ago. The trail to the creek bottom is a bit rough but not impassable. At the creek where the trail turns left, you enter an area of larger timber. After a fairly steep climb of 100 feet with mature trees on the right and young trees on the left, a sign points right to the 1-mile-long rock shelter loop trail and to the left for the natural bridge, 0.25 mile. The trail to the left follows the ridge and is delineated with poles along its edge. In October 1999 I met a couple of hikers coming up the trail at this point who told me that they had just seen 30 wild turkeys crossing the natural bridge.

The trail now swings to the left then winds its way downhill, at first on rock outcrop, then on a wooden staircase. Ahead, below the beech and maple trees of this north-facing slope, the rock bridge comes into view. Take time to explore the bridge from above and below. If you have a wide-angle lens or setting on your camera, this is a good place to put it to use capturing the bridge from different perspectives and angles. Different hours of the day and times of the year provide quite different pictures, with backlit scenes a favorite. If you are fortunate enough to be at the Rockbridge on what photographers refer to as a "cloudy bright" day, especially in early spring or in autumn, you can be rewarded with some very special images. In winter, if the stream has been flowing, there may be a 55-foot frozen waterfall for capturing on film.

The return trip begins by retracing your steps to where you came off the hill, but instead of turning left, go straight ahead up the valley. There is a short bridge over the creek, at the end of which the trail turns left, continuing to parallel the creek. Climbing gently, the trail passes under tall tuliptrees, winding its way to where it crosses a fork of the creek at an oblique angle. Soon it leaves the older woodland and gains 100 feet in elevation among the young trees in a short distance. Ground pine covers much of the ground under sassafras and Virginia pine on this hillside. Eventually the trail turns left, following the south fence line. Mercifully, there is a bench here to provide for rest and contemplation. Two hundred feet beyond is the junction of the trails, with its sign pointing both directions to the natural bridge. A turn to the right leads the hiker down the lane toward the parking area.

No visit to the Hocking Hills area is complete without a walk on the trail at Conkles Hollow. To travel to this state nature preserve and the five areas of Hocking Hills State Park, turn toward Lancaster on US 33 and go to SR 374, the Scenic Route, which many years ago was established as a route for just that purpose. To obtain information about these and the many other attractions of the area, visit the Hocking Hills Visitor Information Center at the intersection of US 33 and SR 664 near Logan.

7

Salt Fork State Park

Total distance: 1.9 miles (3 km)

Hiking time: 1¼ hours

Maximum elevation: 910 feet

Vertical rise: 110 feet

Maps: USGS 7½' Series Birmingham; ODNR Salt Fork State Park brochure

Salt Fork State Park lies north and east of the city of Cambridge in Guernsey County on a 20,542-acre tract acquired by the state in the late 1950s and early 1960s for the purpose of constructing a lake to provide water for Cambridge and to develop a multipurpose park and wildlife area. The dam was completed in 1967, work began on the park in 1968, and the lodge and most park facilities opened in 1972.

The park lies within the Muskingum-Pittsburgh Plateau area of the Allegheny Plateau. It is an area of fairly high relief, with Mississippian- and Pennsylvanian-age sandstones, shales, and siltstones exposed at the surface and Wisconsinan-age sand, gravel, and lacustrine silt deposited in its broad valleys. Beech–maple forests covered the valley floors in presettlement times, and mixed-mesophytic forests dominated the north-facing slopes. Mixed-oak forests were found on the dry ridges and southern exposures. Surely it teemed with wildlife when settlers began felling the timber to carve out farms in the rich bottomlands.

Today Salt Fork is Ohio's largest state park. As such it boasts recreational facilities to suit nearly every taste. There is a beautiful resort lodge overlooking the lake, more than 50 all-season family cottages, a golf course, excellent boating and swimming facilities, a campground, an interpretive program, thousands of acres of wild land on which to hunt, fishing opportunities galore, many miles of bridle trails, and 14 miles of hiking trails. Many of the facilities have been especially designed to be accessible by the disabled.

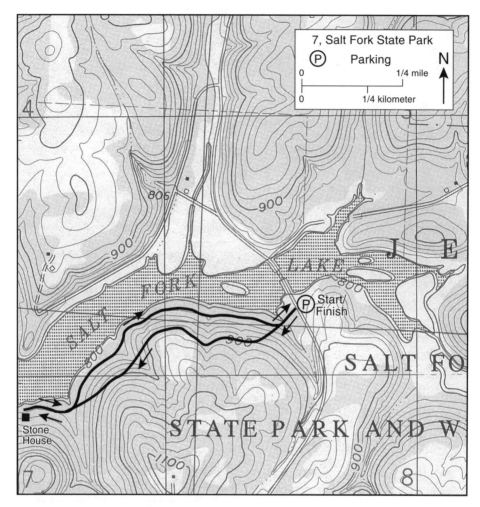

The hiking trails range from 0.3 mile to 3 miles in length. Most, but not all, are loop trails. Many originate within the main camping or cabin areas. One is a connecting trail between the lodge and the amphitheater where evening programs are given. My favorite is the Stone House Loop Trail, accessible from a parking lot alongside the lake on Park Road 1 just over 5 miles inside the park. Though less than 2 miles in length, it will probably require an hour and a quarter to hike, because in some places it is rocky and you will want to explore the environ-

ment. I suggest that you start your hiking on this trail at Salt Fork. If you are staying in the lodge, cabin, or camping area, you will want to add the short loops located close by to your hiking schedule. If you want a more challenging hike, try the short but rugged Hosak's Cave Trail.

How to Get There

To reach Salt Fork State Park from central Ohio, drive east on I-70 to its intersection with I-77 east of Cambridge. Take I-77 for 2 miles north to SR 22, then go 6 miles east to the park entrance. From the Cleveland or Marietta area, travel I-77 to SR 22.

The Trail

The trailhead for the Stone House Loop Trail is across the road from the parking area. Two small bridges span the water running off the hillside. This is a woodland trail with a good mix of hardwood species and, as it is a moist north-facing slope, a nice display of spring wildflowers.

A hundred yards into the woods the trail splits, creating the loop. I chose the uphill trail on the way in, but suit yourself. Immediately there are outcroppings of the fine-grained sandstone so typical of the area. Unlike the Black Hand sandstone of south-central Ohio, this rock does not contain layers of quartz pebbles or display the honeycombed effect of differential weathering. It appears not to have the moisture-retaining quality of the Black Hand; it lacks the mosses, ferns, liverworts, and lichens that characterize the rocks of the Hocking County area.

After the split, the somewhat rocky trail climbs the hill at an angle among 2-foot-diameter trees with a spicebush shrub layer. About two-thirds of the way up the hill, the trail levels off; the trees here are younger, and ground pine covers the forest floor. Beech, sugar maple, white oak, and tuliptree are common on the hillside. Large sandstone slump blocks rest on the hillside below an outcropping layer of the same. There is also a small cave alongside the trail.

As the trail drops toward the lake, evidence of civilization ahead comes by way of the presence of lots of multiflora rose. Planted in the mid–20th century to provide a living fence around pastures, it got transported into the woods by birds that flew there to defecate. The next season indigestible rose seeds complete with fertilizer

germinated and began to crowd out the native plants of the shrub layer of the woods. The red-blazed trail drops to near lake level, crosses two bridges, and continues along the lakeshore, passing a boat dock before reaching the stone house. For a short distance, the trail appears to be shared by horses, leaving it a bit chewed up and muddy.

The presence of the stone house has a startling effect when you come upon it in the wilderness. When it was built by an early Guernsey County resident, David B. Kennedy, in 1837, it overlooked Sugar Tree Creek, not a man-made reservoir. From the front stoop, there was probably a grand view of the crop fields and pastures that made up the Kennedy farm. These hardy pioneers were likely very self-sufficient, producing nearly everything they needed right here on the farm. The 3-foot by 1-foot by 1-foot stone blocks for the house came from a local quarry, and what wood was needed for doors, window frames, rafters, joists, flooring, and roofing probably came off the hillside. The construction of the house is said to have cost a total of $600. It was home to several generations of the Kennedy family, ending with Don Kennedy, the great-grandson of the original Irish immigrant who had it built. After sitting vacant for nearly 30 years, it suffered severe damage when a tree limb fell from a massive pine near the house said to have been planted by Ben Kennedy. Park staff and volunteers have worked to rehabilitate it; the hope is that it can be restored to its original condition. Because of its unique and enduring construction, the house is on the National Register of Historic Places.

When the Kennedys lived in the stone house, the voices of children playing in the yard must have echoed off the hillside. The lowing of cattle and the cacophony of

The solid stone Kennedy house is the destination on a walk on the Stone House Trail.

free-range poultry likely added to the sounds around the homestead. That a house is not a home without a family comes through succinctly in the silence of the site while your imagination tries to tell you what it was like in the horse-and-buggy and ox-and-mule days of yore. Be sure to make images in your mind and on film while you are there, but leave the house as you found it, that those who follow you may also contemplate the past. Joining me in exploring the stone house on a beautiful October afternoon was a small group of ladies from Dublin who, like me, were curious about what was at the end of the Stone House Trail.

The return trip begins by retracing your steps on the trail you arrived on. When you reach a split in the trail, take the left fork.

After passing a couple of grassy lakeshore spots used by fishermen, the trail backs off from the shore and winds its way through sandstone blocks and rubble. Here rockcap fern grows on the sharp edges of some of the sandstone blocks. Though you cannot see them, you can hear the voices of folks following the trail farther up the hillside. Eventually the upper and lower trails rejoin to return to the parking lot.

There is good hiking at Seneca Lake Park southeast of Cambridge, described elsewhere in this book. Wolf Run State Park, located east of I-77 near Caldwell, about 20 miles south of I-70, also has hiking trails. Hikes at Atwood Lake Park and Tappan Lake Park are described in *50 Hikes in Ohio*.

Seneca Lake Park

Total distance: 2 miles (3.2 km)

Hiking time: 1½ hours

Maximum elevation: 1,030 feet

Vertical rise: 165 feet

Maps:USGS 7½' Series Senecaville; MWCD Seneca Lake brochure

The Muskingum River basin is the largest watershed in Ohio. At 8,051 square miles, it drains parts of 24 of Ohio's 88 counties. When the murderous flood of March 1913 occurred, destroying every bridge across the Muskingum south of Zanesville, it devastated homes and especially businesses on low ground throughout the watershed. Civic leaders began considering what could be done to prevent recurrence of such destruction. But a world war, the Roaring Twenties, and the stock market crash that marked the beginning of the Great Depression happened before anything was done. In 1933 the Muskingum Watershed Conservancy District was born; the next year the U.S. Army Corps of Engineers created the Zanesville district and began planning for flood protection in the watershed in full force. Fourteen projects were designed: 10 with permanent impoundments and four dry dams that would impound water only when needed to reduce downstream flooding. Seneca Dam was constructed in 1937 on the Seneca Fork of Wills Creek on the Noble-Guenrsey county line. The district owns the lake and surrounding land, and the Corps of Engineers owns and operates the dam.

Seneca Lake Park is the recreation area developed and operated by the district for use by the general public. Located on the west side of the lake near the town of Senecaville, the park includes a campground, marina, vacation cabins, swimming beach, picnic shelters, nature center, and 2-mile hiking trail. From Memorial Day to Labor Day there is small fee for entry into

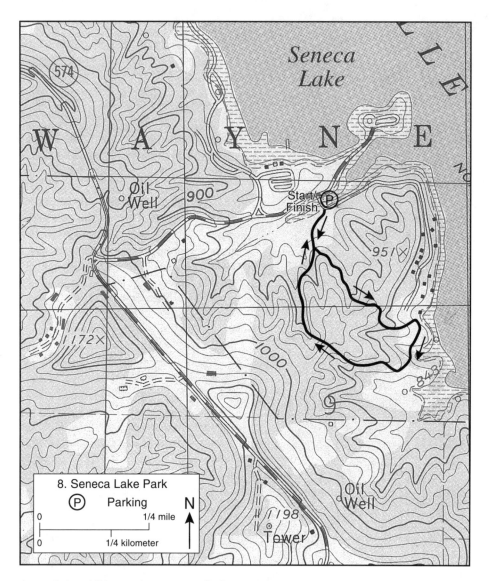

8. Seneca Lake Park
Ⓟ Parking
N
0 ——————— 1/4 mile
0 ——————— 1/4 kilometer

the park. In addition to the nature trail, the Buckeye Trail—Ohio's official hiking trail—passes through the north end of the park on its way toward Headlands Beach on the shore of Lake Erie in Lake County.

This is the high-relief country of the Marietta district of the Allegheny Plateau. The bedrock is Pennsylvanian-age fine-grained sandstone, siltstones, red and gray shales, limestones, and coals. When the Delaware Indians wandered the land, the forests were the blend of hardwoods that botanists refer to as mixed mesophytic, including the American chestnut now gone from the countryside because of a devastating blight in the first half of the 20th century. Game was certainly plentiful at the time, and the unfragmented forest must

Many species of native sunflowers greet hikers in July and August.

have provided nesting territories for many pairs of neotropical birds that came to the temperate climate of Ohio to raise their young. Wildlife populatons have rebounded from their lows of 100 years ago. During the day I spent scouting the Seneca Lake trails, I saw a large flock of wild turkeys, several ruffed grouse, and white-tailed deer. The most exciting sight was watching an osprey harassing a flock of ring-billed gulls over the empty beach. *Columbus Dispatch* columnist John Switzer has been touting Seneca Lake to me for years. Now I understand.

How to Get There

To reach Seneca Lake Park, take I-77 south 6 miles from I-70 to Buffalo. Turn east onto SR 313 and follow it through Senecaville to SR 574. Go right on SR 547 past the state fish hatchery and up the hill where, after traveling about 3 miles, you will find the park entrance on the left.

The Trail

The trailhead for this 2-mile hike is located on the road to the vacation cabins, about 100 feet from its entrance. There is a grass area where a car or two could be parked, but probably a better place to leave a vehicle is on the corner of the large beach parking lot.

The trail starts a gradual climb almost immediately. It winds its way to the hilltops, passing on the way large red and white oaks, tall-trunked tuliptrees, and some really nice sugar maples. At the first junction, take the left fork and head east toward the lake. Soon, at another trail junction, you have the choice of taking the Seneca Loop straight ahead or turning right onto the Grouse Ridge Trail. I suggest the latter, as it will continue on the high ground and make a loop back to the parking lot. The presence of a large number of redbud trees caused me to speculate on the presence of limestone close to the surface. Redbud, a common understory tree in southwestern Ohio, is considered a calciphile, requiring a soil on the alkaline side or at least near neutral.

After passing the end of an old oil field road, the trail crosses an open field before reentering the woods to travel Deer Ridge. Oil is no longer being pumped here, but natural gas is; the park uses it as fuel in their building. Beyond a crossing of a usually dry creek, there is a stand of American elm trees. These magnificent wineglass-shaped trees were a favorite street tree in the Midwest until a disease introduced from Europe killed them in the first half of the 20th century. They show up frequently in wild lands but usually do not get beyond 6 inches in diameter before Dutch elm disease kills them. Occasionally you will see a stand of larger trees that simply by their isolation have reached good size. I well remember when those near my childhood home in Columbus died.

Even more impressed into my memory is the year of the die-off of the hundreds of elms that at one time lined both sides of East Broad Street from Broad and High east to the Norfolk & Western Railroad tracks beyond Franklin Park. What a tragic loss.

The trail now leaves the creek bed and ambles around the hillside, climbing gently. A stand of aspen gives evidence of an earlier fire. After passing a nice stand of stately tuliptrees and an area where running ground pine blankets the forest floor, you'll reach a side trail to the left that leads to an old one-room schoolhouse just beyond the boundary fence. Many of America's most respected and beloved personages of the past received their education in just such an environment; children of all ages under the tutelage of a school "marm," firmly but lovingly directing each child to learn at his or her own speed. On winter days, long before the school door opened, these hardy teachers arrived early to build a fire in the stove so that students would be warm enough to take off their mittens to do their numbers and write their spelling words on slate tablets. Photo opportunities behind, return to the main trail, turn left and cross the ravine on the bridge, then wind your way through the woods to the junction, where a left turn will take you back to your vehicle.

There are good hiking trails at other parks of Muskingum Watershed Conservancy District. Those at Attwood and Tappan are described in *50 Hikes in Ohio,* and one at Charles Mill Reservoir can be found elsewhere in this volume.

9

Shawnee State Forest

Total distance: 6½ miles (10.4 km)

Hiking time: 6 hours

Maximum elevation: 1,210 feet

Vertical rise: 512 feet

Maps: USGS 7½' Pond Run; ODNR Shawnee State Forest Backpack Trail brochure

When I wrote *Fifty Hikes in Ohio* in 1989, I spent nine days of rigorous hiking on the 50-mile Shawnee Backpack Trail. I slept at every campsite and made copious notes and many photographs of my trailside observations. When my manuscript was returned from my editor after her first reading, for reasons of total book length, most of the trail north of SR 125 had been deleted. I understood the need to shorten the chapter but I was a bit more than disappointed. I had been on the trail in the last week of April, that magic time when the vernal wildflowers are near their peak of bloom and the neo-tropical birds are moving through the yet-to-leaf-out trees. It was on this part of the trail that I made my most exciting observations. A male scarlet tanager sat on a branch close to the trail singing at the top of his voice; a zebra swallowtail nectared on long-spurred violets close to my feet on the uphill side of the path; a ruffed grouse brooded eggs a on nest almost at my elbow and at the highest elevation; and a box turtle moved along the trail at about the same speed I was traveling. I recognized that because this part of the trail was the most difficult with steep climbs, it was the logical part to delete, but my travels on it were three wonderful days that I will never forget.

Since that time, the Shawnee State Forest staff has developed a new trail in this part of the forest that offers the opportunity to explore this rugged land without a backpack. The 6½-mile Day Hike Trail travels about the same distance as a day's walk between campsites on the Backpack Trail,

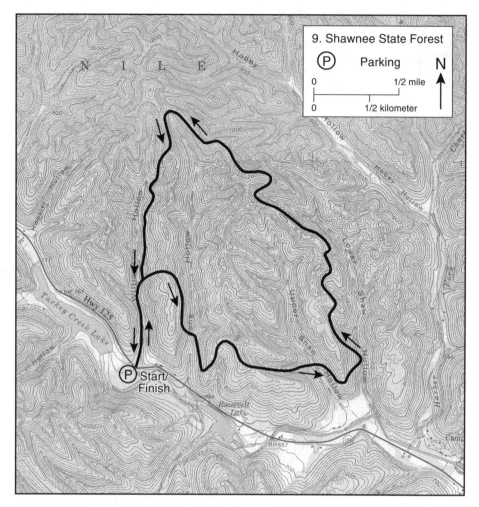

P Start/Finish

but it is a loop trail that begins and ends just across SR 125 from the State Park Nature Center at the spillway end of Turkey Creek Lake. It is, by far, the most challenging trail in this volume as it accomplishes a vertical rise (and fall) of just over 500 feet. There is no potable water available along the trail except near Backpack Trail Campsite #3 several hundred yards off the trail, so the hiker must carry drinking water. This is a trail to be taken by seasoned hikers in good physical condition who understand the challenge that it will present. But walking it will return

rewards far beyond those of most of the other trails presented herein. Enjoy.

At over 63,000 acres, Shawnee State Forest is Ohio's largest state forest. Located mostly in Scioto County in the Shawnee/Mississippian District of the Allegheny Plateau, it is the location of the most deeply dissected high relief terrain in the state. Mississippian Age siltstones, shales, and locally thick sandstones make up its bedrock, with the latter often seen as outcroppings on the hillsides. Mixed oak forests cover its ridges and south-facing slopes. Mixed mesophytic woods occupy the coves and northern exposures. It is the home to many rare wildflowers. The state-endangered timber rattlesnake and the northern copperhead (both venomous) are found in the forest, especially in the vicinity of rock outcrops and shelters and rock covered slopes. Nearly all of the fur-bearing quadrupeds of unglaciated Ohio, including black bear and bobcat, make their home here. Wild turkey are common throughout. Because of the extent of the unfragmented forest, there is probably no better place in Ohio for the nesting of deep forest birds, including the neo-tropical songbirds that fly thousands of miles from Central and South America each spring to raise their young in Eastern North America's deciduous forests. Insect larvae like loopers and inch worms, feeding on the tender young leaves of hardwoods, are pabulum for vireos and warblers. Some of my best observations and photographs of Ohio's flora and fauna, butterflies especially, have been made in Shawnee State Forest, the "Little Smokies of Ohio."

The area's existence as public "natural resource lands" dates back to 1922 when 5,000 acres of cleared and fire-ravaged land were acquired. How it grew to what it is today is a long story, and worth reading in the State Forest brochure. At the beginning of the 21st century, it includes an area designated as a state park within its borders, where there is a resort lodge, cabins, campground, golf course, marina, fishing lakes, nature center, and much more. In addition to harvesting timber on a selected rotational basis, the Division of Forestry maintains several hundred miles of bridle and hiking trails, a system of roads, and a wilderness and backcountry management area. Nearly all of the land is open to public hunting under the management of the Division of Wildlife.

How to Get There

To reach the Shawnee State Forest area, drive south from Central Ohio on US 23 to Portsmouth, then travel west on US 52 to Friendship. There, take SR 125 approximately 5½ miles to the parking lot at the spillway end of Turkey Creek Lake on the left (south) side of the highway.

If you're up for more hiking while you in this special part of Ohio, consider walking the trails at The Nature Conservancy's Edge of Appalachia Preserve near the Adams County community of Lynx about 12 miles west on SR 125. The Lynx and Buzzard-roost Rock trails are described in my book *Walks and Rambles in Southwestern Ohio,* and a recently developed trail in The Wilderness unit of the more than 1,200-acre preserve is described elsewhere in this volume. There are lodge rooms, cabins, and a campground at Shawnee State Park, in addition to good motels and restaurants in Portsmouth along US 23 and US 52 in the town of West Union.

The Hike

To begin a day's adventure in Shawnee Forest, park your vehicle at the east end of the boat ramp parking area near the Turkey Creek Lake dam adjacent to the Nature Center. The entrance to the trail is at a cable gate directly across SR 125 from the parking lot entrance drive. A single sign identifies the start of the trail. Blue paint blazes mark the trail; if you go a considerable distance without seeing a blaze, it's always a good plan to backtrack to the last paint blaze to make certain that you did not inadvertently miss a turn.

The trail leaves the highway on a grassy lane but soon turns into a woodland trail. A short way up the trail you will come to a side trail to the left marked with white blazes.

This is the connecting trail that leads to the Backpack Trailhead located 0.75 mile west along SR 125. Ignore it and continue straight ahead into Williamson Hollow. There will now be both blue and white blazes because this connecting trail utilizes the same tread as the Day Hike Trail in connecting the Backpack Trail parking lot with Campsite #3. After 0.5 mile of hiking, with the trail now following the right bank of the hollow, you will reach another junction with a white- and blue-blazed trail going to the right. This is the Backpack Trail connecting trail and also the returning trail of the Day Hike loop. I suggest traveling the Day Hike Trail in a clockwise direction, thus taking the left fork to walk on the trail marked with blue blazes only. For the next mile, the trail goes nearly due north as it rises 1,200 feet at a fairly steady climb. It's a long, slow trek that will take close to an hour, but when the trail finally makes a hard turn to the right, you will be near the highest point on the hike.

The trail then follows the ridge in a southeasterly direction for about 0.75 mile, then drops 200 feet down the right slope to catch the left side of another ridge at the 1,000-foot elevation level. After more walking near the ridge, you will turn due south and travel on the high land between Upper and Lower Shaw Hollows before dropping into the lower reaches of the latter.

Once at the lower elevation, you will encounter the white-blazed connecting trail exiting to the left that leads to Backpack Trail Campsite #3. The water cistern for that site is along this trail. If you plan to camp overnight in the forest, you must use a designated campsite and register for its use in advance. This campsite is the only one close to the Day Hike Trail. To preregister,

before you start your hike from the Day Hike trailhead, drive to the Backpack Trail registration shelter located about 0.75 mile further west at the intersection of SR 125 and the main park road that leads to the lodge and cabins. The last time I spent a night at Campsite #3, I watched a spectacular thunderstorm pass to the south. I was prepared to pull up stakes and evacuate my hillside site if lightning came too close, but I did not have to do so. If you do plan to camp, in order not to deplete the forest of firewood, I recommend that you carry a portable stove of some sort. In addition to a potable water source close by, there are latrines and a fire ring to contain your campfire at the site. In the springtime, you may drift off to sleep with whippoorwills calling and awaken to the drumming of ruffed grouse or the gobbling of turkeys.

To complete the Day Hike loop, turn west at the trail junction (or return to it if you overnighted at Campsite #3) and follow the trail as it rises then falls into Upper Shaw Hollow. Again, it is blazed with both blue and white. Then, heading west, the trail goes up a side ravine to eventually reach the 1,000-foot elevation before turning south on the first leg of a long switchback that drops into Long Hollow. A steep 150-foot climb up the west slope of Long Hollow precedes a more gentle 300-foot northward ascent to the high ground above Williamson Hollow and the outbound trail. From there, it's all downhill as the trail drops 300 feet to the trail split. A left turn leads you out of the mouth of Williamson Hollow, past the Backpack side trail with its white blazes, and exits right to the trailhead. Across the road is the Turkey Creek Nature Center/Boat Ramp parking lot.

II

Interior Low Plateau–Bluegrass Section

10

Edge of Appalachia Preserve—The Wilderness

Total distance: 2.5 miles (4 km)

Hiking time: 2½ hours

Maximum elevation: 875 feet

Vertical rise: 235 feet

Maps: USGS 7½' Series Lynx; TNC/CMC Edge of Appalachia Preserve brochure

On the east side of Ohio Brush Creek, on the edge of the Appalachian Plateau, The Nature Conservancy and the Cincinnati Museum Center own and manage a magnificent 13,000-plus-acre natural area known as the Edge of Appalachia Preserve. It is home to many rare species of plants and animals and some of the finest wilderness scenery in Ohio. Open to the public year-round, it includes a number of trails that lead to the best places to enjoy the unique flora of the cedar glades and prairie openings that are scattered throughout the preserve. The Lynx Prairie and Buzzardroost Rock Trails are described in detail in *Walks and Rambles in Southwestern Ohio*.

The Wilderness Trail is a recently developed trail in an area of the preserve that has long been referred to as the Wilderness. Use of the name dates back to a visit to the area in September 1961 by the curator emeritus of the Museum of Zoology at the Ohio State University and nature writer for the *Columbus Dispatch* in the company of E. Lucy Braun, a noted botanist. After his visit, the curator described the area as a "howling wilderness," and the name stuck.

The boundary of the advance of the Illinoian glacier lies 7 miles northwest of the Wilderness area. To the west, beyond the valley of Ohio Brush Creek, lie the rolling and fertile lands of the Outer Bluegrass Region of the Interior Low Plateau. To the east is the deeply dissected Mississippian-Pittsburgh Plateau of the Appalachian Plateau. The Wilderness lies in a transition zone between these topographies. The bedrock ranges

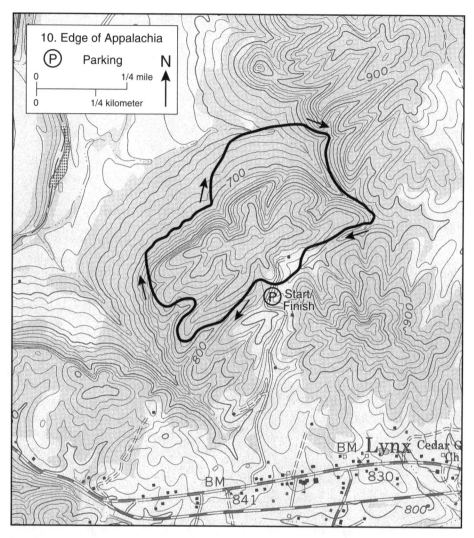

from 450-million-year-old Ordovician to 325-million-year-old Mississippian. In between, massive Silurian-age dolomites are present, forming sharp cliffs and promontories. Soils range from very alkaline to quite acidic. Plants that do well on one or the other or both are found in the preserve.

How to Get There

The village of Lynx and the Edge of Appalachia Preserve are located on SR 125 in Adams County. Travel from central Ohio over US 23, US 52, and SR 125 requires a little over two hours. The trip on SR 125 from the eastern suburbs of Cincinnati takes slightly more than an hour. Finding the trailhead for the Wilderness Trail is a bit difficult. It is located almost at the end of Shivener Road, about 0.3 mile north of Lynx Road. Shrivener Road runs north from Lynx Road at the west end of the community. Lynx Road is the "main street" of Lynx and was once SR 125 before a bypass was constructed south of the village.

Follow Shivener Road north past several houses. After it makes a hard left turn it turns equally hard to the right and descends gently; look for a spot on the left that will hold several cars. A cedar post and barbed-wire fence mark the lot. The entrance to the trail is to the left of this parking area. Do not go farther on the road. There is a steep slope ahead.

The Trail

Enter the woods through the opening in the fence located about 20 feet to the left of the parking lot. The trail is marked with 2-inch by 6-inch yellow blazes painted on trees at slightly above head height. Sometimes they are difficult to see, but they are close enough together that you can usually spot the next one ahead while you stand beside one. Look for them as you walk; and if you fail to see one for more than the usual distance between them, retrace your steps to make certain you have not missed a change in the trail's direction.

With the exception of the cedar glades and prairie openings toward the end of your trek, this is a woodland trail. It is not heavily traveled and has nothing other than the natural surface. The trail is not without poison ivy, and though it has been many years since I have seen one, this is copperhead country—mind where you step. Staff and volunteers try to keep it open and clear of obstacles, but expect an occasional dead-fall. If you would like to volunteer to help maintain this and other trails in the Edge of Appalachia Preserve, call the preserve office at 937-544-2188.

The trail immediately begins dropping into a draw. Follow the blazes to an old road or logging skid on the right-hand slope. After dropping to the creek, the trail begins to climb the right side of the ravine. Occasional red cedar *(Juniperus virginiana)* trees in the deciduous forest indicate that this area was probably cleared early in the last century. These junipers were the first species to invade the area as it began to recover from clearing or pasturing. The hardwoods that followed grew at a faster rate and have now overtopped the evergreens. Because their canopies can no longer get enough light to produce food through their green foliage, they will die, with the needles turning brown. The smaller ones are useful as fence posts. There is a growing cedar products industry in the county, using the rot-resistant wood of these tree trunks for such things as bird-houses and feeders.

As you near the end of this ravine, you will see northern white cedar trees *(Thuja occidentalis)*, also known as arborvitae, along with the red cedars. This species is considered a relic of a time in the immediate postglacial period when the climate of this part of the world was cooler. The trees still persist in Ohio, mostly in cool ravines with dolomite bedrock such as those found in Adams, Highland, and Greene Counties, in a few other areas of exposed calcareous bedrock, and in fens such as Cedar Bog in Champaign County. Their presence here indicates that you are reaching the top of the Peebles dolomite and will soon see an outcrop of this Silurian-age rock around the side of the hill. Redbud and chinquapin oak, species that also grow on calcium-rich soils, give further evidence of dolomite bedrock not too far beneath the surface. An occasional prairie forb, such as tall coreopsis *(Coreopsis tripteris)*, appears along the trail, a vestige of the prairie vegetation that grew on this slope before junipers and hardwoods re-invaded.

The descending trail soon passes through a narrow dolomite cliff edge and past large slump blocks, utilizing an old logging skid. Watch for a double blaze, the traditional way of alerting the hiker to a turn in the trail. At that point, it goes to the right to travel on the level for nearly 0.5 mile, paralleling the broad valley of Ohio Brush Creek. A stand of papaw trees indicates a seepage on the hillside; someone has put short pieces of railroad ties crosswise on the trail to keep feet dry. Tall tuliptrees *(Liriodendron tulipifera)* shade dying red cedars. At a point where for the first time since entering the trail, you see open grassland to the left, the trail crosses a creek then turns east to begin its return. Here you will see some yellow pieces of metal, like pieces of venetian blind slats, nailed to the trees alongside the painted blazes. These are markers for the Edge of Appalachia Trail, which connects many areas of that preserve. It was laid out by the late Richard Durrell, the University of Cincinnati geology professor whose dream and perseverance brought "the Edge" into being.

The ravine the trail now enters is the site of a long-established trail in the Wilderness. The stream is Bread Pan Run, and it tumbles over some beautiful falls and through some small gorges as it drains the hills to the east. The yellow-blazed Wilderness Trail climbs the left side of the valley at an angle before joining an earlier trail blazed with orange metal markers. This is the Knob Trail, a favorite of mine and of many other naturalists for decades. To the left on the orange-blazed trail is a high promontory known as the Knob; it's worth a side trip if you can still discern the trail.

Following the yellow paint blazes to the right, the Wilderness Trail winds its way up the ravine. As you rise in elevation, the dolomite that had been an outcrop on the hillside above on the left becomes the rock of the gorge through which the stream runs

The pearl crescent butterfly, seen here on a wingstem flower of late August, can be seen throughout the state from early May to late September, the result of three or four broods each year.

on the right. Arborvitae grows in this lush, cool environment, and the rare sullivantia *(Sullivantia sullivantii)* grows on the pock-marked face of the Peebles dolomite in the gorge. The distribution of this plant is very limited and spotty; it's found only south of and near the glacial border in Ohio, Indiana, and northern Kentucky. In springtime such wildflowers as large-flowered trillium *(Trillium grandiflorum)* and yellow lady's slipper *(Cypripedium calceolus)* can be found nearby. Soon the trail reaches two small bridges only a short distance apart. In May the columbine *(Aquilegia canadensis)* that clings to a large slump block to the left of the trail attracts ruby-throated hummingbirds *(Archilochus colubris)* to sip its sweet nectar.

Now the trail ascends the creek valley along the right bank. The uncommon green violet *(Hybanthus concolor)* and four-leaved milkweed *(Asclepias quadrifolia)* grow along this trail. Two hundred feet up the ravine, the trail climbs to the right on a switchback to emerge on a prairie opening known as Shivener, for the family who occupied this land for several generations. Interestingly, the late Charles Shivener recalled this hillside prairie at one time being a hillside corn patch. Abandoned crop fields on the thin soil over dolomite take only a few years to revert to prairie. By the same token, it does not take long for red cedar to invade the prairie, in due time to be followed by hardwoods. Maintaining the diversity of habitat that makes the Edge of Appalachia Preserve so unique requires careful management. In the case of the prairie openings, this involves periodic prescribed burning and some removal of woody plants by hand.

The sights and sounds of Shivener prairie through the seasons are something to behold. Big bluestem *(Andropogon gerardii)*, sideoats grama grass *(Bouteloua curtipendula)*, whorled rosinweed *(Silphium trifoliatum)*, dense blazing-star *(Liatris spicata)*, hoary puccoon *(Lithospermum canescens)*, false aloe *(Agave virginica)*, Indian paintbrush (*Castilleja* spp.), oxeye *(Heliopsis helianthoides)*, Seneca snakeroot *(Polygala senega)*, lyre-leaved sage *(Salvia lyrata)*, and yellow star grass *(Hypoxis hirsuta)* are just a taste of what is in store for hikers as they pass through the prairie. In late April and May and then again in July and August, you might want to carry an SLR camera with a 90- to 105-millimeter macro lens to let you capture the blossoms and butterflies of this special natural garden. In spring the prairie warbler *(Dendroica discolor)* can be heard singing its scalelike song from the tops of red cedar trees.

When the trail is about to turn left and leave the prairie, there is short dead-end trail to the left that leads to the best area for Indian paintbrush. If you are traveling the trail in May, don't miss this spot. I often have seen pipevine swallowtail *(Battus philenor)* butterflies nectaring on this striking prairie wildflower. Like the poinsettia (a member of the euphorbia family) of the holiday season, the Indian paintbrush (a member of the snapdragon family) owes it appearance of having a bright scarlet bloom not to flower petals but to a splash of red on the tips of the bracts. When the butterfly seeks nectar from this plant, it must extend its proboscis deep into the top of the blossom to reach the nectaries on the inconspicuous flower hidden below.

Following the trail uphill means leaving the thin, dry alkaline soils of the prairie behind and entering the woodland with its acidic soils derived from the underlying Ohio black shale. It's a different world. Chinquapin oaks *(Quercus muehlenbergii)* are replaced by chestnut oaks *(Q. montana)*. Yellow lady's slippers give way to the pink *(Cypripedium acaule)* ones. The obligate calciphiles (plants that must have alkaline soils to grow) disappear. Virginia pines *(Pinus virginiana)* are the pioneer tree species now.

A short way up the slope, the trail turns sharply to the left to exit the woods onto the Shivener homestead grounds. The house and most outbuildings have been removed, but one building used for educational purposes and latrines remains. To reach your car, walk up the hill on the road to the parking area.

11

Mount Airy Forest

Total distance: 3.5 miles (5.6 km)

Hiking time: 2½ hours

Maximum elevation: 860 feet

Vertical rise: 210 feet

Maps: USGS 7½' Series Cincinnati West; Cincinnati Park Board Mount Airy Forest map

When Cincinnatians think of Mount Airy, the vision that most likely comes to mind is that of the medieval castlelike water reservoir that stands on the top of a hill at the corner of North Bend Road and Colerain Avenue in the western part of the city. That brick structure houses 14 cylindrical steel tanks that hold 8½ million gallons of potable water destined for the homes and businesses of the western hills part of the city. It has been doing so since it first went into operation in 1927. At 960 feet in elevation, the structure is on the highest point of land within the corporate boundaries of the city and is a landmark visible from many directions.

On land directly south and just downhill from the Mount Airy reservoir, in the area between busy I-24 and Colerain Avenue, lies Mount Airy Forest, a 1,472-acre city park. This wooded tract is, literally, just across the road from the edge of the farthest advance of the Illinoian glacier in this part of Ohio. Geologists believe that a much earlier ice advance had at one time covered the Mount Airy property, but since they are not certain which named ice sheet it was, they prefer to describe the area as pre-Illinoian. If you searched hard in the topsoil and subsoil of the Mount Airy Park area and in the colluvium on the surrounding hillsides, you would most likely find fragments of granitic rock that originated far to the north in the Canadian Shield area. But there are no large telltale glacial boulders strewn on the land at Mount Airy that would make it obvious that it had been glaciated like there are farther to the north in Ohio.

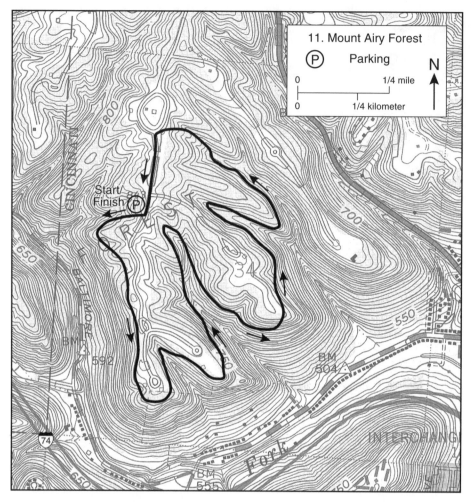

The bedrock under the park is the oldest exposed rock in the state. The Ordovician-age limestone and calcareous shales were formed as a result of the deposition of seashells, shell fragments, and limy muds at the bottom of a shallow arm of the sea that reached into the area from the St. Lawrence River region about 450 million years ago. As the result of millions of years of pressure from other layers of sediment over them, they became the loosely cemented, fossil-filled rock formations that outcrop in the park today.

Because the rivers and streams of the area are at a much lower elevation, the area is subject to the formation of caverns as water finds its way through the bedrock, dissolving and carrying away limestone. Topography of this nature is known as karst, a name derived from a famous cave region along the Adriatic Sea in Italy and Slovenia. Ohio's best-known karst areas are near Bellefontaine and around Bellevue and Castalia. The Mammoth Cave region of Kentucky is probably the most developed karst area in this part of the country.

Because of its soils derived from calcareous bedrock, the Mount Airy area, along with parts of adjacent northern Kentucky, is classified as the Outer Bluegrass Region.

Prior to settlement by people of European origin, Native Americans and their mound-building ancestors had occupied the land here for many centuries. By the end of the 18th century, rapid settlement was occurring and Cincinnati was a busy river town. The upland and ravines at Mount Airy were probably covered by an ancient mixed-mesophytic forest but, because of the crumbly bedrock and weather that allowed frequent windfalls, trees growing on the steep slopes probably did not reach the same size. Though the original timber was likely all removed, large trees still grow in the park. To provide park area, much of the upland is planted to lawn grasses and mowed, thus eliminating the understory, shrub, and herbaceous layers of the forest. In much of the woods, the non-native bush honeysuckle has taken over the shrub layer, replacing native species such as spicebush and, to some extent, even redbud. Nonetheless it is the largest wild area within the city, and its 15 miles of trails offer much good hiking.

How to Get There

The main park entrance is located on Colerain Avenue, about 2 miles west of I-75. To reach it, exit I-75 west onto I-74, then turn right onto US 27 (Colerain Avenue). The park is visible on the left as you travel up the valley toward the water reservoir. Turn left into the park, then go right on Trail Ridge Road. Just over 0.5 mile from the entrance you reach a grassy oval between the lanes of traffic—Picnic Area 20—where there is a shelter house and, to the right of the oval, a rest room. To begin hiking, park near the rest room.

The Trail

The trailhead for the Twin Bridge Trail is to the left of the rest room. On a natural surface, it enters the woods and immediately begins going downhill into the head of Cedar Ravine toward West Fork Road, staying on the right side of the creek. Soon it reaches a junction where the 1.5-mile Furnas Trail exits to the left. Make the left turn across the bridge following the Furnas Trail and continue walking with the hillside above on the left. Very shortly, the trail rises up Hawthorn Ravine and joins a trail coming down the hillside from Picnic Area 20. The Furnas Trail continues on the hillside about 15 feet below the level of the open park area. It crosses several small creeks on bridges, some of which have seen better days. The limestone is very close to the surface here. There are a number of large chinquapin oaks along this trail.

On the September day I walked the trail, white snakeroot was in bloom. This is the relative of joe-pye weed that causes the usually fatal "milk sickness" in people who drink raw milk from cows that have grazed upon it. President Lincoln's mother, Nancy Hanks Lincoln, died from milk sickness in 1818, and many Civil War soldiers on both sides succumbed to it. It was the Michigan-born biologist Edwin Lincoln Moseley—he spent his professional life as an educator in the Sandusky school system and at Bowling Green College—who early in the 20th century made the conclusive connection between white snakeroot and the deadly disease. This was nearly 100 years after Mrs. Lincoln's death. In 1941 Moseley published a summation of his research in a book titled *Milk Sickness Caused by White Snakeroot.*

Along the trail, another side path comes in from the left. A sign points to Picnic Area 21. Just beyond this point, a sinkhole is

The castle-like Mount Airy Reservoir stands at the top of the hill just west of the entrance to Mount Airy Forest, a distinguishing mark on the skyline.

visible alongside the trail. Doubtless, there are some small caverns in the limestone below. Now reaching the end of the ridge (and Trail Ridge Road), the Furnas Trail follows the hillside counterclockwise into Scotch Pine Ravine. Reservable Picnic Area 22 lies between the trail and the turnaround at the end of Trail Ridge Road.

The trail next turns right and, with a steep slope to the right, drops downhill before crossing a creek near the head of the ravine. There is a comfort station nearby on Ponderosa Ridge. Another alien plant, the widespread, obnoxious garlic mustard that covers much of the woodland in southwestern Ohio in spring, is visible in the herb layer along this part of the trail. Hackberry, another tree that does well on limy soils, is common here.

Now headed south-southwest, dropping into the ravine, the trail is lined with large limestone slabs whose surfaces are laden

with fossils. Here the Furnas Trail ends, the Ponderosa Trail (labeled B) goes to the left, and the Quarry Trail (labeled D) goes downhill to the right, clinging to the side of the hill. Take the Quarry Trail as it descends to an area where there was at one time an operating quarry. The walkway soon becomes quite wide, probably a former quarry haul road. As the trail turns gently to the left and around the hillside, it drops into V-shaped White Ash Ravine. The elevation is now around 750 feet, 100 feet below where the trail began. There may have at one time been a bridge across the stream at this point, but there is none now. Crossing on blocks of limestone is not difficult, and soon the trail heads up the valley on a 0.25-mile-long gradual climb. The streambed below is full of limestone slabs.

At another trail junction, the Quarry Trail makes a T with the Ponderosa Trail. A left turn across the creek and a right turn leads to a spur that goes out to Trail Ridge Road. The Quarry Trail ends here. To continue hiking, turn to the right onto the Ponderosa Trail. Following it carries you around the end of Stone Steps Ridge through the woods, slightly downhill from reservable Picnic Area 19 with its shelter, play field, and ball diamond. More sinkholes are visible along this trail. It was along here that I saw young deer feeding on acorns. At the southernmost point of the trail, a sign points downhill to West Fork Road and Picnic Area 26. This is the trail with the old stone steps. Ignore it and continue straight ahead on the Ponderosa Trail as it turns left to enter the Linden Ravine. There is a nice stand of papaw trees on this hillside, as well as some linden trees and one huge bur oak tree. Near the upper end of the ravine are the first beech trees I saw along the trail and a few black walnut trees. At the head of the ravine, a bridge carries the trail to the opposite slope. At both ends of the bridge are side trails that go out to the road if you want to shorten your hike.

To continue on the Ponderosa Trail, cross the bridge and turn to the right, following the white blazes. Soon the trail takes a sharp left turn around the end of Hidden Ridge and enters Red Oak Ravine. It passes through an area where recent blowdowns have opened the canopy, allowing the growth of a patch of white snakeroot. Just beyond there, I found a large concentration of small birds feeding in the understory trees and, once again, I observed a number of yearling white-tailed deer.

About 500 feet from the turn, the trail drops stair steps to a bridge and, just beyond, meets the Red Oak Trail. A turn to the left on this trail, Trail C, leads uphill to Trail Ridge Road near a service building at the oval. From there it is only a short walk across the oval to where the hike began.

III

Till Plains

12

Blendon Woods Metro Park

Total distance: 1.9–4.2 miles (3.0–6.7 km)

Hiking time: 1–3 hours

Maximum elevation: 960 feet

Vertical rise: 100 feet

Maps: USGS 7½' Series New Albany; CMPD Blendon Woods brochure

In an act of Congress passed in 1796, 4,000 square miles of what was four years later to become the state of Ohio was set aside to satisfy certain claims of the officers and soldiers of the Revolutionary War. These U.S. Military Lands, as they came to be known, included the 650-acre tract in Blendon township in northern Franklin township that is now Blendon Woods State Park. The first settlers probably arrived at about the time of statehood.

Blendon Woods was one of the first parks established in Franklin County after the park district was formed in 1945. Though trees had been removed from the area, it had never been clear-cut, and its rolling topography was interesting. Even though situated on the Wisconsinan till plains with glacial drift as the parent material of the soil, there are exposures of bedrock in the ravines running west toward Big Walnut Creek. The Devonian-age Ohio black shale and the lower-Mississippian-age Bedford shale can be seen in the streambanks; Mississippian-age Berea sandstone with ripple marks is visible in the bed of a stream near the east boundary of the park. The origin of these rocks goes back about 350 to 320 million years ago, when muds, silts, fine sands, and gravel washed into Ohio from the Canadian Shield to the north and from the high mountains to the east.

As one of largest and best woodlands remaining in central Ohio, Blendon Woods is a breeding area for many birds. More than 220 species have been sighted in the park.

Till Plains

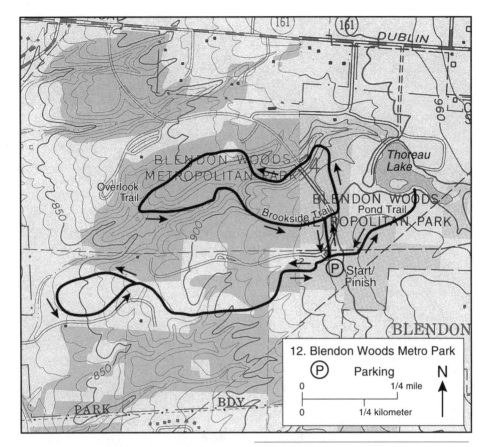

Some of those are, of course, birds of passage on their way to breeding grounds farther north, but others are year-round residents, and many are neotropical songbirds that migrate here each spring to raise a brood of young in the forest or fields before returning to Central or South America to spend the rest of the year. The park staff applies carefully considered ecological management techniques to maintain the habitat diversity needed by butterflies and other insects, amphibians, and reptiles as well as mammals and birds. Special attention is given to providing year-round habitat for aquatic birds at the 115-acre Walden Waterfowl Refuge at the east end of the park.

How to Get There

Blendon Woods, on the northeast side of Columbus, is reached by taking SR 161 east from I-71 or I-270 to the Little Turtle/Blendon Pond Drive exit. Turn south onto Dublin-Granville Road and then west to the park entrance. When the entry road reaches a T, turn left to reach the interpretive center/Walden Waterfowl Refuge parking lot.

The Trail

It is from the refuge/interpretive center parking lot that you begin your hike. There are three good walks originating there. Before you decide which one to start with, check with the naturalist on duty in the center to see if any special species of plants or animals are being seen in the park or refuge. You never know when a quick trip to an observation shelter in the refuge will yield a new bird to add to your life list. I saw my first osprey over Thoreau Lake in 1971. On a day in late October I watched a dozen wood ducks gathered at the upper end of the pond, probably preparing for migration. It was also from one of the Walden observation blinds that I saw a red-headed woodpecker ground feeding on shelled corn that had been put out for the waterfowl. On your way to and from the shelters, look for bluebirds using the nest boxes in the nearby open fields. On a number of occasions, I have been alerted to the presence of a special species of wildflower in bloom somewhere along the park's trails.

Other than the 0.6-mile walk on a paved path to and from Thoreau Pond in the refuge, you also have a choice of exploring a 2-mile unimproved trail through upland that, in season, offers the chance to see butterflies and birds of the open field or an improved (but not paved) woodland trail that follows the ridges, ravines, and streams of the park, affording the opportunity to examine the exposed bedrock. A map of the park and other important information is provided at the parking lot kiosk.

Begin the upland walk directly across the parking lot near the center, where the trail enters an area of what ecologists call old field habitat. Grasses, asters, goldenrod, Queen Anne's lace, and similar perennial forbs abound. After passing through this meadow, the trail turns left and goes through a narrow band of woods where there was once a fence line before crossing the corner of another grassy area. On sunny spring or summer days, this is a good place to observe butterflies. Rail "reminder fence" protects the bluebird habitat from human intrusion.

As the trail next heads straight west, it enters a nice example of a typical central Ohio till plain forest. Large red and white oaks, sugar and red maples, ash, shagbark hickories, and wild black cherries occur here. Soon a ravine begins to appear on the left, dropping toward Big Walnut Creek. Here there is a bench on which to rest and watch the world go by. At the right, there is a fire hydrant along the side of the trail. A large granite boulder reminds us that the Wisconsinan glacier covered this part of what is now Ohio 15,000 to 22,000 years ago.

The trail next heads northwest through younger woods, now on a crushed-rock surface. After passing another hydrant, it crosses a boulder-filled creek on a short bridge. Passing multiflora rose, white and Scotch pine plantings, and both young and mature native hardwoods, it winds its way to a road crossing. From this point, a picnic area and the Sugarbush Day Camp Area can be seen to the southwest.

Fifty yards beyond the road, where the trail splits, a sign identifies the Loop Trail as going either direction. Poverty grass, salmon colored after frost, grows here on thin soil over the Ohio black shale. It makes no difference which way you walk this loop. I choose my direction of travel on the basis of what position I want the sun in photographs I might take. The trail has a mowed grass surface here. A small thicket is being allowed to grow in the center of the meadow. With the proliferation of multiflora rose, this should be a good place to look for mockingbirds and brown thrashers.

More granite boulders are visible in the trail. With the wind coming from the west on the day I scouted the trail, I could clearly hear the rush-hour traffic on the freeways in the distance. Walking clockwise, as you near completion of the loop, the trail will pass close to many mature hardwoods, a single

Large rectangular holes chipped into tree trunks indicate the presence of pileated woodpeckers—probably searching for carpenter ants, a favorite food.

young shingle oak that will have either green or tan leaves most of the year, and a stand of young sycamores. Even though your hike will conclude using the same trail you came out on, you will see the natural world quite differently from the other direction.

Once back at the lot, you can add another 1.9 miles to your day's travel or save the other loop for another day. The trailhead for the Hickory Ridge Trail is directly north of the lot, diagnally across the road. Very soon after entering the trail you will reach a major intersection. The Overlook Trail goes left, the Hickory Ridge Trail continues straight ahead, and the Ripple Rock Trail goes right. Take the latter and head up the rise to cross the road and turn left, parallel to the high fence that surrounds the refuge. A sign discusses why hawthorn trees, a pioneer species in old fields of the area, are present in this young part of the woods. There is soon another sign, this one noting that thin soil on top of bedrock was why so many of the trees in this particular area of the woods blew down in the blizzard of 1978. The trail next swings left. Beyond a rail fence, Berea sandstone ripple rock is visible in the streambed. In the far streambank you can see the thinness of the drift (the glacier-deposited parent material out of which soil is formed) in this area. Is it any wonder that a strong wind easily toppled these trees, or that species with taproots do not grow here?

After passing a sign that explains more of the geology of the area, the trail climbs past a bench, crosses the road, and, about 75 feet into the woods, reaches another intersection. To the left is the Hickory Ridge Trail, which goes back toward the center parking lot. Straight ahead, the Overlook Trail moves west along the watercourse that has created the main ravine in the park. A sign warns of the presence of steps ahead, making the trail inaccessible to people in wheelchairs or strollers. A sign discusses the difference in the vegetation on the north-facing versus the south-facing slopes. Forty-five steps carry the trail to the valley floor. Note the use of gabions, stone-filled wire baskets, to stabilize the streambank. Now both sandstone and shale outcrop on the streambank.

After crossing the stream, the trail climbs the hill at an angle to the right. In wintertime the reservable Shadblow Picnic Area is visible through the woods on the right. A side trail connects with the Cherry Ridge program area.

Again the trail begins to drop, with a ravine on both sides. A bench beckons the weary walker. Beneath large white oak trees, another sign tells the story of how the granite boulder and, perhaps, the nearby bed of red clay arrived here with the last glacier and how the clay was used by Native Americans. Signs discuss the presence of sycamore and buckeye trees in the riparian corridor. Note, too, the sandstone slabs that have moved down the creek and arranged themselves in the streambed like roof shingles. The unusual characteristics of the black walnut, another species of this beech–maple forest, are spelled out on yet another trailside interpretive sign.

At the next trail junction, a turn left onto the Brookside Trail will begin to close the loop on this hike by taking you back up the creek valley. Here you see more exposed Ohio black shale. This is a massive formation that can better be seen in closer to its entirety near the east end of the Cheshire Road and US 36 causeways, where they cross Alum Creek Reservoir, or along the east bank of the Olentangy River from the overlook in Highbanks Metro Park.

The trail now crosses the stream twice. A sign directs attention to an oak tree with a bent trunk and explains how it got that shape and why it is not an "Indian Tree." The trail begins a slow but steady rise to a flat beech woods where once more there is a bench on which to rest. While you are walking this trail, watch for the rectangular holes chiseled by the crow-sized pileated woodpeckers in their constant search for carpenter ants and other insect "goodies." Pileateds nest in these woods and are often heard calling.

Perhaps the most important trailside interpretive sign of the hike aids in the identification of poison ivy, the nemesis of the eastern hardwood forest. If you do not know how to recognize this plant by its leaves or woody parts in winter and summer, take time now to learn. Look around for more "P.I." vines in this part of the woods.

In this flat area of the park there is an impervious layer of sandy shale near the surface of the ground through which water will not pass. The woods remain swampy nearly year-round. Most trees that can survive here have shallow roots with no taproot, making them susceptible to blowdowns. There are always fresh examples of "tipped-up" trees to be seen as you walk through here. Papaws are often an understory tree in areas of moist soil in the park.

Arriving back at the trail intersection where you earlier turned right to follow the Ripple Rock Trail, now turn right onto the Hickory Ridge Trail. The parking lot and interpretive center are just a short distnace ahead. There are rest rooms and a small volunteer-operated nature gift shop in the center. Elsewhere in the park are facilities for picnicking and other passive recreation activities. There is good hiking at Highbanks and Slate Run Metro Parks, also described in this volume. Trails at Battelle-Darby, Clear Creek, and Chestnut Ridge Metro Parks are featured in *50 Hikes in Ohio*.

13

Deer Creek State Park

Total distance: 3.5 miles (5.6 km)

Hiking time: 3 hours

Maximum elevation: 870 feet

Vertical rise: 30 feet

Maps: USGS 7½' Series Five Points; ODNR Deer Creek State Park brochure

Ohio's Darby Plain is a vast area in the west-central part of the state bounded on the north by the Powell Moraine, on the west by the Cable Moraine, on the south by the Reesville Moraine, and on the east by the increasing slope to the Scioto River. It's an area of often flat, sometime hummocky Wisconsinan-age ground moraine where poorly drained soils held prairies, oak–hickory forests, and bur oak savannas in pioneer days. When its high-lime soils were drained by ditches and tiles, it became some of the richest farmland in the state. It is drained by several large streams, including Big and Little Darby Creeks (designated state and national scenic rivers) and Deer Creek.

Though not thought of as an area of great scenic beauty, the Darby Plain has long been attractive to naturalists who seek out pockets of prairie plants in cemeteries and along railroad rights-of-way and populations of prairie creatures such as badgers and short-eared owls and other birds of prey in meadows. Before settlers reached the area in the 18th century, Native Americans are known to have lived nearby in the Scioto River bottoms and to have hunted extensively on the Darby Plain. There is at least one written account of the use of grass fire to drive game, including the great cloven-hoofed animal of the American plains, the bison. The greater prairie chicken, another prairie animal now extirpated from Ohio, was also at home on the Darby Plain. Present, too, were the badger and its frequent prey, the 13-lined ground squirrel, both still found in limited numbers in some areas of western Ohio.

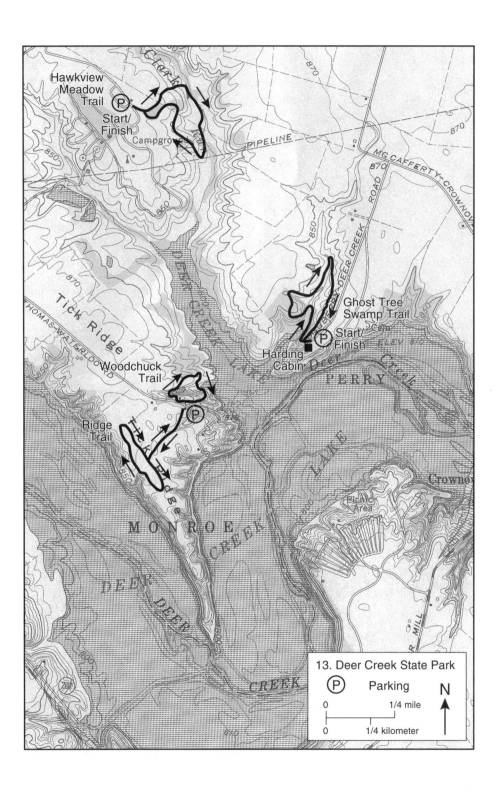

Hawkview
Meadow
Trail
℗
Start/
Finish
Campgro

PIPELINE

MG CAFFERTY-CROWNOV

870

870

870

850

850

850

Tick Ridge

HOMAS-WATERLOO RD

Woodchuck
Trail

Ridge
Trail

Ghost Tree
Swamp Trail
℗ Start/
Finish

Harding
Cabin

PERRY

850

℗

MONROE

DEER

CREEK

CREEK

CREEK

850

950

Crownov

Picnic
Area

R MILL

207

13. Deer Creek State Park

℗ Parking

N

0   1/4 mile

0   1/4 kilometer

Deer Creek originates on the east slope of the Cable Moraine near the intersection of Champaign, Clark, and Madison Counties and flows southeast to join the Scioto River east of Yellowbud just inside Ross County. En route, it cuts through the London and Bloomingburg Moraines, but nowhere does it create any spectacular gorges such as those of the Little Miami River to the west. In western Pickaway County, where the creek makes a wide meander, the U.S. Army Corps of Engineers completed construction of 1,277-acre Deer Creek Lake in 1968 as part of the flood-protection plan for the Scioto and Ohio River basins. In 1973 the Ohio Department of Natural Resources opened the area to the public as Deer Creek State Park, a major recreation area with a campground, vacation cabins, a resort-type lodge, a swimming beach, a golf course, and riding, boating, and picnicking facilities. More than 8 miles of foot trails have been established, providing great hiking opportunities for long-term or day visitors to the park.

How to Get There

Deer Creek State Park is located about 30 miles southwest of Columbus astride the Pickaway/Fayette County line, about 6 miles south of the Madison County community of Mount Sterling. From either Columbus or Cincinnati, travel I-71 to exit 84 (London/ Mount Sterling). Follow SR 56 east for 4 miles to Mount Sterling. Go to the second traffic light and turn right on Columbus Street (SR 3). Follow it south for one block to a fork where there is a BP station. There, turn left on SR 207 and follow it for approximately 4 miles. Turn left onto Cook-Yankeetown Road and follow it to the park entrance on the right side of the road. It is 3 miles to the park resort lodge at the end of the road. The park office, open during normal business hours, is located just inside the park on the right side of the road.

The Trails

Two of the trails start from the lodge parking lot, located about 3 miles within the park. On the west (right) side of the lot, a sign announces the 1.5-mile Ridge Trail. If you are from a hillier part of the state, you may get a chuckle out of this name, but for decades the low ridge east of Deer Creek just west of here has been known as Tick Ridge, and the name still shows on the USGS map. That name is not used on the trail for the obvious reason that it would likely scare away the casual park visitor. But most seasoned hikers know that ticks are present in much of Ohio during the warm part of the year, and they are prepared to deal with them.

Park by the trailhead sign and begin hiking by following the mowed path to the west, across the cabin area entry road and along the north edge of the ball field area. There the trail enters young woods on a low ridge and winds its way west toward the lake. Along the way it passes a wildlife observation blind where bird feeders and salt attract birds and deer. Winding its way south along the slope to the lake, the trail passes red cedar trees, chinquapin oaks, hackberry trees, and the alien bush honeysuckle, which indicate that limestone bedrock is not far below the surface. But the presence of granite boulders reminds you that 15,000 years ago the glacial ice, with its load of rocks, grit, and boulders from the Canadian Shield, covered this land.

On the upland, slowly disappearing plow furrows under the young trees tell of crop fields that were here half a century ago. Along the hillside where cattle once grazed are 150-year-old oaks among the young ones, tree that somehow got spared when the land was cleared. In the gullies on the slopes to the lake are piles of rocks, hauled off the upland so farmers wouldn't break the blade of the steel moldboard plows used to till the land.

The Ridge Trail travels south on the narrowing ridge that protrudes between the loops of the river's meander. Then it turns on itself to return to a spot where, with a right turn, you can return to the trailhead. It's not a deep-woods trail or one through deep ravine gorges, but its late-summer flowers attract monarchs and milkweed beetles; an occasional red-tailed hawk makes a scream overhead that gives the rabbits hidden in the grass a bit of a fright.

Back at the lodge parking lot, find the entrance sign for the 1-mile Woodchuck Trail about 100 feet to the east of the Ridge Trail sign. It is to the left of the tennis courts. The entrance to the Rolling Hills Trail is also located here. That trail is 2.5 miles one way and leads to the campground. It is intended primarily for those who want to commute between the lodge and the campground by foot.

The Woodchuck Trail leaves the parking area by dropping precipitously to a footbridge across a deeply cut stream. Note the dark, deep loamy prairie soil and the presence of more glacial erratics in the creek. Beyond the bridge, the trail heads north then turns east to make a loop around to the sides of a small pond. Until 2000 this was a "fitness trail" with exercise stations; you can see places where those stations were removed in its conversion to a nature trail. The trail turns left and leaves the pond through thicket and young woods. I did not discover any woodchucks (also known as groundhogs) or woodchuck holes along the trail, but I have no doubt they are there and that the early-morning or evening hiker will see them calmly munching grass near the pond.

The glacial drift of western Ohio makes for easy digging by these common creatures of woods and field.

Now the trail winds its way around the upper end of several ravines that lead to the lake, passing within sight of the lakeshore before turning to the west to cross the earthen dam of the pond. Soon a turn to the left leads to a crossing with the Rolling Hills Trail. To the right leads to the parking lot; left, to the campground. The red blazes of the Woodchuck Trail lead straight ahead, carrying you downslope toward the lake. Before getting to the shore, however, the trail makes a 180-degree swing to the right to return to yet another corner of the lodge parking lot. It is a short walk to where you are probably parked. Rest rooms, a gift shop, and food facilities are at hand in the lodge for your comfort and enjoyment.

There is more to explore at Deer Creek. Next drive to the campground and park in the visitors lot outside the welcome station. From there, walk past the office on the park drive; across the road to the left is the entrance to the 1-mile-long Hawkview Trail. After crossing the dip between road and sign, head straight ahead, following the yellow arrow on a post inside the woods and blazes on the trees. Very soon the trail angles to the right and travels down a ravine to an open field area perhaps 2 acres in size. It follows the outside of the field alongside a stream traveling in a clockwise manner. Two butterfly boxes stand in the field. Don't expect to see butterflies hovering about them. They may have been used by some of the angle-wing butterflies such as the comma or mourning cloak that overwinter as adults—but I seriously doubt it. Such boxes are really intended for yard and garden, where there are no natural spaces such as hollow trees and loose bark for use as insect hibernating sites. I have never seen such boxes used; nor has anyone with whom I have ever discussed it.

The trail reenters the woods alongside a creek. At one point, two steps provide access to explore the stream. Still in the woods, the trail next climbs the hillside, switching back to take the slope more comfortably. Soon it travels on the hillside back toward the slope at the upper end of the meadow. A bench provides rest for the hiker. It is from this point that a red-tailed hawk has often been seen in the meadow below. Red cedars, thicket, and young hardwoods stand on the hillside above. Pass the entrance to a trail to the left; it would take you to the amphitheater near the nature center. Now heading at an angle downhill, the trail passes a grove of young shingle oak trees. When I hiked the trail in late March, the leaves from the previous season still hung on these trees. Moving on down the hillside, the trail soon crosses a short bridge before entering the more mature woodland that fills the ravine. Back among larger trees, it turns uphill past shagbark hickory and white oak trees on a ridge between two ravines. Now on high ground, the trail leaves the mature trees toward the nature center. A side trail to the right leads to a program site at the creek.

The main trail heads through the thicket and splits once again, with the yellow-blazed Hawkview Trail continuing to the right, winding past nice shagbark hickory trees. Shortly it joins the inbound trail at what looks like a twin-trunked tree but is actually a hickory and an oak growing very close together. On the side of the oak away from the trailhead is an owl box not visible when you are entering the woods. Back at the campground road now, it is a short walk past the welcome station to the parking lot. At the time I hiked this trail there were a number of well-written but unfortunately vandalized interpretive signs along this trail. I was told by park personnel that they are to be removed because of the difficulty in maintaining them. This trail requires about 45 minutes to walk.

The last trail to walk at Deer Creek is connected with a bit of history from the early 20th century. In 1918 Harry M. Daugherty, later the attorney general under Ohio-born president Warren G. Harding, built a one-and-a-half-story cabin on land overlooking Deer Creek now within the park. President Harding is said to have visited this cabin, which now bears his name. It has been restored and can be rented by parkgoers.

The 1-mile Ghost Tree Swamp Trail is located near the Harding Cabin. It originates in the center of the north side of the large parking lot there. A sign to the right in the woods announces ROAD CLOSED AHEAD. This trail is also blazed with yellow paint marks. It begins by dropping to the old bed of Longberry-Deercreek Road, which has been abandoned for many years. From there it drops steeply to the left and downhill toward a small embayment of the lake made by the flooding of the mouth of a Deer Creek tributary. Close to the lake's edge, the trail turns right, rises to move upstream through woodlands, then returns to the water's edge.

When I walked this trail the lake was down several feet, having been drained to make room for expected late-winter rains. Dozens of granite boulders and large areas of glacial gravel were visible on the muddy lake bottom. As the trail moves closer to the lake's edge, it crosses a side stream on a 10-foot-high bridge. Beyond, it again climbs the hillside, with red cedar being overtopped by native hardwoods on the uphill side and a stand of 25-year-old red pine along the trail ahead.

The trail next crosses the stream on a bridge at the upper end of the embayment before passing between two very thorny

This massive glacial erratic lies deep in the woods on the Ghost Tree Trail.

honey locust trees as it turns downstream along the hillside. Notice the tree covered with holes made by a yellow-bellied sapsucker on the left side of this hill-hugging trail. Now curving to the right and climbing the hillside, the trail makes a 180-degree turn and enters a nice mixed-oak woods, heading northwest. In the middle of this woods, look for a bench at about the spot where the trail arcs right to move toward the ravine it just left. Turning left now along a creek cut in very deep glacial drift, the trail moves upstream until, at a severe meander, it drops off the high ground to cross the small waterway then climb the opposite bank. Glacial erratics protrude from the soil in the strreambank.

Now the trail turns back toward the lake with an old field on the left and red pines alongside. Dropping into the head of an-

other ravine, the trail arrives at what must be the Ghost Tree. A huge old oak hugs one of the largest granite glacial erratics I have seen in Ohio. It was worth a picture taken from a camera carefully balanced on my hiking stick/monopod jammed into the soil.

From here the trail makes its way back to the trailhead, remaining mostly on the high ground along the edge of the wooded ravine. The vegetation is a combination of old field, thicket, pine plantings, and native hardwood. The park and the lodge are almost 3 miles from the entrance.

The Harding Cabin is reached by going farther east from the park entrance on Dawson-Yankeetown Road to Deer Creek Road. Turn right, then—after making a sharp left—turn right again onto a dead-end park road that leads to the cabin parking lot and a boat-launch area.

14

Fowler Woods
State Nature Preserve

*Total distance: 1.3-mile (1.73 km)
accessible boardwalk*

Hiking time: 1 hour

Maximum elevation 1,190 feet

Vertical rise: 20 feet

*Maps: USGS 7½' Series Olivesburg;
ONDR Fowler Woods
State Nature Preserve brochure*

One of the most popular nature preserves in Ohio for viewing spring wildflowers is Fowler Woods, situated in northeastern Richland County, 10 miles north of Olivesburg on the west side of the Olivesburg-Fitchville Road. This 133-acre tract includes about 50 acres of old-growth forest, with the remainder rapidly returning to forest. What makes it especially good for spring woodland wildflowers is the diversity of habitat within the forest. The higher sites are beech–maple woods; in the wetter situations red maple–ash swamp forest dominates; and where standing water remains throughout most of the year, there is buttonbush swamp. Apparently the old-growth woods have never seen the ax, and they don't appear to have been grazed.

Fowler Woods is in the Galion Glaciated Low Plateau physiographic region, a transitional area of gently rolling hills between the till plains to the west and the Glaciated Allegheny Plateau to the east. Deep beneath many feet of late-Wisconsinan-age drift lies Mississippian-age sandstone. At the surface the ground moraine is a very gently rolling silty clay till; there is also an east–west hummocky low-end moraine with clayey till, which is very poorly drained. The woods are located on the divide between streams that drain to Lake Erie through the Vermilion River and those draining to the Ohio River via the Mohican/Muskingum River.

This part of Ohio was congressional land, sold to settlers at a government land office. The settlers were, for most part, of Scottish and Irish descent, arriving from the

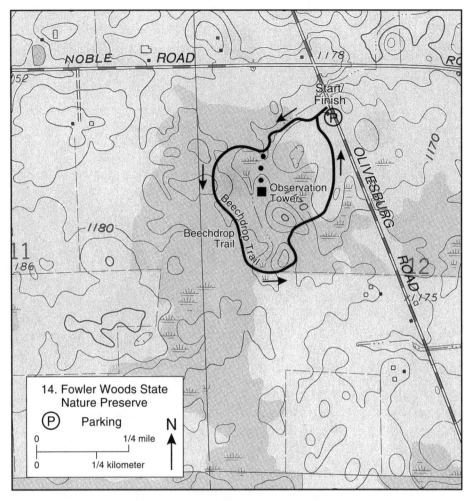

14. Fowler Woods State
Nature Preserve

Ⓟ   Parking   N

Middle Atlantic coastal area. In 1832 the section of land that includes what is now Fowler Woods State Nature Preserve was purchased from the U.S. government by John Dobbin. He probably had to go to Bucyrus to file his claim, as the there were no closer land offices. Prior to 1832, congressional land in Ohio had to be purchased in a block of at least 640 acres at a minimum of $2 per acre. It did not sell well, and land offices were closed down. In 1832 the minimum size was reduced to 40 acres, the price was lowered to a minimum of $1.25 per acre, and a land office opened at Bucyrus.

After changing hands several times, the land that now includes the preserve was purchased by Chester and Hettie Fowler in 1917; they resided on the farm until 1970. The Fowlers loved and protected the woods. After their passing, their heirs respected the Fowlers' love of woods and resisted attractive offers from timber buyers. In 1970 Ohio service forester Jack Basinger inspected the woods at the request of the Fowler family. He was so impressed that in

1971 he contacted the newly created Division of Natural Areas and Preserves. Based on his recommendations, the division purchased it as one of Ohio's first state nature preserves.

The spring floral display gets under way in April, when the wetter portions of the woods are blanketed with a golden display of marsh marigold. The remainder of the forest floor springs to life shortly thereafter with wildflowers in bloom continuously through late May. The blooming of wildflowers is accompanied by the arrival in the woods of vireos, warblers, and other neotropical migrants, many remaining there to raise young. Frogs, toads, and salamanders reappear as the temperatures rise and the days lengthen. Even an occasional harmless snake can be seen in the preserve.

How to Get There

Reach Fowler Woods by taking I-71 to the Ashland exit, US 250, then traveling west into Ashland on US 250 and taking SR 98 west to Olivesburg and Olivesburg-Fitchville Road. It goes north from SR 96 just to the west of the SR 546 intersection. Be on the lookout for slow-moving Amish horse-drawn carriages and children on bicycles on the road in this area.

The Trail

Travel in Fowler Woods is via a 1.3-mile-long handicapped-accessible boardwalk. Signs along the self-guided trail point out some of the natural history highlights. Benches are provided at frequent intervals to encourage study and contemplation while hiking in the preserve.

Shortly after you head out from the parking lot in the young woods at the front of the preserve, you'll spot a bulletin board, and the trail splits to become a loop. Heading right takes you very quickly into the more mature woods. The trail soon crosses a small stream. This is the area of the best display of marsh marigolds in early spring. The trail begins to rise gently and soon reaches a juncture where a short side trail to the left leads to an observation tower overlooking a buttonbush swamp. If amphibians are singing when you reach this point, they likely will stop as you approach the tower. When you get to the tower, stop talking and stand quietly and they will begin calling once more: A single frog at first, then a few more will join, and then the entire population will set up a cacophonic chorus.

Back on the main trail you will notice an occasional small pit with a low mound of earth alongside it, usually on the east side. These are places where a tree blew over, tilting up a rootball with soil. After the trunk and roots rotted and returned to the earth, the pit and dirt pile remained, creating breeding places for amphibians and insects.

The trail continues in a counterclockwise manner, circumnavigating the preserve. As the trail rises in elevation, beech and maple trees are joined by oaks. In a swampy spot along the west boundary of the preserve there is a nice stand of pumpkin ash, an uncommon swamp forest species. After reaching higher land at the farthest point from the parking lot, the trail slowly drops to where the swamp can be seen on the left. At a point where a hill lies directly ahead, the trail turns left to begin its return to the parking lot. Look for the place where it passes through a former fencerow. It is easy to spot because of the granite boulders piled to the right of the trail. These glacial erratics, hunks of the bedrock of the Canadian Shield that were carried into Ohio by the Wisconsinan glacier around 15,000 years ago, had to be cleared from the former field beyond this fence line before it

Massive beds of marsh-marigold are a spectacular sight along the trails.

could be cultivated. It was usually the chore of the boys in the family following plowing to hitch up a draft horse to a stone boat (a large, flat wooden sled) and walk the fields, gathering rocks that had been turned up by plowing. These were usually taken to a fencerow or ravine and dumped.

Where the farm field once was, young hardwoods are now reaching for the sky. Among them are tuliptrees, the tall magnolia family tree of Ohio's mixed-mesophytic forests. For the first few years of ownership by the Division of Natural Areas and Preserves, this area was mowed. Since the intention was to preserve the spot as a mixed-hardwood forest, it was decided to let the fields return to woods through natural secondary succession. You can observe all levels of this process in this part of the woods. In recent years biologists have come to realize that the larger a tract of unfragmented forest is, the greater its utilization for nesting by the neotropical birds. Because of the hazards of nesting near edges—where you're more likely to find predatory mammals such as raccoons, and birds such as jays, crows, and the parasitic cowbird—birds from South and Central America seldom nest closer than 100 yards from the forest edge. Remember, take away only photographs and memories and leave the beautiful wildflowers for those who follow to also enjoy.

Depending upon how much time you spend taking pictures, watching birds, or just enjoying the ambience of the mature woods, you should be back at the parking lot inside of an hour. A right turn will take you to Olivesburg, where the ice cream cones served at the country store are the main attraction. I seldom pass up mint chocolate chip.

15

Gahanna Woods Park and State Nature Preserve

Total distance: 1 mile (1.6 km)

Hiking time: 45 minutes

Maximum elevation: 905 feet

Vertical rise: 12 feet

Maps: USGS 7½' Series New Albany; ODNR Gahanna Woods State Nature Preserve brochure

On a cool, blue-sky March 22 morning, I went to Gahanna Woods to see if, as the calendar indicated, spring had returned. It was still a black-, gray-, and straw-colored world, but the vernal equinox was behind so spring must be making an appearance somewhere, or so I reasoned. As I sloshed along a wet path on last year's fallen leaves, I caught a glimpse of something in the air close by. Then there it was, a mourning cloak butterfly, perched on a twig not 3 feet in front of me, having just flown in from my right. Slowly it moved its wings from flat to a sun-catching angle, the better to warm its thorax and wing muscles. I whipped out my new point-and-shoot camera and clicked off a photo from where I was standing, just in case the Camberwell beauty—as the British call this butterfly—took off before I could get to the minimum focusing distance my camera would allow. Then slowly I moved in. Click went the P&S and away went the butterfly, on down the trail. If I saw nothing else that morning, my day was made.

As an airliner made its noisy approach to nearby Port Columbus, a beautiful orange-and-brown comma butterfly made an appearance on the trail ahead of me. More skittish than the mourning cloak, it did not sit for a portrait. Both of these species overwinter as adults, hidden in a tree cavity or under bark waiting for just such a morning.

Once inside the woods, spring made itself known through another sense. Even as an emergency vehicle sirened its way along a nearby road, the sound of male western chorus frogs calling from the buttonbush

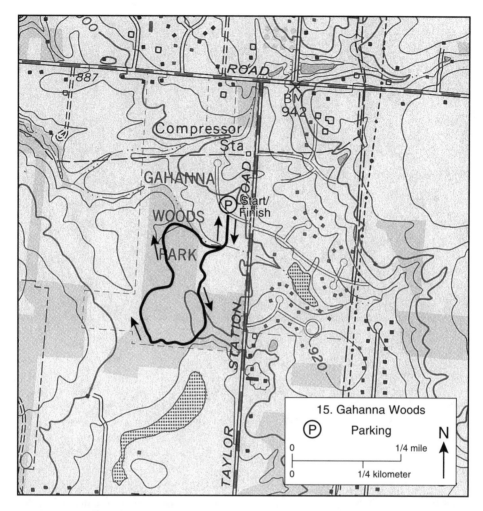

15. Gahanna Woods
Ⓟ   Parking   N

0   1/4 mile

0   1/4 kilometer

swamp was overwhelming. I walked as slowly and silently as my old legs will allow, moving to the point where the boardwalk crossed the neck of the hourglass-shaped pond. Dozens of the impossible-to-see 1 ¼-inch-long amphibians kept right on making their finger-on-the-teeth-of-a-comb song. To a female chorus frog, that translates into something like "aren't I the strongest, hand-somest, sexiest frog in the pond, won't you come mate with me?" In the pond to my right I heard a single spring peeper making its bird-chirp-like call with the same

intended message for the females of his kind. Indeed! Spring had arrived in central Ohio. All the skunk cabbage, chickadees, cardinals, or even pileated woodpeckers of that morning could not top the frog chorus that had greeted me.

Farther along on the woodland trail, my presence forced a pair of geese to move from land to water and a pair of wood ducks to take flight. A year or two earlier, on a sim-ilar spring "swamp stomp," I had spotted a great horned owl in a still-leafless tree about 100 feet off the trail. At this time of year,

In spring this pond in Gahanna Woods comes alive with chorus frogs and spring peepers.

with about the only leaves on any tree being those rattly yellow ones still hanging on the young understory beech trees, it is still easy to see anything that wings its way through the woods. In the warm days of May come the warblers, vireos, orioles, and tanagers—but with them the new foliage that makes it a challenge to sight them.

Gahanna Woods was one of the earliest aquisitions of the Division of Natural Areas and Preserves. A 50.77-acre tract acquired in cooperation with The Nature Conservancy was dedicated in 1973. The city of Gahanna, which owns adjacent land, dedicated an additional 3.126 acres in 1992. It is managed by the Gahanna Park and Recreation Department as Gahana Woods Park and State Nature Preserve.

Located on the eastern edge of what is called the Columbus Lowland district of the interior plains, this is land reshaped by the glaciers. The presence of large granitic boulders, the hummocky land with shallow

water-filled depressions, and the deep loamy soils visible at the stream crossing tell the story. The Wisconsinan glacier covered this part of Ohio as recently as 16,000 years ago, and the shape of the land is a result of its scraping over the countryside as it advanced then depositing the material as it melted. This area features the confluence of ground moraine, lateral moraine, and outwash. Beech–maple forest grows on the drier sites in the woods, with swamp forest containing such species as pin oak, swamp white oak, and silver maple in the low wet area. One pond contains a good stand of buttonbush. Outside the woods, an old field is overgrown with weedy shrub species such as privet and multiflora rose in some places; in others, native hardwoods are beginning to take over.

The well-developed natural-surface and boardwalk trail system offers a mile of hiking. Spring is an especially rewarding time to explore the area, but fall and winter offer a new look at raw nature. Mosquitoes are always part of the food chain of wetlands, so be adequately prepared during the warm months.

How to Get There

From Columbus, take I-670 east. Beyond I-270, it turns into US 62 east, taking you into the center of Gahanna. Go straight ahead, leaving US 62, which turns left. When you leave the city, you will be on Havens Corners Road. About 1.5 miles east of the center of town you will come to Taylor Station Road. Turn right. The park/preserve is on the right just beyond the water tower.

The Trail

The entrance to the trail system is directly south of the parking lot, to the right of the playgound equipment, where there is a bulletin board. Cross the bridge toward the ODNR sign, turn right, then turn left to begin hiking. The state guidebook describes this as field, but it is now thicket fast becoming young woodland. The grassy trail can be wet in spring as the snow is melting away. After about 600 feet, the trail enters the woods, where it is generally better drained. The total relief of the preserve is not more than about 12 feet, but that makes a great deal of difference in the vegetation. There is a pond to the left of the trail just as you enter the woods. At a junction with the Woodland Pond Trail, keep going straight ahead on the Beechwoods Trail. It rises into the higher part of the woods almost to the southern boundary before swinging north, then east toward the other area of ponds. A boardwalk keeps you dry as you move across the narrow neck between ponds. To the east is the stand of buttonbush. Watch for wood ducks in any of the ponds. They are tree nesters whose precocious young readily skydive when it's time to leave home.

At the next junction, turn left and follow the Woodland Ponds Trail across the boardwalk, past a bench toward the other end of the woods. A large pond lies to the west.

Before reaching the creek, the trail swings to the right to exit the woods and travel through thicket to the entry area. Close to where it leaves the woods, it passes a pile of rock rubble—perhaps the remains of the fireplace of an early cabin?

If you live or work on the east side of Columbus, Gahanna Woods is a nice place to spend an hour, stretching your legs while taking in the sights and sounds of the natural world. Put it on your list of those places to visit each season of the year.

16

Green Lawn Cemetery and Arboretum

Total distance: 3.75 miles (6 km)

Hiking time: 2½ hours

Maximum elevation: 735 feet

Vertical rise: 25 feet

Maps: USGS 7½' Series Southwest Columbus; Green Lawn Cemetery & Arboretum map

The National Geographic Society lists it in its *Guide to Bird Watching Sites.* Birders have identified somewhere around 200 different species there. It's the location of seven state champion trees and many more outstanding specimens of native and exotic trees and shrubs. Founded in 1848, it is the final resting place for more than 145,000 of central Ohio's captains of industry and captains of war, poets and peasants, entertainers and entrepreneurs, founders and philanthropists, scientists and sorcerers; people rich and poor from all walks of life. Originally 83 acres in size, it now covers 360-plus acres.

Located in the Columbus Lowland region of Ohio's till plain, Green Lawn Cemetery lies along the western margin of Wisconsinan-age valley outwash deposited in the southern part of what is now Columbus between 15,000 and 14,000 years ago when the last ice sheet was melting. For more than a century sand and gravel have been commercially removed from land close by, and similar material likely lies close to the surface in the nearly level eastern part of the cemetery. The base of the hill and the higher ground in the cemetery appear to contain larger-sized glacial gravel—baseball- to softball-sized well-rounded pieces of limestone and granitic material—along with the usual larger glacial erratics.

My introduction to the natural qualities of Green Lawn came in the spring of 1947 with the late Donald Borror's ornithology class field trips. As April turned into May, birds from warblers to warbling vireos,

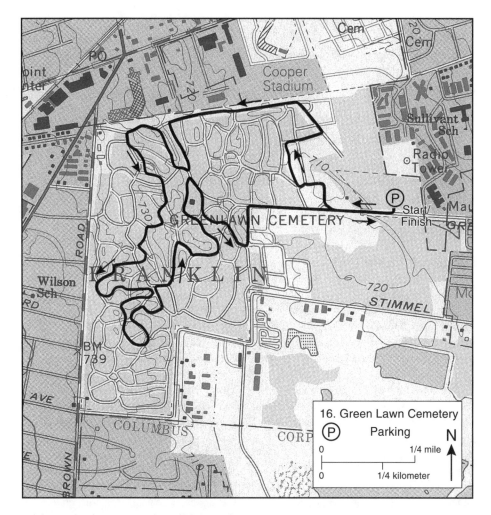

16. Green Lawn Cemetery

P Parking　　　N

0　　　　　　　1/4 mile

0　　　　　　　1/4 kilometer

orioles to owls, appeared as if by magic each Saturday morning in the trees and shrubs of the cemetery. It has continued to be an oasis for weary-winged travelers of the Scioto River corridor as they hie their way north toward the wilderness nesting areas of Canada and beyond.

As for the trees and shrubs, I spent nearly a week roaming what is now called Green Lawn Cemetery and Arboretum in preparation for writing this chapter, and I was continually bedazzled by the size and beauty of what I saw. Early records suggest that this area was on the border between beech and maple forests and, on the higher sites, mixed-oak forest. Even with the many ornamental trees from around the world that have been planted at Green Lawn, you can still feel the presence of those early woodlands. Watch for 4-inch by 4-inch posts with slanted tops next to trees. Those with green plastic labels identify specimens of unusual trees or unusually good specimens of usual trees. Gold labels identify state champion trees of a particular species, either native or non-native. There are too many to insert into this text or locate on the map, so keep your eye peeled for them as you explore.

Perhaps wandering through a graveyard isn't your idea of excitement, but I find it peaceful and educational. I learned a great deal about the history of Columbus and Ohio by reading the tombstones and monuments. And I would be remiss if I did not add that I was able to pay my personal, private respects to those I did not know but whom I know helped our great community grow and prosper, as well as to colleagues, mentors, acquaintances, relatives, ancestors, and many dear friends and family members who are among the 145,000 lying beneath the sod in this restful setting.

How to Get There

The entrance to Green Lawn is at the end of Green Lawn Avenue, 0.75 mile west of I-71. The Green Lawn Avenue exit from the interstate is the first one on I-71 south of its separation from I-70 on the west side of the Scioto River 70/71 bridge. It can also be reached by traveling south of SR 315 to where it joins I-71; again, take the first exit to the right past that point. The cemetery gates are open seven days a week, November through April 7 AM to 5 PM; May through October 7 AM to 7 PM. The management encourages passive recreation activities such as walking and birding in the cemetery. They do request that you show respect for the interred by not walking directly on graves and, of course, by leaving no litter. If you park at places other than the lots, they ask that you keep all wheels of your vehicle on the pavement in order not to destroy the turf.

Park in the lot on the west side of the office, which is located on the right side of the road just inside the cemetery. Before you leave the lot, check the trees on each front corner of the building to get an idea of what the label posts look like. A large thornless honey locust is on the west corner; a lovely small sweet bay magnolia was in full bloom on the east corner when I was there on D-Day (June 6), 2001.

There are approximately 25 miles of roads in Green Lawn Cemetery. The main thoroughfares are marked with centerlines of red, white, or yellow. The 3.75-mile walk suggested here avoids these roads as much as possible and, instead, uses the less traveled tracks. It may, at times, seem circuitous, but it is designed to take you past special points of interest and through interesting habitat.

The Trail

Walk west from the parking lot and turn right at the first opportunity. At the next corner, where the road swings west, to the left in the distance is a sign interpreting a butterfly and hummingbird garden established there by the Columbus Audubon Society in 1996. Both native and exotic plants attractive to larval and adult butterflies and to hummingbirds have been planted there. You will recognize butterfly bushes (provided by Wild Birds Unlimited), purple coneflower, prairie gay-feather, and many other nectar-producing perennials. Notice, too, the beautiful specimen shingle oak tree growing in an unmowed area just north and west of the garden.

West from this point you will see the mass graves of those who fought and died in World War II. Pass the road to the right and walk to the Section 104 sign (looking like a street sign). Turn right at that point and walk north past the anti-tank weapons and flagpole. From here you can see the skyline of downtown Columbus to the northeast. Walk clear to the road beyond the rows of government-issue grave markers, then turn right.

Follow the road to the east as far as it goes. In Section 105 on the right side of the road are the graves of veterans of more recent conflicts. Markers are of bronze and lie flush with the earth for easier maintenance. There are always more decorations on this section than any other. The heroes are leaving widows and children. There were three freshly dug graves awaiting interments on my last visit. Yes, old men still send young men off to war.

A turn to the north affords a full view beyond the cemetery fence of Cooper Stadium, the home of the Columbus Clippers. Not many remember it as Jet Stadium when the local teams carried that name because of the city's pride in the air force jets that North American Aviation build on the eastern edge of the city. Fewer still remember it as Redbird Stadium, named for the St. Louis Cardinals triple-A farm club that played there when I was a lad. With 25 cents in my pocket, I could spend two nickels to ride the streetcar to and from the stadium. It took a dime to get in if I remembered to carry my "Knot-hole Gang Card." With the other nickel, I could buy a Vernor's Ginger Ale or hot dog. That was 15 cents more than the Saturday matinee at the movie theater, but a whole lot more entertaining.

As you near the fence, make the sweeping turn to the left. To the right are single burial plots. Don't fret that there is little shade here. Soon you will be walking entirely beneath towering trees.

As you walk west, notice several tall ginkgo trees with distinctive fan-shaped leaves in Section 106 on the left of the road. This is the single surviving species of a coniferous plant family, the Ginkgoaceae. It represents an ancient line that is unlike any other living conifer. Though native to southeastern China, it has been widely planted as an ornamental in North America.

It's a dioecious tree—there are both male and female plants. The females bear a yellow to orange fruit, circular or globular, with a thick fleshy layer surrounding the seed. When these fruits ripen in autumn, they fall and split, giving off a strong unpleasant odor that some call putrid, so few females are deliberately planted. In recent years ginkgo has gained notoriety as an herbal medicine. There is also an especially tall, straight sycamore to the right as you near the end of Section 106.

At the end of Section 107 beneath huge native hardwoods stands a caretaker's building from earlier years. Jog slightly to the right here and continue walking west, against the one-way designation. As you move uphill, you enter an older part of the cemetery. The road drops again and under tall maple trees continues west. After passing Sections S and Q, where the road once again begins to rise, turn left toward the Green Lawn Garden Mausoleum. Just beyond this hillside structure is an Ohio historical marker discussing Civil War veteran Ovid Smith, who earned a Congressional Medal of Honor by being with the Union outfit that captured "the General," a Confederate locomotive. He had enlisted under an assumed name at the age of 16. He died of pneumonia at 22 and is buried here. Until 1985 he was the only one of the 24 raiders whose whereabouts were unknown by historians.

A few steps beyond this sign, if you look to the left and slightly to the rear, you can see in the distance what is considered one of the more distinctive monuments, the Reese woman and child. Now continue south with Section Q on the right. At the white-striped road, turn right, uphill, and cross the road to immediately turn left. On the left is a large monument honoring Lyne Starling, one of Columbus's pioneers, who with a gift of $35,000 founded the hospital that grew into the Ohio State University Medical Center.

Just beyond the Starling monument are those of the Sullivant family. Lucas Sullivant, a surveyor born in Mecklenburg, Virginia, laid out the village of Franklinton (later incorporated into Columbus) on the west bank of the Scioto in 1797. It was the first settlement in the area. With statehood and the establishment of Franklin County in 1803, it became the county seat and remained so until 1824, when it was moved to Columbus, on the opposite bank of the river. Lucas's son, William Starling Sullivant, whose monument lies to the south along with tombstones of members of his family, was a prominent Ohio botanist. The saxifrage family plant sullivantia *(Sullivantia sulivantii)* was named for him by John Torrey and Asa Gray from a specimen collected in Highland County around 1840. For interesting reading about the life and times of the younger Sullivant, see *Frontier Botany: William Starling Sullivant's Flowering-Plant Botany of Ohio (1830–1850)* by Stuckey and Roberts. Many other members of the family were also involved in scientific pursuits.

On your hike, I suggest you now turn about and walk north, crossing the road with the white line where you will have Section C on the right. Almost immediately you will pass the dark stone monument to W. B. Hubbard and his family, all with matching headstones in rows facing one another. Hubbard was the founder and first president of the board of the nonprofit Green Lawn Cemetery Corporation. In the distance in this section is a monument with a sleeping child figure and the inscription LITTLE IDA. Directly behind the Garden Mausoleum is a monument to Nathan Goodale, an officer in the Revolutionary

War, that tells a story of migration to Ohio, then capture by Indians and death. Alongside is the monument to his brother, Dr. Lincoln Goodale, who at the time of his death was thought to be the oldest Ohioan. The Goodale name still lives in Columbus through the north-side park bearing the name.

Continuing north, you soon pass beneath the deep shade of a state champion native black maple tree. About 50 feet to the left stands the state champion Douglas fir tree, a native of the American West. At the end of Section C stands a large American beech tree and, behind it, a ginkgo with the Lazell family stone grouped around an open book.

As you turn west at the road, a large monument to the right commemorates prominent Worthington citizen Orange Johnson, whose home is now a museum. As you walk west, the original gate to the cemetery, off Brown Road, lies in the distance. The oldest graves in the cemetery are between here and the gate on the right side of the road. As I explored along here, I discovered gravestones with my family name that will prompt me to do more genealogy research.

In the middle of Section A, at the Deering tombstones, turn left and head south, following the white-lined road for a short distance to where it turns left. There go straight ahead on an old gravel road. At the base of the hillside to the left are several beautiful white oak trees. To the right in Section X, facing the next road to the right, is the well-known statue of five-year-old George Blount that is often adorned with a new cap and scarf during the winter months.

Walk past Sections F and H, then turn left with H still on your left, Section I on the right. There is striking specimen chinquapin oak on the left. Follow the curve to the right with Sections I and K on the right. As you do so you will pass the final resting place of P. W. Huntington, the founder of the bank that bears his name, and the Neil family monument. At the neoclassical-style statue to Gustavus Swan, turn right, with Section K on your right and N on the left. Follow the road alongside Section N, now heading south. In the woods to the left is an obelisk marking the grave of former governor Alfred Kelley, considered by many the Father of the Ohio Canal System.

Directly ahead is an unnumbered area of Civil War graves arranged in concentric circles. Walk clockwise around this section, noting that many markers on the far side are of unknown soldiers. Many families from the border state of Kentucky pitted brothers against brothers in the tragic conflict. Behind the plot and mausoleum of the Lazarus family, the founders of the Lazarus Department Stores, stands the state champion Oriental spruce tree. This species has the shortest needles of all the spruces.

Leave the Civil War circle on the grass lane just east of the Lazarus mausoleum, heading due west. When you reach the yellow-lined road, turn left, then immediately turn right to pass between Sections 36 and 37. Walk straight on across the next intersection until Section 42 is on the right and 43 on the left. Walking with Section 43, you now approach another area flying the national emblem. Directly ahead are buried those who fought and died in the Spanish-American War. Though the 1898 conflict was short in duration, fathers, sons, and brothers from Ohio and the rest of the nation found themselves fighting on foreign soil in the heat of the tropical summer. Looking back from more than 100 years later, it appears now to have been a case of rich old men sending poor young men off to war. Some paid the ultimate price for a victory that brought the country insular possessions, a newfound "world power" status, and a new hero, Rough Rider leader Teddy Roosevelt. A hundred years later we still salve and soothe our children with stuffed toys in the shape of stylized bear cubs named for the mustached soldier-politician who liked to shoot bears.

Turn right and march up the hill (seems appropriate) past the veterans. Look to the left to see an old iron bridge hidden in the woods. Stay to the right of the Hannah family monument and continue west, arcing to the south, with Section 58 on your left. At the first triangular intersection on the right there stands another state champion tree. It's easy to see how the cut-leaf European beech received its name. It turns golden-brown in autumn. Continuing on the curving road under the tall sugar maple trees alongside Section 68, you will soon be greeted by the smiling face of Captain Eddie Rickenbacker, a hometown hero, on his tombstone along the left side of the road. This World War I flying ace who grew up in Columbus went on to accomplish many things, including founding the now-defunct Eastern Airlines.

Continue walking with Section 58 on your left, turning onto the gravel road that goes to the left into a ravine between 58 and 54. Underfoot you can see the kind of large gravel that was quarried in the cemetery for use as a road base. These large pieces of round limestone and granite washed to the side of the Scioto outwash when glacial meltwater was carrying sand and gravel south from the edge of the melting Wisconsinan ice sheet. You will see the same kind of stone in the road base throughout the older part of the cemetery and even in the fill for new graves.

Pass the Smith family plot on the hillside before passing under the old bridge. Likely this ravine was made when gravel was removed for roads, at the same time creating a landscape feature. As you continue east beyond the bridge, stay right while noting the huge glacial erratics to the left. By now you have probably seen other small granite boulders throughout the cemetery, usually in the triangular intersections or on section corners.

Circle right and climb the hill headed west, keeping Section 55 on the right. A multitrunked specimen of a Scotch pine, with its orange upper branches, stands in the intersection ahead. Off to the right is the other end of the iron bridge, should you wish to explore it. Otherwise continue west to the next intersection, then make a hard left with Section 63 on the right and 64 on the left. Head toward a triangle where a group of spruce trees grow. Stay to the right of them and head due south past the old iron hand pump with Section 62 on the right and 69 on the left. Immediately ahead are the graves of those who died fighting in World War I, "the war to end all wars." Turn left past the row of birch trees guarding the final muster of our grandfathers and uncles who gave their all in the trenches of France. The grave markers pitch a bit, and fewer flowers adorn their resting places each Memorial and Veterans Day as those who remember also answer the call.

Heading east now, keep Section 70 on the left while you curve to head north with Section 68 on the left. Continue north then east alongside Section 68 until the road runs into Section 67. Henry Waldschmidt, one of the last blacksmiths in the German Village area of Columbus, my wife's grandfather, lies buried not far from this point alongside his own wife, who outlived him by 46 years.

Turn left with Section 57 on the right and Section 64 on the hillside on the left, heading north. Continue with 57 on the right, curving toward the east. Once again back at the yellow-striped road, cross it headed east so that Section 66 is on the right and M on the left. Turn left almost immediately, with Section 60 now on the right. On the left there is a stone bench carved to appear as if it was made from branches; the John Beales Brown mausoleum sits on the opposite corner. Here and elsewhere in the older part of the cemetery you may have noticed that some plots have curbstone steps to allow visitors to make a graceful step down from a carriage.

Near the end of Section 60, just beyond a tall stately tuliptree, you will pass the final resting place of the *New Yorker* writer, cartoonist, and best-selling author James Thurber, who died in 1961. It is marked with an unpretentious headstone matching those of others in the family.

The quarry or "pit"—short for gravel pit—lies ahead behind the trees and shrubbery. This has been a favorite haunt of birds and birders for as long as anyone alive today can remember. When the cemetery was established in 1848, it was the source of much of the gravel used to build the roads, but it has not been used for that purpose since the 1920s. The pond is kept filled naturally by the aquifer that exists in the outwash valley.

The "pit" is generally the first place birders go. In recent years the Columbus Audubon Society has worked with the cemetery to enhance the area as a special sanctuary for birds. There is a bulletin board there where bird sightings can be posted and several feeders that visitors frequently refill, especially during the winter months. Dr. Edward S. Thomas, the late curator of natural history for the Ohio Historical Society, often wrote of the birds he saw at Green Lawn in his weekly *Columbus*

Dispatch nature columns. He and his wife are just north of the area.

Turn east to circle the quarry pond counterclockwise. Some of the most striking monuments, mausoleums, and tombstones are in this area. Immediately around the corner from the Thurber graves is the beloved statue of Emil Ambos, candy maker and amateur fisherman, sitting with pole in hand ready to make another cast. This bronze likeness is also at times enhanced with additions such as a fishing lure, scarf, sandwich, or cap.

Across the road is the Wolfe (publishing and banking) family grouping, including John W. Wolfe, with whom I played when I was young. Just east of that is the beautiful aboveground vault of Frederich Schumacher, a major contributor to the Columbus Museum of Art. On the corner across the road stands yet another state champion tree—a Chinese catalpa, with fruits longer and narrower than those of our native species and leaves with "devil horns" toward their tips. When I was a youngster, I liked to pull off the corolla of the catalpa flowers from the tree alongside our home and suck sweet nectar from within. On around the pond are the plots of the Jeffrey family (mining equipment manufacturers), the Schoedinger family (funeral homes), the Vorys family (law firm and U.S. congressman), and the Pace family, which includes a close personal friend.

Continue around the pond with Section 85 on your left, touching the red-lined road only momentarily as you do so. Amid the tall shade trees you will spot the neo-Egyptian mausoleum of well-known Columbus architect Frank Packard. Beyond that is the mausoleum of Gordon Battelle, a Columbus industrialist whose lasting legacy is the Battelle Memorial Institute where, among other things, the "xerography" process was developed. Next is the Howald mausoleum.

Like Schumacher, he was a major contributor to the Columbus Art Museum. On the corner, facing the chapel, is the large C. H. Hayden mausoleum, the final place of peace for the son of financier Peter Hayden.

Moving to the right clockwise on the road behind the chapel, you will pass the headstone of Samuel Bush, Columbus industrialist, president of Buckeye Steel Casting Company, and great-grandfather to President George Walker Bush. On the west side is a road of early-20th-century headstones of the Bancroft family with one military stone in the row, that of George Dallas Bancroft, Co. D, 16th Reg., Ohio Volunteer Infantry, July 9, 1869, aged 26 years, 1 month, and 27 days. The circumstances of his death remain to the imagination, but his next of kin obviously wanted him buried on their plot rather than in the military burial ground.

Back in Section 56, just before the chapel there is group of three dawn redwood trees, the attractive deciduous conifer from China grown widely as an ornamental. As I passed behind the chapel, the carillon started to play as it does each hour during the day. Beethoven's "Ode to Joy" from his Ninth Symphony rang out, lifting my spirits as it never fails to do. As you pass behind the chapel, note the exquisite stained-glass windows. Across the road on the hillside are some very old headstones, and up the hillside near the end of Section O is the very unusual Tallmage grotto. He was a stagecoach "king" in Lancaster, Ohio.

Follow around Section 34, momentarily along the right side of the busy white-striped road, to approach the front of the chapel. Across the road on the corner of Section 32 is the cottagelike Gay family mausoleum, with its beautiful stained-glass window visible as you approach it. Just before you reach the chapel, adjacent to a large specimen of the Ohio native cucumber tree stands the monument to Peter Sells, co-owner of the Sells Brothers Circus that operated out of Columbus during my childhood.

When W. B. Hubbard addressed the cemetery board at its founding in 1848, he announced his intention "to erect a neat and permanent stone chapel" on the grounds. It was 54 years later, in 1902, when the Frank Packard–designed Roman-style marble structure was opened. Tiffany's of New York designed and installed two mosaic murals below the dome, representing "truth" and "wisdom." Peletiah Huntington gave two stained-glass windows, one picturing Peggy Thompson, first resident of Franklinton to die, and the other a representation of Isaac Dalton, who, too old to fight in the Civil War, cared for the sick and wounded of that conflict. When little use was made of it for services, it was remodeled to add burial crypts and a columbarium. Additional crypts were added later and the chapel was converted to a lounge with chairs and sofas and opened for meditation.

Still other improvements have been made through the years. It is open from 8 AM to 4:30 PM Monday through Friday and from 8 AM to noon on Saturday but closed Sunday and most holidays. As you exit the driveway to the south of the chapel, there is a European horse chestnut tree of about 30 inches in girth.

From the chapel driveway, cross the road, passing the Powell monument on the left, and head east between Sections 39 and 47. Beyond there, stay to the right of the spruce tree in an intersection triangle and cross the busy red-lined road to head southeast between Sections 77 on the right and 112 on the left. As you approach the Marks-Frank mausoleum you may see to the left the low pink marble Waldschmidt-Ramey monument where Carolyn Ramey is interred and her mother and father will someday join her.

Continue counterclockwise with Section 122 on the left and you soon will be walking directly north with recent burials on the right. At the stop sign next to a specimen native hackberry tree at the busy red-and-white-striped road, turn right onto the sidewalk. The hackberry is an important larval food species for a number of native butterfly species. Heading east now, notice the large round glacial stones in the base of the road. To the right in Section 120, about 60 feet from the road, stands a beautiful statue of a Native American with tomahawk in hand. The family name is Gabriel; I have no knowledge of the story behind the monument.

My wife's father was raised in a home adjacent to the present-day Schmidt's Sausage House in the German Village area. He lost his own father when he was seven. The family story is that his mother frequently walked to the cemetery via Greenlawn Avenue, two children in tow, to sit on an iron bench by their father's gave. The bench now sits on our front porch, and instructions from my wife's father before he died were something like "don't spend time sitting at my grave site." Time only will tell whether the nearly 100-year-old bench will find its way back to Green Lawn Cemetery. I visit there often, mostly to walk and watch birds. I hope you will join me.

17

Highbanks Metro Park

Total distance: 4.75 miles (7.6 km)

Hiking time: 2½ hours

Maximum elevation: 910 feet

Vertical rise: 110 feet

Maps: USGS 7½' Series Powell;
CMPD Highbanks Metro Park brochure

The 100-foot-high shale bluffs that overlook the Olentangy River from the east in southern Delaware County have long been known as the Highbanks—hence the name of the 1,050-acre park that lies between US 23 and the river south of Powell Road. The bluffs are mostly composed of the massive formation called Ohio black shale that is also exposed at Alum Creek State Park, but the much-thinner Olentangy shale can be seen at the bottom near water level. Concretions—unique round rocks formed around an organic object in the shale—are found in the bluffs and in the rivers and streambeds below and downstream in the area. The Wisconsinan-age glacial till of the area is relatively thin, so the shale is also exposed in the deeply cut ravines that carry streams draining to the river from the east. Because central Ohio's bedrock dips to the east, not too far to the west of the Highbanks area the limestone rises closer to the surface, above the drainage system, giving rise to some solution caves.

Prehistoric Indians used the area, building mounds and earthworks. Later, with the arrival of settlers—many from Virginia redeeming warrants issued in payment for service in the War of Independence—the beech forests of the uplands and much of the oak—sugar maple woodland of the ravines fell to the ax. Crop fields, pastures, meadows, and orchards took their place. Through the decades of change, many folks simply enjoyed the beauty of this part of the Olentangy River Valley, choosing to make their homes in the area.

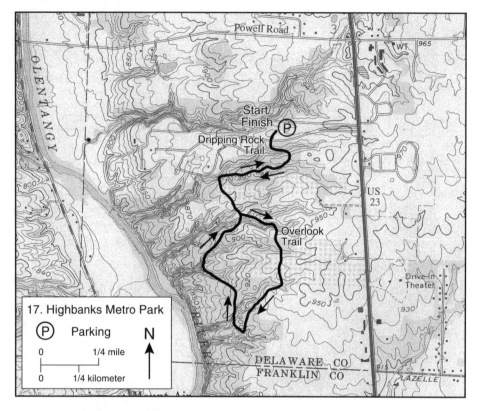

The Columbus and Franklin County Park District acquired the land in the 1960s and opened Highbanks Park in the early 1970s. Play fields and picnic areas were laid out, shelters built, and an extensive trail system established, making the park a favorite of hikers. In the late 1990s, in pursuit of the park district's educational goals, a nature center was built. Programs for school groups and the general public are now offered throughout the year. A 206-acre plot within the park is registered as a national natural landmark and dedicated under Ohio law as the Edward F. Hutchins Nature Preserve.

How to Get There

To visit Highbanks Metro Park in the Columbus area, travel 2 miles north from I-270 on US 23. The park entrance is on the west side of the road.

The Trail

The nature center is a good place to begin hiking at Highbanks. After viewing the exhibits telling of the park's natural and cultural history, take the Dripping Rock Trail just west of the building and turn right to head into the woods toward the river. Here the trail enters the largest and most heavily wooded ravine of the park. Notice the shale exposed in the ravine as the stream cuts its way downhill to the Olentangy. After crossing the stream, the trail climbs the north slope to eventually reach an observation deck designed for viewing such wildlife as white-tailed deer and red-tailed hawks.

Ancient earthworks are visible from the trail.

From there, the trail continues a brief distance north to an educational study site, intersecting along the way with the pet/ski trail. To continue hiking, follow the Dripping Rock Trail signs as the trail heads south then west toward the Big Meadows play area. As it exits the woods, it intersects with an unpaved trail that goes to the right by the sledding area to join the paved Big Meadows Path at a parking lot to the north. Follow the Dripping Rock Trail to the left along the edge of the woods; it soon meets a paved connector going right to the Big Meadows Path. Rest rooms and drinking water are available at this area.

The Dripping Rock Trail next reenters the woods and heads south to pass under the main park road. Then, following another ravine, the trail begins the slow 100-foot climb back to the upland area. Just after touching a parking lot and returning to the woods, the Dripping Rock Trail meets the Overlook Trail, leaving to the right. For a view

of the shale bluffs of the Highbanks and a look at the earthworks, follow this trail.

Soon the trail passes through an area that is deliberately kept open as a habitat for nonwoodland wildlife. Beyond, the trail forks to make a loop. Going to the right, you will soon see on your left a fenced area with tombstones within. During the development of the park, these tombstones were found together, having been moved many years earlier. Likely they were cleared from an old family graveyard to make way for agricultural activity after a farmstead had disappeared. The park district found it fitting to memorialize this pioneer family by re-erecting the stones at this new location.

The trail continues toward the overlook, soon entering the E. F. Hutchins Nature Preserve. Before long you find yourself traveling alongside what looks like a ditch or trench, sometime water filled, on the right side of the trail. This semi-elliptical earthwork is considered to be a protective or defensive feature associated with the Late Woodland, or possibly Cole culture, Indians. The blufftop fortification has walls about 3 feet high; the depth of the ditch varies from 3 to 7 feet. There are three openings in the embankment. It is thought to have been built between A.D. 800 and A.D. 1300. The Overlook Trail is joined by an outgoing trail as it turns west to carry you to a wooden platform overlooking the banks of the Olentangy River.

On the return trip from the overlook, take the right fork in the trail to continue walking on the deep-woods trail. You will pass the 0.41-mile Wetland Spur Trail, leaving the Overlook Trail to the right. A side trip will take you to a man-made wetland with a viewing shelter, another opportunity to see native wildlife close up.

Back on the Overlook Trail, continue through the woods to close the loop and return to the intersection with the Dripping Rock Trail. After turning right onto that trail, you will find that it moves away from the congested picnic and playground area to continue into the woods. To the right, another side trail leads to Highbanks Park Mound II, also known as the Orchard Mound (there was an orchard there in the middle of the 20th century) or the Selvey Mound for the name of an earlier landowner. This subconical, 2½-foot-high earthen burial mound is, because of its shape and upland location, presumed to be of the Adena culture.

Return to the Dripping Rock Trail, turn right, and in a few moments the trail will take you to the main park road and a crosswalk to the nature center and your vehicle.

The other parks of the Columbus Metro Park System offer excellent hiking opportunities. Chestnut Ridge, Battelle-Darby, and Clear Creek are described in detail in *50 Hikes in Ohio*. Blendon Woods and Slate Run are included elsewhere in this volume. Enjoy them all.

18

Indian Lake State Park

Total distance: 2 miles (3.2 km)

Hiking time: 1¼ hours

Maximum elevation: 1,025 feet

Vertical rise: 10 feet

Maps: USGS 7½' Series Waynesfield; ODNR Indian Lake State Park Trail Guide

When the Wisconsinan glacier was melting from west-central Ohio 14,000 to 18,000 years ago, most of the time it did so at a fairly steady rate, leaving behind a flat to gently undulating ground moraine of clayey nature. Sometimes the melting of the glacier's leading edge halted for a long enough period of time that there occurred a buildup of glacial debris, the mineral material that was continuously being transported south in the moving ice sheet. When the climate again warmed to the point that more ice was melting annually than falling and being transported south as glacier, the edge of the ice sheet again moved north. When it did so, it left behind at the point at which it had been stationary a ridge of mineral material that was higher than the surrounding land—what geologists call an end moraine.

In the high country north of Bellefontaine, a series of about half a dozen such general east–west end moraines were deposited upon on the land. They are still visible in this area, referred to as the central Ohio clayey till plain. As the glacier continued to melt, water was often trapped between some of these ridges, leaving areas of silt and sand. In some places, especially where ice had been trapped in the drift, then melted, small lakes occurred. Streams and rivers eventually developed to drain most of the land, but poorly drained areas remained. Some of the intermorainal areas drained to the west through the tributaries of the Wabash River. Others drained east and south to the Scioto River. In the southern edge of the area, west of Bellefontaine, the highest point in the state, the meltwater cut new channels through the moraine and made its way to what we now call the Great Miami River and its tributaries.

Even in historic times many shallow lakes remained in the area. The poorly drained land was covered with elm–ash–maple swamp forest, with an occasional grassy marsh. Before white settlement, Native American tribes lived and hunted in the area. Because not too many miles distant the rivers flowed north, the Natives could easily paddle and portage their way from the Ohio to Lake Erie. Early French and British traders took advantage of this fact, and many skirmishes between settlers and the Natives occurred in this area. Though the 1795 Greeneville Treaty between our new nation and the Indian tribes prohibited settlement in most of this area, part of it had already been claimed by the state of Virginia as land to be used to compensate its underpaid Revolutionary War soldiers. By 1803 it became part of the new state of Ohio, and the floodgates on settlement were opened. In 1800 Ohio claimed 45,365 residents. By 1850 there were nearly 2 million.

Transportation was a major problem for the new state so, following the example of New York, Ohio began building a system of canals to get products and people to markets and faraway places. The shortest way from Cincinnati, Lake Erie, and its connection to the east through the Erie Canal was the route the Indians used. In 1851, during the building of the Miami & Erie Canal that would connect the Ohio River with Lake Erie along a north–south line about 23 miles to the west, it was determined that additional water was needed if the canal was to be operable year-round. Work was begun on expanding the largest of the lakes in northwestern Logan County,

one known as Old Indian Lake, for use as feeder lake to supply the needed water to the canal. By 1893 the lake, then known as Lewistown Reservoir, covered 6,334 acres with 29 miles of shoreline. In 1898 the Ohio General Assembly dedicated the lake as a recreation area by the name of Indian Lake. Soon after, the canal was completely out of operation, replaced by trains and, later, motor vehicles. But Indian Lake lived on.

For the next 50 years Indian Lake was a popular resort area, with an amusement park and many private cottages. During the summer season, steam and electric railroads brought visitors from far and wide. Though most of the land near shore was private, beginning in 1939, the lake and recreation facilities were operated by the old Ohio Division of Conservation and Natural Resources. When the Department of Natural Resources was created in 1949, the area was assigned to the new Division of Parks and Recreation as Indian Lake State Park.

Many improvements have been made in the intervening years, including the creation of new public land by dredge-and-fill operation and the construction of modern park facilities. The center of activity is now the campground on the north side of lake, many miles from where the amusement park once drew crowds. About 6 miles of trails have been developed, giving access to much of the park. Three miles of the distance is a paved bike/hike trail along the shoreline in the southwestern corner of the park near Lakeview. The remainder is divided between two hiking trails: the 2-mile Cherokee Trail located just west of the campground entrance area and the Pew Island Trail in the center of the lake, reached from the south side of the park. The multipurpose trail is in an area of mowed lawn with no shade trees. For pushing a stroller or using a wheelchair it would be fine, especially if you don't mind the sun. To explore on natu-

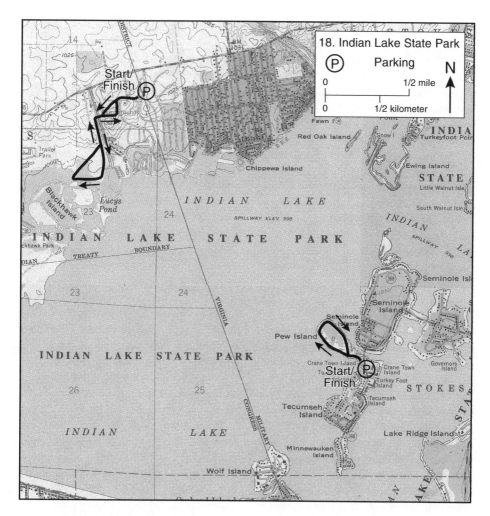

ral turf and in a natural setting, you can include both of the footpaths in your plans for hiking at Indian Lake.

How to Get There

Reaching the 6,000-plus-acre Indian Lake Park is relatively easy. Travel US 33 northwest from central Ohio or SR 235 north from the Dayton area to the village of Lakeview. From Lakeview, follow SR 235 north to the campground entrance.

The 0.7-mile Pew Island Trail is more difficult to find. From the campground or park office, follow SR 235 south for 1 mile to SR 366, where it curves to the east along the water. (It passes by the area of the 2.5-mile Indian Lake Bike Trail.) In 6 miles, after going through the community of Russell's Point, turn north (left) onto SR 368. Follow it 2.5 miles north to Logan County Road 286. Turn left onto CR 286 and the parking lot will be 0.75 mile ahead on the right. Don't miss the hard left turn to Cranetown Island.

Park under the tall oak trees and head past the trail sign, across the short causeway to Pew Island. The trail follows the west shoreline of the island to where there is a fishing pier. There it turns right, then right again as it follows an elevated boardwalk through a cattail marsh. This island was created many years ago by pumping dredge spoil inside a wall of limestone riprap. In some places the silty material from the lake bottom has dried in tall piles. Elsewhere it settled, leaving areas of wetland. Tall cottonwoods ring the island, and young red maples grow with the cottonwoods in the interior wet woods. Ducks nest there. The trail returns to the parking lot through woods, alder thicket, and a grassy area. Keep your binoculars handy for waterfowl, woodpeckers, and other woodland species.

The Trails

The Cherokee Trail begins at the edge of a pine planting just west of a pumphouse near the campground welcome station. Park at the south end of the nature center and visitors parking lot just outside the park campground. Walk west around the south edge of the recently constructed pond and past the small pumphouse. A one-board sign across the mowed area near a pine planting to the west of that building identifies the trail entrance. If you are camping, there is an entrance to the trail behind the playground in the A area.

This is a level trail and quite easy walking. Most of the vegetation is pine planting or thicket, but there are some large trees near the lakeshore. In spring carry your binoculars for a closer look at the small birds that nest in the area. This is a poorly drained low-lying area where mosquitoes are likely to breed, so application of a repellent or the wearing of some sort of protection is appropriate during late spring and summer.

The trail crosses a small wooded bridge as it heads west; you can see the end of the campground through the shrubbery on the left. On the right is an old field with an occasional young pine plus naturally invading hardwoods. There is a stand of giant ragweed at this point, so if you suffer from hay fever, you may want to walk the trail before ragweed season or after frost. The trail makes a sharp left turn and, after about 100 feet, turns right, where it is joined by a path coming in from the left from the campground. This is what naturalists call thicket. In summer it's good habitat for birds like brown thrashers and butterflies like monarchs and silver-spotted skippers.

A second trail comes from the left from the campground as the trail heads west toward Cherokee Road. An interpretive sign notes that the best way to attract bluebirds is to erect boxes. This is true, and this was probably good bluebird habitat when the sign and box were installed, but due to encroaching thicket it has lost its appeal to America's favorite songbird. Other species such as chickadees and tree swallows do use them.

Beyond the road, the trail crosses a ditch and reaches a junction where a side trail leads right to a wildlife observation shelter, a good place to see small birds if it is being maintained. Turning left, the Cherokee Trail winds through thicket then enters secondary woods growing on silty soil that looks like dredge spoil. In late summer the blue blossoms of great lobelia greet you. The trail soon arrives along the lake's edge, where tall cottonwoods grow on the old spoil. For many decades, a suction dredge nicknamed the Chief operated on Indian Lake throughout the warm months, keeping boating channels open. Long pipes supported on the water by floats carried the spoil to an area where "new land" was being made. There are some old dredge pipes off to the side of this trail.

Riprap protects the trail at Pew Island from erosion by storms. The island was created from dredge spoils many years ago.

Several interpretive signs along the trail help you learn more about this man-made natural environment. The trail follows the lake's edge west to where there stands a large eastern cottonwood tree. A sign tells the story of this denizen of the Ohio swamps.

Several hundred feet of boardwalk now carry the trail to the northwest through what must be a very wet woods at some times of the year. Great patches of spotted jewelweed or touch-me-not lend a dash of color. When the boardwalk runs out, the trail becomes a bit more difficult to discern. I expect that more boardwalk is planned. As the land gets higher and drier, ironweed is present, offering its nectar to butterflies.

Soon the trail rejoins the outgoing trail to complete a triangular loop. Following the trail back to the origin is not difficult. On the morning I walked it, more butterflies showed up as the sunned warmed things. For a different look at things, after crossing the road, go directly east on the left fork of the trail. When you reach a trail going left, follow it north to where it intersects the entry trail. I carried a single-lens reflex camera with a 100-millimeter macro lens when I was exploring and was able to take close-up photos of several butterflies and a spider on its dew-dampened web as I traveled these trails.

A trail in another canal feeder lake park, Lake Loramie, is located south of Minster in nearby Shelby County. It is described elsewhere in this volume. A trail in Shelby County Park District's Lockington Reservoir near the historic village of Lockington is described in *50 Hikes in Ohio*.

19

Kendrick Woods Metropark

Total distance: 3 miles (4.6 km)

Hiking time: 2 hours

Maximum elevation: 810 feet

Vertical rise: 20 feet

Maps: USGS 7½' Series Spencerville; JAMPD Kendrick Woods South Trail Guide

When, in the spring of 1794, the army commanded by "Mad" Anthony Wayne moved down the valley of the Auglaize River to its confluence with the Maumee River, they were moving through virgin forest. Where they passed the mouth of Six-Mile Creek, where Kendrick Woods Metropark is located in what is now western Allen County, they were traveling through spectacular beech–maple forest on rich glacial till.

By the time they reached what was later to be called Six-Mile Creek, the small stream that empties into the "Glaize" at Kendrick Woods, the army was already north of the major recessional moraines left 10,000 years earlier by the receding Wisconsinan glacier. Only a few miles farther north the going would get more difficult as they encountered the mire of the Great Black Swamp. Occupying the old bed of one of a series of lakes that developed in front of the glacier as it melted from the Ohio countryside, the swamp forest consisted of elm, ash, and soft maples, along with swamp white, bur, and pin oak—all trees that grow well with their roots close to the water table. When the troops reached the Maumee River, the main stem of the river system that drained the Black Swamp, they built Fort Defiance then moved downriver to do battle with the Indians. The rest, as they say, is history.

The Greeneville Treaty that resulted as a result of Wayne's victory at Fallen Timbers did not immediately open this part of Ohio to settlement. But less than 10 years later, Ohio became a state and settlement began to occur in waves all across its territory.

Lima was surveyed in 1831 and from 1835 to 1843, the federal government had a land office there, in the heart of the congressional lands of this part of Ohio, making it easy for settlers to file land patents. In 1846 Allen County was created. Timber was an impediment to progress, and logs went to the sawmills by the wagonload. In 1884 oil was discovered by a man drilling for gas. A year later Lima found itself at the heart of the largest oil field on the globe. Thousands of oil wells were drilled, and the earth's largest oil refinery was built in Lima by the Standard Oil Company.

As the 21st century gets under way, the largest contiguous tract of woods extant in Allen County is the one preserved as Kendrick Woods. Though the USGS Kendrick Woods topographic map still carries the label "oil field," the oil is depleted and the wells are capped. The beech and maple trees that Wayne and his men passed beneath were felled for firewood and construction timber centuries ago. With tile fields and ditches drying out the land, young oaks and hickories now dominate the upland forest. Fortunately, more than a dozen huge white oak trees, estimated to be near 300 years old–trees that likely were growing saplings when General Wayne and his men passed nearby–still grow in Kendrick Woods. Through all the clearing and row-cropping, drilling and pumping, successive generations of landowners did not clear-cut this woods. Strayer's Woods, as it was called locally, stood when the local park district was born.

In 1976 the district received money from the estate of Florence Kendrick to be used to buy land to serve as a memorial to her late husband, Raymond W. Kendrick. An avid outdoorsman who loved the woods and wildlife, Kendrick felt a personal closeness with the out-of-doors, and Mrs. Kendrick wanted the gift to be used to

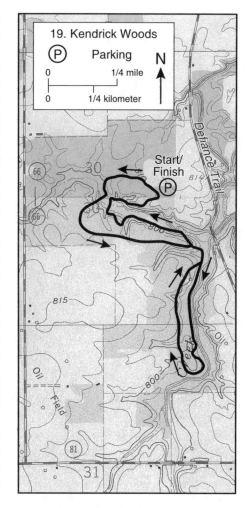

share this feeling with others.

It took 10 years to acquire the needed titles and easements to protect this 218-acre tract, but in 1987 it was opened to the public as Kendrick Woods. In May 1992, when I was serving as chief of the Division of Natural Areas and Preserves, Kendrick Woods was dedicated as a state nature preserve. Interestingly, the purchase of the original 182 acres in 1976 specified no development or disturbance of the woods. The people who owned the land at the time it was bought were planning to develop a mobile home park there and had to be persuaded by local conservationists to sell the woods to the park district.

How to Get There

The entrance to Kendrick Woods is on the west side of the Defiance Trail less than 1 mile north of SR 81 and approximately 12 miles west of Lima. The open area in front of the woods includes rest rooms and picnic and play facilities. There are said to be a total of 5 miles of trails within the park. The best access is just beyond the bulletin board, which is located at the far corner of the first parking lot. *Note:* From mid-May until mid-September, this woods is generally full of mosquitoes. The park district does not run programs during that period of the year. If you plan hiking then, be very well prepared.

The Trail

Begin walking on the All-People's Trail, a boardwalk of less than 0.25 mile that is accessible to those with wheelchairs and walkers. My late daughter, Carolyn, lived most of her 42 years in a wheelchair, so I am particularly pleased to find more of these sorts of facilities in Ohio's outdoor recreation areas. Just inside the woods, a monument notes that this trail is the gift of the Lima Rotary Club. There is also a plaque alongside the trail illustrating the layout of the trail system. I suggest that you begin walking by turning left to travel the boardwalk in a clockwise direction. That way, at the first place a trail exits to the left, you can pick up a trail guide from a dispenser, then turn left and follow the earthen trail and read the interpretive material in the guide in the proper sequence. Posts numbered from 1 to 10 along this trail are keyed to the trail guide; you will find the first one alongside the trail shortly after you leave the boardwalk.

White, red, and occasional bur oak and

shagbark hickory stand close to the wide winding boardwalk. Almost immediately into the woods I encountered a fat fox squirrel, as might well be expected given the abundance of what is called mast—acorns and hickory nuts. In some parts of the woods there are large trees; in other areas they look to be 50 to 100 years old. There is a good understory and, in some spots, a good layer of spicebush and other native shrubs. The spring wildflowers of these woods are spectacular. I do not remember seeing large-flowered trillium blossoms this big anywhere else, and the abundance of wild blue phlox reminded me of that which grew in the wet beech forests of eastern Franklin County during my youth. How well I remember the day when workers began digging a hole for the basement of a home in the exact location of my favorite patch of "sweet williams." Unfortunately, the invasive alien garlic mustard is present in a growing number of places along the trail, probably brought in on the soles of hikers such as we.

Upon leaving the boardwalk, the trail tread is unimproved forest floor. Watch out for the occasional protruding root. It drops into the valley of Heidlebaugh Creek, the small stream that drains the northern part of the park, then climbs the hillside gently before dropping to a trail intersection. The park people have made navigation in Kendrick Woods easy by placing at strategic points small plaques with a map carrying a red dot indicating your location. You have already passed one numbered post; to continue past them in succession, turn left. A humpback bridge carries the trail across the major channel, and a smaller plant bridge across a lesser channel. Then the trail climbs and winds its way to the east on high ground.

At the next intersection, go straight ahead. The trail to the right is the Hickory

Trail, which circles the west end of the park and returns to the All-People's Trail. If you were to take that, you would miss the interesting South Loop Trail. Continuing ahead, you soon come to a trail exiting to the left. It goes back to the parking lot (in case you need to abort your hike). The trail continues east then swings south to join with a trail coming in from the right. On a single trail, continue south, traveling downhill to cross a small bridge and travel upstream on the floodplain of Six-Mile Creek. (Incidentally, the name of this creek probably dates from after 1812. In that year Colonel Poague of General Harrison's army built a fort that he named Fort Amanda in honor of his wife, along the Defiance Trail 6 miles upstream from here.Travelers coming north likely put the *six-mile* name on the stream because of its location 6 miles up the trail from Fort Amanda.) Note the absence of glacial gravel and boulders in this stream. At one spot, the trail goes very close to the stream edge. Channel posts have been installed with brush tucked in behind in an attempt to halt erosion with natural material. By now, the trail has passed five of the numbered posts.

Your nose probably tells you that post 6 is not far ahead. You will pick up the smell of the sulfur-bearing artesian spring before it comes into sight off to the right of the trail. Like the water, the origin of the spring is not very clear. Either it was formed when an aquifer was drilled as the area was being explored for oil, or the aquifer naturally meets the surface here. In either case, there is a spring flowing from the broken upturned end of what looks like a buried concrete tile. It is surrounded by an area of wetland that is fed by natural seeps rising out of the ground year-round. The spring flowed at a considerably faster rate before the city of Delphos developed a well field directly west of the northern part of the woods. At one

time the spring was used to water cattle that grazed nearby. A similar spring close by along the Auglaize River was formerly called the "Fountain of Youth"—visitors filled bottles with the sulfur water thinking that it possessed medicinal qualities. At the outflow for the spring there is a sluice and some instruments, which of course should not be disturbed.

Beyond the spring the trail crosses another small side stream on a bridge that looks as if it has a bite out of its right side. It is, of course, a circle cut out of the deck to accommodate a tree that's no longer there. The trail next moves closer to Six-Mile Creek on what looks like dredge fill from a channelization project. Off to the right is what appears to be the natural channel.

As the trail rises from the flood, a large stump to the right gives you some indication as to the size of trees that stood in this part of Allen County at the time of settlement. Beyond, on the higher ground, the trail passes the large white oaks mentioned earlier. These scattered forest-grown trees must be close to 300 years old. Imagine what this area must have looked like when trees like these were widespread across the landscape. One early Ohio settler, writing in 1817, reported that "The white oak is the glory of the upland forest. I measured a white oak by the roadside, which at four feet from the ground was six feet in diameter and at seventy-five feet is measured nine feet around." If you look closely at some of these trees, you can see a faint blue color. Sometime in the not-too-distant past, these trees were probably marked by a timber buyer to be cut. How fortunate we are that someone felt these woodland monarchs were worth saving for future generations to see and admire.

The trail remains now on the high land. Groundhog burrows give evidence to the

The author gets a close up look at one of the large oak trees along the trail at Kendrick Woods.

ease with which a critter can dig into this deep glacial till. Traveling parallel to the edge of the woods, the trail now begins its return to the northern part of the park, crossing several small bridges across streams that drain the farm fields to the left. More oaks and hickories dominate the woods, with sugar maples in the understory. As the trail drops to the valley of Six-Mile Creek, it passes a big honey locust, one you would not try to climb. Here there is a side trail to the right that leads to an area where skunk cabbage and marsh marigolds grow. I suspect a small hillside spring provides water year-round.

When you reach the trail you came in on, continue north, turn west to rise and fall, then cross a bridge. After turning toward the west, the trail arrives at a split. If you want to cut your hike short here, go right, then take

the next right across a bridge to the parking lot. Otherwise, turn left and head due west on a wide trail that looks like a former farm lane. Kendrick Woods is like most parks and natural areas: Tucked into a corner is the spot where former occupants of the land disposed of unwanted appliances and equipment. Nature hides it during the green time of the year, but not so in winter.

After a good distance, the South Loop Trail meets the Hickory Trail coming in from the right. Continue west on the Hickory Trail to where, at a park bench, the trail turns right. This section is one of the best places to photograph spring wildflowers without leaving the trail.

At the bench, look due south across the fence. There lies the only glacial erratic that I found in the area. What a contrast with the "boulder belt" areas of the moraines of west-central Ohio, where granite boulders are everywhere. From here the trail travels to the north on flat ground, then turns east and drops to broad floodplain—Heidlebaugh Creek (named for the owners of the land to the west) in the deep woods. After crossing another bridge, the Hickory Trail reaches a T. Turn left amid tall oaks and hickories and follow the trail as it arcs right to meet the All-People's boardwalk. A left turn and a short walk soon bring you back to the bench and monument area near the trail-head and parking lot.

It was fall the first time I walked this trail, but I was so impressed by the quality of the forest that I returned at the end of the following April. I was rewarded with a beautiful display of spring wildflowers in a woods very different from those I more frequently walk in central Ohio. I believe that you will share my enthusiasm for Kendrick Woods Metropark and the 150-acre state-designated Kendrick Woods Nature Preserve that it includes.

20

Kiser Lake State Park and Kiser Lake Wetlands State Nature Preserve

Total distance: 2.5 miles (4 km)

Hiking time: 2 hours

Maximum elevation: 1,150 feet

Vertical rise: 80 feet

Maps: USGS 7½' Series St. Paris; ODNR Kiser Lake State Park brochure

I knew I was in for a special treat the moment I set foot on the Kiser Lake wetlands trail. It was a warm cloudy-bright early-April morning, and 20 feet down the trail I was greeted by the sunny face of a marsh marigold in full bloom. As I hit the boardwalk, I thought I heard the call of a single western chorus frog, so I began a slow, stealthy walk along the edge of the wetland. At the end of the short section of boardwalk just inside the preserve, the trail returns to a dirt track and follows the east bank of Mosquito Creek upstream. I could see a huge bed of marsh marigolds (really a species of buttercup) across the creek where I could only enjoy them from a distance. Then it happened. The lone frog I had heard earlier turned into a full chorus of them. I froze, for the slightest movement will often return them to silence. As their confidence grew, their numbers did too. Soon they were joined by the chirping of male spring peepers also advertising their presence to would-be suitors. As if that weren't enough, from deeper in the wetland came the trilling voices of male eastern American toads singing of their readiness to mate. The final member of this anuran symphony, a single northern leopard frog, began its snorelike calls from across the waters, hoping that some lady-in-waiting leopard frog would choose him. It was almost too much: four of the nine species of frogs and toads known from Champaign County present and singing in one place. Anything that was to follow would be anticlimactic.

The wetland that I was exploring may

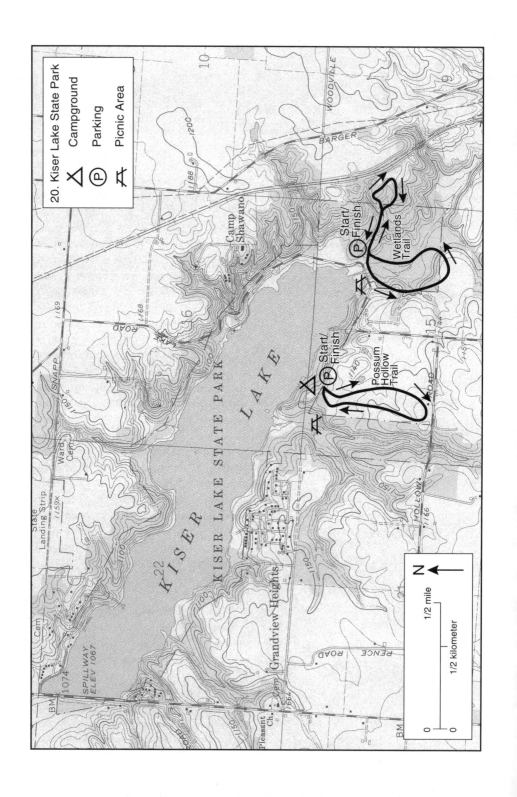

20. Kiser Lake State Park

△ Campground
Ⓟ Parking
⋔ Picnic Area

well have resulted from the work of humans—flowage from springs being blocked by road fill or stream-dredging spoil. But this wetland has been here in one shape or another since soon after the melting of the last ice sheet. Mosquito Creek drains the runoff and seepage from springs from the western side of a large area of hilly Wisconsinan-age moraine along the western edge of Champaign County, carrying it northwest to eventually empty into the south-flowing Great Miami River near Sidney. The moraine east of Kiser Lake is the divide between the Mad River drainage to the east and the Great Miami. Mosquito Creek, nestled in a valley between the moraines, was a slow-flowing stream fed by numerous hillside springs as well as runoff. It created a wetland known as the Mosquito Creek Swamp in the valley now occupied by the lake. It was the dream of local resident John W. Kiser and other members of his family that the area be dammed and made into a lake.

In 1932 the Kiser family offered several hundred acres in the Mosquito Creek Valley to the state. In 1939 a dam was constructed at that time, creating the 396-acre Kiser Lake, which became part of the state park system operated by the former Division of Conservation and Natural Resources. A bronze plaque commemorating the gift of the lake site by John W. Kiser and his mother, Thyrza Kiser, is attached to a large glacial boulder in the picnic area on the south side of the lake. As a part of the terms of the gift, motors are not permitted on Kiser Lake, so it has always been a popular place for enjoying small sailboats, rowboats, and canoes.

This area of the southern Ohio till plain lies within what geologists refer to as the boulder belt, where large glacial boulders of Canadian Shield origin were found in abundance at the time of settlement. Fencerows and gullies are full of them hauled from farm fields, and great piles can be seen near barns. No creekbed or stream cut is without them. Beech forest, with its many other associated species such as oak and maple, covers the well-drained land, with swamp forest occurring in the poorly drained areas.

Opened to the public for purchase in the first decade of the 19th century, this part of Ohio was formed as a county two years after statehood, with Urbana early on becoming an important jumping-off spot for exploration farther north. The Shawnee Indians lived in the area before being forced north by the Treaty of Greeneville. Legendary frontiersman Simon Kenton also made his home in Champaign County for a number of years.

How to Get There

The Kiser Lake area can be reached by taking SR 235 north from I-70 north of Fairborn to Possum Hollow Road, a distance of about 24 miles. There turn east, drive 1.5 miles to Kiser Lake Road, and then turn north to the park and preserve. An alternate approach is to take Kiser Lake Road from the center of St. Paris, which is located on US 36 about halfway between Urbana and Piqua.

The Trails

Begin hiking, as I did, by parking on the grass next to the bulletin board and trailhead just east of the sign identifying the Kiser Lake Wetlands State Nature Preserve on Kiser Lake Road at the southeast corner of the lake. The best way to reach this point is by driving east from SR 235 on Possum Hollow Road (located just over a mile south of the lake dam). SR 235 dead-ends into Kiser Lake Road. Turn left and follow the road as it heads north toward the lake, then

The trail into Kiser Lake wetlands moves onto a boardwalk to pass through a patch of cattails in the marsh.

turns right (east). At the bottom of the hill you'll find a short side road, along with the entrances to the wetlands trail and the state park's Red Oak Trail.

Enter the wetlands trails on the right side of the bulletin board. A boardwalk carries you across the seepage area and outlet to the marsh; then the trail uses a dredge spoil on the left bank of Mosquito Creek to head south adjacent to the wetland. Another section of boardwalk, this time plastic, bridges a seepage as the trail works its way upstream. Other bridges span small outlets from the marsh to the stream. After a turn to the east along the meandering stream, the trail makes a sharp left turn to travel a long, winding boardwalk northeast across the wetland to the base of the moraine.

At the end of the boardwalk it looks like the trail goes both left and right. It really doesn't. Go left as the arrow on the Carsonite post indicates. Follow the trail as

it climbs over and winds its way between the loam-covered piles of gravel that constitute the moraine. As you approach the end of the trail, it dead-ends with the Red Oak Trail. If you have time, turn right and follow this 0.7-mile-long trail as it climbs the moraine to the right and loops south along the park boundary before returning to this intersection. As you go to your parking area, there is an old cellar hole uphill and to the right among a large patch of daylilies. Scramble up there, taking a moment to examine the stone foundation and, perhaps, to contemplate what living in small house on this site might have been like 100 or more years ago, looking out not onto a beautiful lake but toward the well-known Mosquito Creek Swamp. I suspect that making a living and raising a family was tough.

To continue exploring the Kiser Lake area on foot, drive due west on Kiser Lake Road to the spot where it makes a right turn up the

Till Plains

hill toward St. Paris. Instead of turning, take Park Road 7 straight ahead for about 0.5 mile to signs on the left introducing the 0.7-mile Possum Hollow Trail and the 0.5-mile Pine Tree Trail in the state park. Then explore this habitat, which is very different from the wetland. The trail follows the high bluff to the east of Possum Hollow then returns via the valley floor. Huge patches of blue cohosh, skunk cabbage, and many other woodland wildflowers, including the uncommon twin-leaf, grow near the trail. When I walked it on Earth Day 2001, the shrill voices of tree frogs echoed throughout the valley at high noon.

Kiser Lake has a pleasant campground with about 100 campsites where you may want to overnight. Boats are available for rent at two locations, and there is a swim-ming beach on the north side of the lake. During the warmer part of the year, interpre-tive programs and exhibits are offered at a small nature center and amphitheater near the campground.

While you are in Champaign County, you might enjoy hiking at other state nature preserves. Siegenthaler-Kastner Esker is located on Couchman Road between Calland and Church Roads in Harrison township. Davey Woods is located off Lonesome, Smith, and Neal Roads north of US 36 in Concord and Mad River town-ships. Cedar Bog State Memorial, with its mile-long boardwalk, is reached by travel-ing west on Woodburn Road from US 68 south of Urbana. Walks in all three are de-scribed in *Walks and Rambles in South-western Ohio.*

21

Lake La Su An
State Wildlife Area

Total distance: 5 miles (8 km)

Hiking time: 4 hours

Maximum elevation: 990 feet

Vertical rise: 60 feet

*Maps: USGS 7½' Series Nettle Lake;
ODNR Lake La Su An Wildlife Area map*

Lake La Su An sits high on the edge of the Wabash End Moraine in the northwest corner of the state, only a stone's throw from Michigan. The Wisconsinan-age loamy till soil of the hummocky terrain lies atop Mississippian-age Coldwater shale. It features rolling hills, closed depressions, wetlands, few streams, deranged drainage, and interspersed flats. Beech forests dominate the uplands, with swamp forests present in the poorly drained areas. It is land like none other I have seen in Ohio.

Most of this Steuben till plain, as the geologists call it, is located outside Ohio in Indiana and Michigan. In fact, at one time the area where Lake La Su An Wildlife Area is today was claimed by the state of Ohio and the territory of Michigan. It lay between what was known as the Fulton Line—the line Michigan claimed as is southern boundary—and the Harris Line, which Ohio was certain was its northern border. War almost broke out over the conflicting claim in 1835. The dispute over the 8-mile strip was settled when the Upper Peninsula was added to Michigan in return for it giving up its claim on the disputed turf.

Hardly anyone lived in this far corner of the state until the 1830s, when people from the Middle Atlantic area began to settle the western end of the Michigan survey lands. Timber was cleared, and subsistence farming began. I suspect that the rolling land was used for grazing livestock.

Much of the land along the West Branch of the St. Joseph River that is now the 2,280-acre Lake La Su An Wildlife Area was

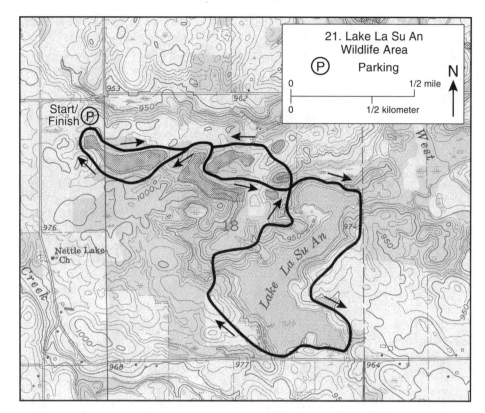

first purchased and developed as a fishing area by people in the private sector. The name honors members of the family that was involved. In 1981 the Division of Wildlife began acquisition of the original development. As funds and land become available, the area is being expanded. Former wetlands are being restored and management techniques applied to maximize the wildlife diversity of the area. From the outset it has been a limited-access fishing facility. Advance reservations are needed to go after the largemouth bass, bluegills, and other native fish that are abundant in the small lakes of the area. Public hunting and trapping are also allowed on some parts of the area. Information can be obtained from the area office or from the Division of Wildlife in Columbus. Hikers must, of course, be aware that hunters may be present during open season, though I have hiked the area in fall and found no one around but me.

How to Get There

This unusual wildlfie area is located approximately 60 miles west from Toledo, 41 miles north of Defiance, 1 mile south of the Ohio-Michigan state line, and 5 miles from the Ohio-Indiana state line. To reach it, take US 20 west from Toledo to SR 15 in Williams County. Turn north and go 1 mile to the center of Pioneer. To reach the headquarters of the area, turn west on County Road R and travel 7.5 miles. To reach the parking lot suggested above, drive 1 mile farther north on SR 15, then turn west onto CR S and travel 8 miles. The entrance to the Area A parking lot is on the south side of the road.

Plan to spend a day hiking and a day fishing and/or canoeing (you must bring your own).

The Trail

I suggest that you begin your hiking at the Area A parking lot outside the gate on Williams County Road S. That is the northwest corner of the property. As I assembled my kit to begin walking on a beautiful May morning, a male eastern bluebird flew to the top of a post close to my car. Eastern towhees were singing their drink your tea song from nearby established territories. And a chorus of frog calls was coming from the closest lake.

Head into the area on the entry road and turn to the left, uphill, to continue on the gravel road overlooking Lake LaVere off to the right. There are 14 lakes in the area, many of which you will pass on your hike. The clockwise direction of travel is my choice to give me some backlit scenes of the lakes and possibly some pictures of wildlife with the sun behind me. The shagbark-hickory-dominated woods between the road and the lake along this first part of the walk are full of yellow trout lilies in spring. A first-hatch tiger swallowtail butterfly flew alongside me here on a May day, nectaring on dandelions beside the road.

At the east end of Lake LaVere, continue walking east on the service road with fields to the left and woods to the right. The road rises then turns right and drops to a parking lot sitting between Lake Sue on the right and her smaller sister, Lake Ann, on the left. There are wood duck nesting boxes on nearly all of these lakes, so keep your eyes open for these spectacular woodland waterfowl.

Beyond the parking lot, follow the deteriorating old road as it makes a long climb through the woods, past an old field at the summit, and descends to another pair of ponds. These are the much-smaller Hogback Pond on the left and Lou's Pond to the right. There are several clumps of a white-barked birch growing in this area. Not native, they may be either the European white birch or the paper birch found farther north on this continent. Some old apple trees alongside the trail must surely be enjoyed by the white-tailed deer of the area.

With Lake La Su An directly ahead through the woods, the service road turns left. A side road goes left toward the Hogback Pond dam, and another heads to the right around the west edge of Lake La Su An. Don't take it; continue straight ahead, traveling east parallel to the north shore of the lake, which is about 20 feet below the trail to the right. This is a nice wooded trail with a good show of spring wildflowers. Off to the left is buttonbush swamp. The endangered copperbelly water snake is a known resident of this part of Williams County. This is the kind of habitat it prefers. It is, of course, illegal to collect or harm these creatures. Like their cousins the common water snakes, they are aggressive when encountered, but not poisonous.

Trees obviously felled by beavers give away the presence of a bank den along the lakeshore downhill from the trail. It was also here that I found American columbo growing. This rosette-producing perennial member of the gentian family has not been reported in the literature as occurring in this part of the state. When seen in spring before it sends up its flowering stalk, it has a resemblance to a cultivated tobacco plant. When it blooms in late spring, it has large paniculate clusters of four-lobed, purple-spotted greenish yellow flowers on stalks about 6 feet tall.

Soon the trail makes a right turn to cross the dam and, heading south now, begins its ascent to the high open land east of Lake

La Su An. As I traveled this area, I was not alone. Several unnamed dragonflies and a six-spotted (green forest) tiger beetle moved along the trail at about my pace. Both are predators, carnivores if you will; they were looking for other flying insects upon which to feed.

It is about a 75-foot rise from the dam to where the gravel service road turns 45 degrees to the right to travel a ridge through open grassland above the lake. There is a mowed trail parallel to the fence if you prefer, but I chose the route closer to the lake. There was a male prairie warbler singing his up-the-scale song as I passed through. From here you get the best view of Lake La Su An. The track you are following begins dropping as it swings to the left to cross the dike to Ed's Pond. A single redbud tree was in full bloom down the hill toward the lake during my hike.

A sign indicates that this is the nesting area of an endangered species. Upon inquiry, I learned that the Henslow's sparrow nests here. To the right of the trail is a planting of several acres of big bluestem grass, a native of Ohio's tallgrass prairies. Short-eared owls are seen in this wildlife area during the winter months. This crepuscular species occasionally nests in Ohio, but most of those seen are winter migrants from farther north. They fly low to the ground in the early-morning and late-afternoon hours, hunting meadow voles.

Another bird that is considered uncommon in Ohio but is occasionally seen here during migration is the sandhill crane. They breed not far to the north in Michigan then fly south to spend the cold months in Florida and other Gulf states. Their breeding range seems to be expanding, so it is not unlikely that they may be seen nesting here in the not-too-distant future.

As the trail makes its way around the upper end of the lake, you are about as far

American Columbo, with its tobacco-like basal leaves, is found along the trail.

from where you started as you will get. After passing a pump, the old road you have been following goes by a dock, then heads to the area checking station, where fishing permits are issued and catches checked.

After a short rest, it's time to begin the return leg of the hike by heading west along the road, then turning back into the wildlife area to follow a mowed path uphill among pines and open meadow. As I crossed the area, a tree swallow emerged from a bluebird box, a brown thrasher entertained with its mocking song, and a towhee sang from a branch close by.

At the end of the pines, the trail passes a large sycamore that seems out of place so far from the water's edge; then, after a short stretch of more old field, it enters the woods. As the trail drops rapidly toward the lake level, it passes another small pond, this one through the woods to the left. The trail is surfaced with crushed gravel in this area. In this more mesic woods, there were some large patches of wild blue phlox in bloom when I walked the trail. Among the oaks, hickories, and maples, the wide trail heads east on the level. To the left and right you can see where the road was located in an earlier time. Spring beauties and large-flowered trilliums, Ohio's official state wildflower, were in full flower in mid-May. A little-used track heads off to the right toward Lake La Su An, but do not follow it. Though this is not one of Ohio's boulder belts, an occasional glacial erratic sticks up though the surface of the ground.

After crossing another ravine, the trail returns to high ground and heads east once more. You can see Lake La Su An through the trees to the right and another small impoundment, Clem's Pond, to the left. The trail makes a hard left turn to cross in front of Clem's Pond. This is a picturesque spot where I could not keep the camera in my pack. The first green frog I had heard that spring gave its banjolike call from the water's edge, and male toads were trying hard to seduce the opposite sex. Set a good many feet higher than La Su An, Clem's Pond is several acres in size. A blue jay scolded as I moved on down the trail; the shadow of a turkey vulture passed over the trail, as it had many times that day.

As the trail nears the top of yet another rise, the presence of old-fashioned garden iris in the young woods seems to indicate the presence of a homestead in earlier years. A sign on the right identifies Lake La Su An, and the trail has returned to a familiar intersection. The outbound trail route has passed from left to right. Turn left, if you wish, to return to your vehicle by the route you entered.

Or you can go straight across the intersection and cross the dike of Hogback Pond, which lies to the left. I interrupted a common

water snake's sunbath on the dike but enjoyed watching it navigate through the water. This pond has been stocked with amur carp to try to control aquatic vegetation. At the far end of the pond, a pair of Canada geese took to the water from their nest.

Next, follow the road uphill to where you can see Jerry's Pond on the right. There is a tower here that looks like a nesting tower for ospreys. These have been successful in many places around the country and should work here. There are a couple of other small ponds beyond this point, but they are neither accessible or visible from the trail. Take the grass trail to the west to head through the woods past the construction disposal area and reconnect with the service road to the parking lot. Lake LaVere is visible to the south.

When you reach the mowed path to the Lake LaVere dam, turn left and walk to the dam. In spring you will likely be greeted by Canada geese using the earthen dike for nesting. Follow the trail beyond the dam and into the woods. American columbo also grows among the oaks and hickories on the slope. Eventually the trail comes out into a grassy field where there are more towers. Walk past them, heading northwest, to reach a service road that will lead you to the parking lot.

Camping is not permitted at Lake La Su Ann, but Harrison Lake State Park, which has a fine campground, is located about 20 miles to the east just inside Fulton County.

22

Lake Loramie State Park

Total distance: 4 miles (6.4 km)

Hiking time: 2¼ hours

Maximum elevation: 960 feet

Vertical rise: 3 feet

Maps: USGS 7½' Series Fort Loramie;
ODNR Lake Loramie State Park brochure

Loramie Creek is a small tributary of the Great Miami River that formed in front of the melting Wisconsinan glacier many thousands of years ago. It drains a short, narrow northeast–southwest strip of land east of Fort Loramie between two end moraines—the St. Johns and the Mississinewa. Nearly the entire watershed is in Shelby County. To the west of Shelby, the land between these two moraines drains to the west to the Wabash River, then into the Maumee, and, eventually, into the Atlantic Ocean. Less than a mile south of Shelby County, in Miami County, Loramie Creek joins the Great Miami River to start runoff from this area on its way to the Gulf of Mexico.

The Loramie Creek watershed is just barely south of the divide on quite level ground moraine. The watershed on the north side of the St. Johns Moraine also flows to the Atlantic, only first via the St. Marys River to the Wabash, then joining the Maumee in the vicinity of Fort Wayne, Indiana, before traveling through Lakes Erie and Ontario and on to the ocean.

When the route of a Miami (later Miami & Erie) Canal connecting the Ohio River with Lake Erie was planned, the flat land near Loramie Creek was chosen as the place for the summit. It was the easiest route from the Ohio River watershed to that of Lake Erie. Native Americans had known that for years. They had made thousand of trips, or portages, as the French voyageurs called them, between the two stream systems. That is why in about 1769 the French Canadian Pierre Loramie established a

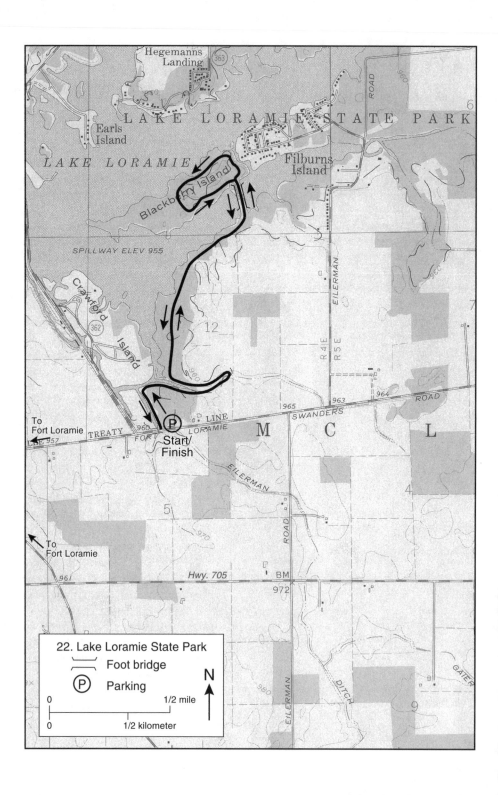

Hegemanns
Landing

363

Earls
Island

L A K E   L O R A M I E   S T A T E   P A R K

6

L A K E   L O R A M I E

Blackberry Island

Filburns
Island

SPILLWAY ELEV 955

Crawford Island

362

7

EILERMAN ROAD

12

R 4 E
R 5 E

960

ROAD

960

965   963   964   ROAD
SWANDERS

M   C   L

To
Fort Loramie
LINE 957   TREATY   960   FORT   LORAMIE   LINE
P
Start/
Finish

EILERMAN

ROAD

5

970

To
Fort Loramie

961   Hwy. 705   BM
972

GATER

DITCH

EILERMAN

960

9

22. Lake Loramie State Park
Foot bridge
P   Parking
N

0   1/2 mile

0   1/2 kilometer

trading post along the banks of the creek that still bears his name. The trading post burned down in 1782 and Loramie fled west with the Indians, but in 1794 or 1795 a fort was built on the site by federal troops. By 1812 it was no longer in use, but the name and a small community at that site still exist.

By 1840, when the Miami & Erie Canal was completed, an 1,828-acre reservoir had been built on Loramie Creek to collect and feed water into the north end of the 23-mile-long Loramie Summit section of the canal. (The 14-mile-long Sidney feeder brought water from the Great Miami to the canal just south of the summit to help float boats toward Cincinnati.) But each time a lock was used to move a canal boat in either direction from the Loramie Summit section, water was lost downstream. A renewal supply of water was critical to continued operation.

The canal era was pivotal in Ohio's growth, especially the agricultural sector, but it did not last long. The rise of the railroad, financial difficulties, and natural disasters spelled its demise. The legislature lost interest in spending any more money on the canal in 1920, and the massive flood of March 1913 brought operation to an end.

In 1917 action by the general assembly ensured the creation of Lake Loramie State Park. It was being managed by the old Division of Conservation and Natural Resources when in 1949 it, like other canal lakes, became a part of the new state park system.

With the privatization of some areas of the old reservoir and an almost continuous dredge-and-fill operation, the size and shape of the lake and park area have changed over the years. Now with 1,955 acres of water, 30 miles of shoreline, and 400 acres of land, the park boasts a fine campground, many picnic areas, good boat-launch ramps, and 10 miles of hiking trails.

How to Get There

To reach Lake Loramie State Park, travel to Shelby County from the Dayton or Toledo area on I-75. At Sidney, take SR 29 northwest to Fort Loramie–Swanders Road, then travel west to the park and the Lakeview Trail parking lot. From the Columbus area, travel I-70 west to SR 29, go northwest through Urbana and Sidney to Fort Loramie–Swanders Road, then west to the park.

The Trail

A good place to start hiking at Lake Loramie is at the Lakeview Trail parking lot just east of SR 362 on the north side of Fort Loramie–Swanders Road on the south edge of the park. A sign indicates that Blackberry Island is 1 mile away. By my calculations it is a little farther than that; if you follow the trail in exploring the island, this hike should be closer to 4 miles in distance. It is not difficult. Although it is level for most of the way, it is not adapted for wheelchair use.

The trail heads northwest along the water's edge. To the west, across a narrow arm of the lake, is a picnic area under tall trees. The trail soon makes an abrupt right turn to move due east, still paralleling the lake's edge and traveling through thicket. Second-growth swamp forest typical of this poorly drained part of the state lies to the right. Pin oak, swamp white oak, ash, and red maple are common. When the trees run out, continue hiking east with a ditch on the left. When you reach a culvert, turn left across the ditch and left again to continue on the Lakeview Trail. On the August afternoon when I walked this trail, dozens of dragonflies were patrolling along here, looking for flying insects for a meal on the wing.

A pontoon boat quietly cruises off Blackberry Island.

As you would expect, mosquitoes were also present in good numbers.

The trail reenters the woods, turning to the right. Follow the trail as its travels north about 15 to 20 feet inside the woods. Black walnuts, shagbark hickories, locusts, and an occasional buckeye are in the forest mix. After turning northeast, the trail soon reaches an intersection where walking straight ahead will take you to a parking lot at a turnaround at the end of a park road. Going left will cut through the woods and head between the water and the woods toward the bridge to Blackberry Island.

Once on the island, choose which way you want to walk the loop trail. It is quite well defined as it passes through bush honeysuckle thicket and stands of young trees circumnavigating the island. There are areas where boardwalk has been built to save the trail surface. This appears to be a man-made or, at the least, enhanced island; it's probably the recipient of many yards of

dredge spoil during past efforts to keep the lake deep enough for recreational boating. A suction dredge has been in use almost continuously for close to 50 years removing silt that is carried into the lake from nearby agricultural fields. Some of the dredge piping can be seen in the woods on Blackberry Island.

The trail traverses only the east half of the two-part island, turning and returning to the bridge after it travels along the bisecting channel. After returning to the mainland on the Blackberry Island bridge, turn right and follow the trail back to the isolated parking area. A sign directs the Lakeview Trail hiker back into the woods. Red cedars attest to the high lime content of the soils of the area. In this area I heard a pileated woodpecker calling on the warm summer day when I was exploring. At a split in the trail there is an option to follow a different trail, closer to the lake on your return trek. If you do so, after the trail has gone southwest for a while then swings toward the south, be sure not to accidentally take a trail to the right that leads across a narrow arm of the lake to the campground. Continue south until you turn left to emerge from the woods at the same point as the inbound trail. Travel east along the ditch to cross the culvert and turn right to return to the parking lot by the route you used to enter.

The Buckeye Trail, Ohio's official hiking trail, passes through Lake Loramie State Park along SR 362 near the campground and picnic area. In this area it follows lesser-traveled road and parks of the canal system as it works its way around the state. This is a linear trail, and hiking it requires either hiking two directions or arranging a two-car shuttle in advance. While you are in the area, consider hiking the trails at Lockington Reservoir near the village of Lockington. The hike is described in *50 Hikes in Ohio*. Miami & Erie Canal locks numbers 1 through 5, which stepped boats down from the Loramie Summit to the valley of the Great Miami River, are in the center of Lockington and well worth a visit. A few miles south of there, on Hardon Road just off SR 66 northwest of Piqua, is the Ohio Historical Society's Piqua Historical Area. Its museum features emphasizes the story of Indian tribes present in Ohio at the time of settlement. There is also the restored home of a government Indian agent and a restored section of the Miami & Erie Canal, with an authentic canal boat operating between May and October.

23

Lawrence Woods
State Nature Preserve

*Total distance: 1.1-mile (1.8 km)
accessible boardwalk*

Hiking time: 35 minutes

Maximum elevation: 1,065 feet

Vertical rise: 5 feet

*Maps: USGS 7½' Series Mt. Victory;
ODNR*

The locals called it the Devil's Backbone, but geologists refer to it as the St. Johns Moraine. It is one of several recessional moraines that stretch across the Wisconsinan till plains of northwestern Ohio and was likely named for the small community of St. John that sits astride it in eastern Auglaize County. It reaches clear across the southern part of Hardin County, blocking any southward drainage from the lowland that lies between it and the Wabash Moraine to the north. Runoff from that area—including the north slope of the St. Johns Moraine—is via the Scioto River system, which drains the south-central part of the state. The Scioto River originates in the Scioto Swamp at the western end of that intermoraine area, only a few miles southwest of Kenton, the Hardin County seat.

Lawrence Woods State Nature Preserve lies right square on the St. Johns Moraine 5 miles south of Kenton, in the Scioto River drainage system. Several plant communities can be found in the 500-acre wooded part of the preserve: oak–hickory forest, beech–oak–red maple forest, elm–ash–pin oak swamp forest, mixed-hardwood swamp forest, and buttonbush shrub swamp. Though part of the woods has been grazed in the past and hardwoods have been selectively harvested during the past half century, this is a good example of an old-growth forest. Several species of rare plants occur there and, because of its size, it is a good nesting area for neotropical migrant birds such as vireos, warblers, and orioles. In several recent seasons there has been a small great

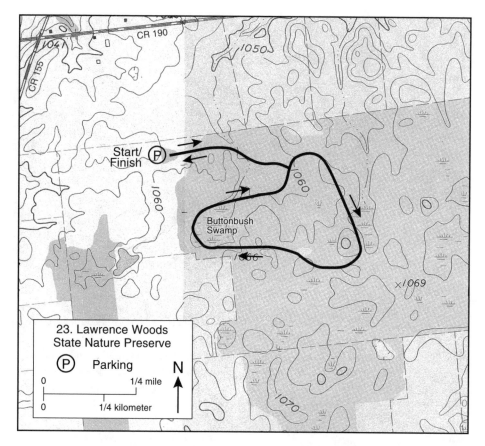

Map legend:

23. Lawrence Woods State Nature Preserve

(P) Parking

N

0 — 1/4 mile
0 — 1/4 kilometer

Labels on map: CR 190, CR 155, 1050, 1060, 1066, 1070, 1069, Start/Finish (P), Buttonbush Swamp

blue heron rookery in the woods.

Lawrence Woods was purchased in 1997 from the Augustine Family Limited Partnership. It is named in honor of the Honorable William Lawrence and his descendants. The judge was a prominent political figure in the formative years of the community and state. He was an author, statesman, banker, and cofounder of the American Red Cross. He served as U.S. congressman at the end of the Civil War. Many of descendants gathered at the woods on May 1, 1999, when the preserve was dedicated, pleased to see that the woods will be preserved in perpetuity as a state nature preserve.

The entrance to the area and the trail-head is from CR 190 near the northwest corner of the 1,059-acre parcel. The drive goes to the south from the road, passing a barn and making a left/right jog before passing through a cultivated field. When it reaches the south edge of farmed land, the road turns left into a parking lot. There is a bulletin board with an area map near the lot. The recycled plastic boardwalk is accessible from the lot by people using wheelchairs or walkers, but there are no sideboards, so caution is required.

How to Get There

To reach Lawrence Woods, travel US 33 northwest from the Columbus area to Marysville. Then go north on SR 31 through

Visitors have likened this contorted tree to a rhinoceros.

Mount Victory to CR 190. Turn left (west) and go approximately 3.5 miles. A sign identifies the entrance to the preserve on the south side of the road.

The Trail

Almost immediately the trail enters the woods, where it passes a number of very large-boled trees, perhaps 42 inches in diameter at chest height. These are trees that grew deep in some virgin forest, for they have the low-spreading branches so characteristic of trees that have grown in the open, perhaps at the edge of pasture or along a fence line. Around them the trees are all much younger—trees that began growing in the area perhaps 10 years after the grazing stopped.

The white oak referred to as the Rhino Tree is very obvious when you come to it. It's easy to see where the name came from. A bench, albeit a rather high one, is provided for rest and relaxation. The trees are species common to the wet woods of the till plains of northwestern Ohio: bur oak, red oak, swamp white oak, red maple, ash, and even elm. The latter continues to grow in swamp forests from seeds in the soil (what is often referred to as the seed bank). They seldom grow to more than 5 or 6 inches in diameter before Dutch elm disease kills them.

Where the ground is just a little higher in elevation, you'll find large beech trees with no hearts or initials carved in their bark. The trail twists and turns to avoid large trees, coming, eventually, to a junction where it splits to make a loop through the woods. There are numbered stations along the trail, which is set up for a self-guided trail brochure. If you obtained one, continue walking clockwise on the loop to follow the numerical sequence.

If you look into the woods away from the trail, you will see some very large stumps remaining from one of the late-20th-century selective cuts. After the spring rains, you will see some vernal ponds, the breeding habitat of the amphibians of Lawrence Woods.

Lawrence Woods is one of just a handful of locations in Ohio where heart-leaf plantain, a threatened species, grows. It is a plant of cold, clear streams flowing over a limestone substrate, a condition that is apparently found in Lawrence Woods. The bedrock beneath all of Hardin County is Devonian-age limestone.

On the early-March day when I last walked Lawrence Woods, I needed no sign to tell me when I was approaching the buttonbush swamp. Western chorus frogs were in full voice, the males making what biologists like to call the advertising call. It's the full-blown "come hither" call for thsee thumb-sized amphibians. Unlike some of the Rana group of frogs such as the bullfrog and green frog, which call on into the summer months, the chorus frogs call only during mating season. Lawrence Woods looks like it would be good habitat for the eastern wood frog, but the *Ohio Frog and Toad Atlas,* published by the Ohio Biological Survey in 2000, shows no records for Hardin County.

The last two weeks of April and most of the month of May is the time to visit Lawrence Woods if you are especially fond of wildflower and birds, as I am. Midsummer is butterfly time in the old fields of western Ohio, so if you enjoy stalking the "wildflowers of the air" with camera or binoculars, don't overlook the edges of the fields near the parking lot.

24

Morris Woods
State Nature Preserve

Total distance: 1.5 miles (2.4 km)

Hiking time: 1 hour

Maximum elevation: 1,250 feet

Vertical rise: 30 feet

Maps: USGS 7½' Series Johnstown

James W. Abbott loved the woods, and he loved birds. In 1957 he purchased a 104-acre tract of land along Dutch Lane in northeastern Licking County that was probably 65 percent woods and 35 percent abandoned farmland. What woods existed were by nobody's definition old-growth forest. Down through the years many trees had been removed, though apparently the area had never been clear-cut. It may even have been grazed back in the days when it was not uncommon for farmers to turn cattle or swine loose in a woods. But even so, it was a nice woods with some large forest-grown trees. Mr. Abbott apparently saw in it great potential.

From then until the time of his death in 1979, Mr. Abbott spent a great deal of his time planting and nurturing the land into a wildlife sanctuary. He believed that this could educate the young and old, but especially the young, in the ways of nature. He built two small ponds to attract migrating wildlife: Lake Helen, named after his mother, and Abbott's Pond. He named his sanctuary Morris Woods after his father. Following his death, the land came to the state to be used as a wildlife sanctuary.

James Abbott especially wanted the area to be used as a bird sanctuary. He would be pleased to know that more than 40 species of birds have been recorded as nesting there; many more use the land as a resting and feeding area during migration.

Morris Woods in located in the eastern part of Ohio's till plain, in an area known as the Galion Glaciated Low Plateau. It's an area of rolling upland that is transitional

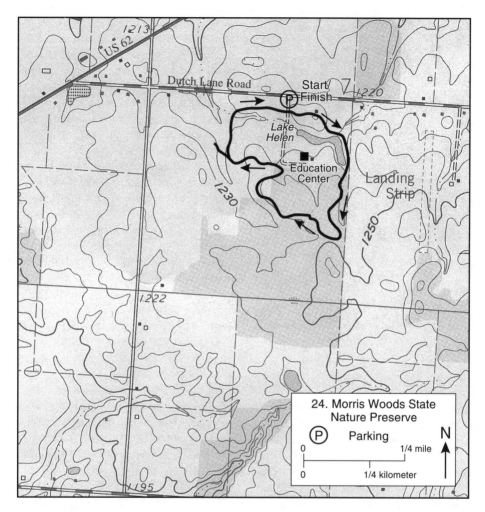

24. Morris Woods State Nature Preserve

Ⓟ Parking

N

0 — 1/4 mile

0 — 1/4 kilometer

between the gently rolling till plain to the west and the hilly Glaciated Allegheny Plateau to the east. The drainage from Morris Woods is both to the north and to the south, but it all eventually flows east and into the Muskingum River system. The till has the medium to low lime content of Wisconsinan-age over Mississippian-age shales and sandstones. The land was covered with hardwood forest at the time of settlement: beech–maple on the better-drained sites and elm–ash–maple–pin oak swamp forest in the poorly drained places.

Lying south of the Greeneville Treaty line, this part of Ohio was being settled as the 19th century was being born. Licking County was formed in 1808, only five years after statehood. From 1804 until 1840 the government had a land office just down the Licking River at Zanesville, not a far walk or ride to make to file for a land patent. The western part of the county soon became farmland, and the Ohio Canal that ran through the county seat, Newark, provided a way to get agricultural products to the market. The till plain and moraine of western

In late summer, cardinal flower blooms close to the trail.

Licking County still produce good crops from farm and orchard.

Had it been clear-cut and drained, Morris Woods would not have been good farmland. Wisely, subsequent owners kept it for the lumber, firewood, and maple syrup it could provide the farm family. The hummocky land with its wet areas and hardwood forests is a good place to explore.

How to Get There

Morris Woods is easy to reach from the central Ohio area. Take US 62 east through Johnstown. Dutch Lane Road is the second road to the right after leaving the city limits. The preserve is no more than a mile to the east on the south side of the road.

The Trail

Park at the lot just inside the entrance off Dutch Lane Road. After checking out the map on the bulletin board, begin hiking by

taking the trail directly across the driveway (east) from where you parked and locked your car. It's a grassy trail that winds its way between ornamental evergreens planted by Mr. Abbott. You soon come to a rise known as the Lighting Knob where there is a bench. This is a good place to sit on watch or "pssh up" the birds of the thicket. The bush honeysuckle and multiflora rose often attract many cardinals and other birds such as the brown thrasher and mockingbird. From the grassy knob, the trail arcs to the right to a narrow boardwalk that leads around the east side of Lake Helen. Like all wooden boardwalks, this one can be very slippery when wet or frosty. The trail along the east boundary can also be quite wet after a rain as the water from the field next door drains into the pond.

A short wooden bridge carries the trail over an inlet to the pond coming from the edge of the woods. The trail rises as it enters the woods. The trees are not huge, but the fact that the area has been protected from timber harvests for at least 45 years has allowed a good shrub layer of spicebush to develop; stumps from earlier cutting are no longer visible. At a trail junction, a sign points to the Abbott's Pond Trail to the right. Continue on into the woods on the Woodland Trail. Oaks, sugar maples, and beech trees dominate the canopy.

As the trail nears the south boundary of the preserve, it turns right and drops to a wetter part of the woods where there is a short section of boardwalk. Here it is passing through an area that returned to woods through natural succession after Mr. Abbott purchased the land. Going north back on natural forest surface, the trail winds its way to an intersection with the other end of the Abbott's Pond Trail. When the leaves are off the trees, you may be able to see a low building to the north that was built by Mr. Abbott as a place to stay when he was working in the woods. It is now used as a site for educational programs offered by Division of Natural Areas and Preserves staff or by visiting school groups.

Just before the reaching the road to the program building, the trail (now the Abbott's Pond Trail) turns sharply to the left. It passes through a grove of mixed evergreens planted by Mr. Abbott: white pine, hemlock, and spruce. Beyond, it enters a thicket composed largely of small trees and shrubs that spread from government-agency-supplied wildlife planting packages of earlier years. A sweep to the right with old field alongside brings you to the entrance of the trail that goes left to Abbott's Pond. Be sure to take this trail to the vicinity of the pond. This is where, in late summer, cardinal flower grows in the low grassy vegetation. If it has been a well-watered summer, it will be very visible above the other vegetation. If has been a droughty season, you may have to hunt for it low in the grass. As the name implies, it is bright red, and one of fewer than a dozen red-colored wildflowers that grow in Ohio.

Back on the main trail, go left to continue a loop hike. A bridge spans an outflow from Lake Helen as the trail moves into an area mowed annually to keep it as old field habitat for birds that require that kind of landscape. Beginning in mid-July, I find it a great place to photograph butterflies in the wild. In rainy seasons the trail can be soggy, so be prepared with adequate footwear. In midsummer milkweeds, attractive to monarchs and many other butterfly species, hang over the trail, and thistles seem to always have a great spangled fritillary posed ready for your long lens. At the east end of this field, the trail returns to the parking lot. Morris Woods is a good trail to walk at various seasons of the year—one to get to know in its many garbs.

25

Mount Gilead State Park

Total distance: 2.52 miles (4 km)

Hiking time: 2 hours

Maximum elevation: 1,197 feet

Vertical rise: 101 feet

*Maps: USGS 7½' Series Mt. Gilead;
ODNR Mt. Gilead State Park brochure*

The county seat town of Mount Gilead sits on high land where three Wisconsinan-age glacial end moraines converged, leaving distinctly rolling terrain in the glaciated low plateau region at the eastern limit of the till plains. Whetstone Creek courses along the western edge of Mount Gilead State Park, separating it from the town, then runs south and west of the community to eventually drain into the Scioto River basin of central Ohio. Its tributary, Sams Creek, has cut a deep valley in the moraine as it drains a small area on the very eastern edge of the Scioto watershed. Less than 4 miles to the east of the park, the headwaters of the Kokosing River drain the runoff to the east into the huge Muskingum River watershed of eastern Ohio.

The first settlement in the area began shortly after the War of 1812, probably with the establishment of a gristmill on Whetstone Creek. Some say the community was at first called Whetsom (whetstone) after the name of the stream, but from 1824 to 1832 it was generally referred to as Youngstown, after Jacob Young who had laid out the town. In 1834 it was incorporated as Mount Gilead, apparently honoring a similarly named town in Virginia. Morrow County, with Mount Gilead as its seat, was established in 1848, taking its name from Jeremiah Morrow, governor of Ohio from 1822 to 1826. Over the years the area has been one of mostly small farms, though in the 1960s there was a small oil boom that lasted a little over a decade.

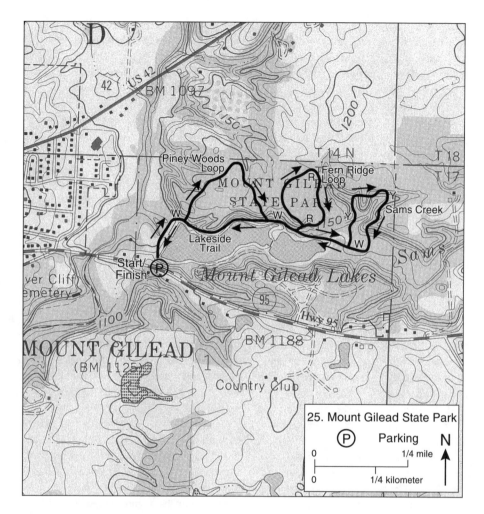

In 1919 a small lake was built on Sams Creek, still in existence as the upstream lake in the state park. In 1930 a larger lake was completed just downstream from the original. At that time the property was under the supervision of the state Bureau of Engineering. In 1949, when the Department of Natural Resources was formed, the land was turned over to the new Division of Parks and Recreation to be maintained as a state park. Since then it has been a popular area for family camping, fishing, picnicking, and hiking. Over the years about 3.5 miles of hiking trails have been established, and with the recent purchase of additional land, more trails are under development. Though the original forest cover was removed a long time ago, the park had good secondary hardwood forest and nice 50-year-old pine plantings.

How to Get There

To reach Mount Gilead State Park, travel north from Columbus on I-71 to the SR 95 exit. Turn west and travel to the office parking lot about 0.5 mile beyond the park entrance.

The Trail

From the park map, it might seem that a good place to begin hiking would be at the parking lot at the spillway area at the narrow neck that separates the two lakes. However, there is no bridge at that location, which means to reach the trails on the far side of the lake you must walk on the spillway. This can be slippery and, in times of high water, dangerous. Instead, I suggest that you bypass the main park entrance and drive 0.5 mile farther west on SR 95 to park at the lot next to the office.

Walk downhill across a play field to reach a bridge that crosses Sams Creek downstream from the dam. In the distance you will see a sign pointing toward the Piney Woods Trail. The trail that you are embarking on is actually the Lakeside Trail, a footpath that goes completely around the lake. It is blazed with white paint. The four other named trails of the park all originate off the Lakeside Trail and are blazed with different colors.

At the end of the bridge turn right and climb onto the earthen dam, heading toward the far side of the lake. On the warm August day when I walked the trail, Queen Anne's lace was still in bloom, and ironweed and tall green-headed coneflower were just coming into flower here. Dragonflies, in their stark-colored beauty, were abundant. A pileated woodpecker called from the tall timber on the distant hillside.

At the far end of the earthen dam, there is a trail junction. The Maple Grove Trail, blazed with green paint, leaves to the left and drops into the valley of Whetstone Creek. It goes about 1,000 feet upstream on floodplain before turning right and climbing a ravine to join the Piney Woods Loop near what used to be the north boundary of the park. In addition, a new trail that will continue along the river to reach land recently acquired to the north is under development as I prepare this narrative.

My preference is to follow the Lakeside Trail with its white blazes to where, about 100 feet into the woods, it reaches a junction with the blue-blazed Piney Woods Loop. The latter leaves the Lakeside Trail at a right angle to the left, heading uphill. The white-blazed trail continues along the lakeshore. Presently the Piney Woods Loop is the longest trail that ventures away from the valley, though that might not be so when more trails are opened to the north.

On the Piney Woods Trail you will gain about 100 feet in elevation in a fairly short distance. As you make the initial climb, you can see the deep valley of the Whetstone to your left; for a short time there are ravines on both sides. The trail circles clockwise through the beech–sugar maple woods for a little over 0.3 mile before it rejoins the white-blazed path just above the lakeshore. You will see the junction with the Maple Grove Trail close to the northernmost point in the loop. Be careful as you descend toward the lake. Steps, waterbars, small bridges, and even the trail surface on this and other trails in this hilly park are in continual conflict with the runoff from the steep slopes, but the trails are quite passable, and volunteers have been working hard in recent months to improve their condition.

Back on the Lakeside Trail, head east (a left turn coming off the hill). You may see a trail that exits right toward the lake and the spillway of the upper lake. Park officials discourage the use of this trail because of its sometimes slippery condition. Continue on the white-blazed trail until you see another trail exiting uphill to the left. Blazed with red, this is the Fern Ridge Trail—and in fact you will see more fern along this woodland path than anywhere else in the park.

The 0.5-mile-long trail begins by climbing steeply then reaching a split to make a

In late summer, giant puffball mushrooms seem to appear overnight.

loop. I suggest that you follow it in a clockwise manner. Once at the junction, the trail travels on a fairly flat hilltop, making a broad loop to then return to the junction. As you turn back toward the lake, the trail is bordered on the left by first a deep ravine and then the steep slope to the lake. By the way, the park map being distributed at present shows a connecting trail along the north fence between the Fern Ridge Loop and the Sams Creek Trail; this no longer exists.

Once again at the Lakeside Trail, turn left to follow the white trail east to its intersection with the Sams Creek Trail. Also about 0.5 mile in length, blazed this time with yellow paint, this trail uses a boardwalk at one end and a long set of steps at the other as it leaves and returns to the Lakeside Trail. It was developed many years ago as a self-guided nature trail with a well-written and illustrated booklet available that interpreted objects or areas of interest along the trail identified by numbered posts. At my last walking, most of the posts were gone or in a bad state of repair, but it is a lovely section of trail that winds its way among large trees on the hillside above two side ravines and the Sams Creek Valley.

As the Sams Creek Trail comes off the hill, it meets the Lakeside running in either direction. At high noon as I descended the steps here, a wood pewee was calling even though it was mid-August, long after it needed to advertise for a mate or mark a territory with a call. Could it be that birds sometime just sing because they enjoy doing it or hearing the music? I don't know why not. I also heard the town noon whistle blow and chimes in a church tower playing a hymn. I preferred the pewee.

To the left the trail crosses Sams Creek upstream from the lake and goes to the campground. Though it does not show on the park map, there is a white-blazed route that will lead you on around the lake to where you can return to the park office lot.

I am an advocate of returning along the north shore of the lake on the white-blazed trail you have been traveling intermittently. It's farther from the picnic and fishing areas and is not a mowed grass trail. Besides, the scenery will be entirely different when viewed from the other direction. And maybe the pewees will sing for you, too.

26

Paint Creek State Park

Total distance: 4.75 miles (7.6 km)

Hiking time: 3 hours

Maximum elevation: 865 feet

Vertical rise: 55 feet

Maps: USGS 7½' Series Bainbridge; ODNR Paint Creek State Park brochure; USACE Paint Creek Lake brochure

A floodplain is, by definition, an area of low-lying land that a river flows across and that is covered with sediment as a result of frequent flooding. It doesn't sound like a good place to build permanent structures such as homes, factories, and businesses. But build them there we humans have done. The availability of water for power generation, transportation, temperature reduction, and to quench our thirst has made the advantages of living alongside a river seem to outweigh the risk of occasional flooding.

The years 1913 and 1959 brought walls of water down the Scioto River Valley, inundating Chillicothe and Portsmouth. Lesser floods have happened in the area in many of the years between. The simple solution of the 20th century seemed to lie in building dams across rivers in their upper reaches to contain heavy torrents of water, to be slowly released in measured amounts at a later date. We now know that the problem of periodic flooding is more complex, requiring a multifaceted approach, but in 1962 the Army Corps of Engineers proposed to build three new dams in the Scioto River watershed to help prevent flooding in the lower end of the valley. Whether cost effective or not, the figures do show that much flooding has been prevented by the building of Alum Creek, Deer Creek, and Paint Creek dams (Delaware dam on the Olentangy River had been completed in 1951).

Nine-thousand-acre Paint Creek State Park on the Highland-Ross county line 21 miles west of Chillicothe is operated by the Ohio Division of Parks and Recreation on

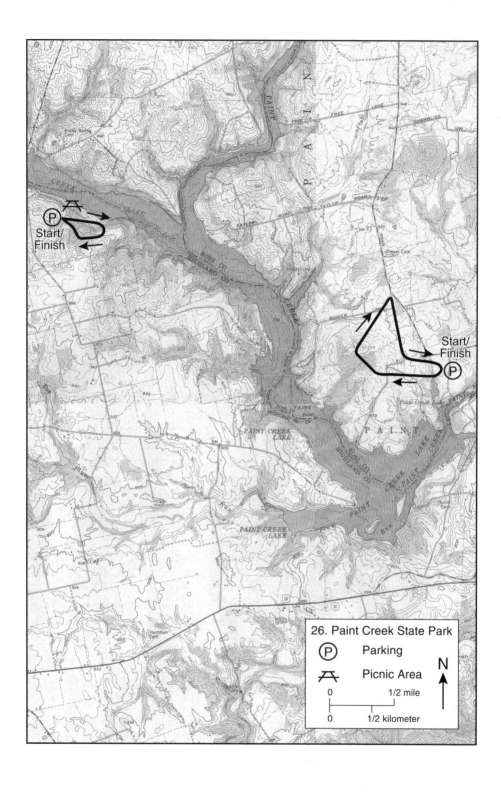

Start/
Finish

Start/
Finish

26. Paint Creek State Park

Ⓟ   Parking

🛆   Picnic Area

N

0   1/2 mile

0   1/2 kilometer

The dam and spillway structure and a favorite fisherman's cove are visible from the trail.

Paint Creek Lake, the 1,190-acre body of water that now occupies much of the lower valley of Rattlesnake Creek and part of the valley of upper Paint Creek. The Corps operates the dam, controlling the lake level and downstream flow, while ODNR manages the recreation facilities and wildlife resources.

Paint Creek is virtually astride the Allegheny Escarpment and very close to the end moraine marking the farthest reach of the Wisconsinan ice sheet into this part of Ohio. For that matter, well-weathered moraine left by the farthest reach of earlier glaciers in Ohio lies only a few miles to the southeast. Paint and Rattlesnake Creeks drain the Wisconsinan-age southern Ohio loamy till plain and the southern part of the Darby Plain in Highland and Fayette Counties, flowing south between the north–south moraines of that region.

Elm–ash swamp forest once covered the river bottoms and rich, mixed-mesophytic forests blanketed the uplands.

Though apparently not an area used by Adena and Hopewell Indians, the valley of Paint Creek north of Greenfield is said to have been the location of many Indian villages during the 1780s and 1790s.

White settlers likely ventured into the area even before the signing of the Greeneville Treaty in 1795. Virginians especially flocked to the area when land became available in exchange for vouchers given as compensation for service with the Virginia Militia in the Revolutionary War. In the opening years of the 19th century Chillicothe was the cradle of statehood for Ohio. Politicians from there vied with those from Cincinnati and Marietta for positions of power and leadership in the state that was to come into being in 1803. Ross County was an important center of influence on the fledgling western frontier.

How to Get There

Paint Creek State Park is located just north of US 50 approximately 24 miles west of

---

Paint Creek State Park

Chillicothe off Rapid Forge Road. It can, of course, be reached via US 50 from the Cincinnati area.

The Trails

Begin your exploration of Paint Creek Park by taking a quick walk on the 0.75-mile-long Harmony Trail below the spillway. Turn north from US 50 at Rapid Forge Road. It parallels Paint Creek heading north, then makes a wide sweep toward the west. The entrance to the dike and spillway area is on the left, just before Rapid Forge Road turns back to the north. Turn south and cross over the spillway bridge. Just before you reach the headquarters building, turn left and follow the driveway to a large parking lot at the river level. Here you will find the Harmony Trail, which makes a loop upriver to just below the spillway and back. This may or may not be an exciting area, with the sound of lots of rushing water possible, depending upon the weather.

Return to your car and take the driveway to the entry road, turn right across the spillway bridge, then park in the lot on the left side of the road. There you will find picnic tables, a shelter, and playground equipment. Drinking water and rest rooms are accessible during the warmer months only. A sign introduces the Little Pond National Recreation Trail. The water in the pond in the distance around which the trail travels is at a different level than Paint Creek Lake off to the left. There are some large beech, maple, and oak trees here. At this point, the trail is about 8 feet wide with a crushed-limestone surface. It crosses a knoll between the pond and the lake then begins to drop toward the pond. The trail splits, forcing the counterclockwise-or-clockwise decision upon you. I chose the latter. Taking it, you turn left and head for a cantilevered bridge that carries you across a deep gorge that connects the pond with the lake.

A rise off the other end of the bridge leads to a T in the trail in an area of old field vegetation. The trail to the right leads around the west shore of the pond and back to the parking lot. To the left, the trail climbs among young hardwoods and red cedar to a knob overlooking the lake. Behind a three-rail fence, the trail travels around the perimeter of this knob back from the edge of a precipice above the lake. (I estimated that it was close to 25 feet down to the water on the November day when I walked the trail. A fall drawdown had already lowered the lake by 10½ feet to its winter level of 787½ feet above sea level. This provides the lake with a large storage capacity in the event of a major storm.)

The trail leaves the knob by dropping into a lower open area then climbing the hillside. A hundred yards up the trail there is a cut back to the right toward the pond. It goes downhill past a trash drum, then reaches a T. After a left turn, the trail descends immediately to a bridge then rises and continues around the pond about 25 feet back from the shore. A wide side trail to the left looks to be a part of the mountain bike trail system. Ignore it, remaining within sight of the water. Occasionally moving closer to the shore, then again climbing the hillside, the trail eventually emerges from the woods at a point where you can see the rest rooms and the parking lot.

There are two other foot trails and many miles of bridle and mountain bike trails in the park. The 1-mile loop Milkweed Meadow foot trail is located at the campground on Taylor Road close to the amphitheater. It's a good open field trail to walk in late summer if you're interested in summer-blooming wildflowers and butterflies.

Yet another trail, the 1.5-mile Fern Hollow Trail, is a woodland path located on the west side of the Rattlesnake Creek arm of the lake. To reach it, it's necessary to return to US 50 and drive west to Rainsboro. There, turn right onto SR 753 and follow it through New Petersburg (where it makes a right turn) to its intersection with Snake Road. Turn right and immediately left onto a park road leading to a picnic area where there is a fishing pier and a rest room. The Fern Hollow Trailhead is at the far right corner of the parking lot. The trail makes a loop up a small hollow in second-growth woods, returning to the parking lot on the same path.

While you are in the Chillicothe area, you may want to explore any of several trails at Great Seal State Park, described elsewhere in this volume. A good hiking trail at Scioto Trails State Park south of Chillicothe is described in my earlier guide *50 Hikes in Ohio*.

27

Sandusky State Scenic River—Howard Collier Area

Total distance: 1.5 miles (2.4 km)

Hiking time: 1 hour

Maximum elevation: 810 feet

Vertical rise: 60 feet

Maps: USGS 7½' Series Tiffin South

The Sandusky River arises on the central Ohio clayey till plain between the Fort Wayne and the Defiance Moraines, both late-Wisconsinan age; it lies north of the divide that separates rain running off the land to the Atlantic Ocean via the Gulf of Mexico from rain that travels via the St. Lawrence River. It drains a 1,421-square-mile triangular piece of northern Ohio, with the mouth of the river flowing through the eastern part of the Black Swamp to reach Lake Erie at Sandusky Bay through one corner of the triangle.

Beneath the mantle of glacial till and moraines on the watershed lie Devonian and Silurian limestones and dolomites that in places outcrop along the river. The northern third is flat to gently rolling, with shorelines from ancient lakes that formed as the glaciers receded visible on the land. The southern two-thirds is relatively flat except where it cuts through the Defiance Moraine, with its 10- to 50-foot-high hills. Beech forests once covered the well-drained upper reaches of the watershed, but elm–ash–maple swamp forest prevailed in the poorer-drained land north of the Defiance Moraine and on to Sandusky Bay.

In January 1970 a 70-mile reach of the Sandusky River from near Upper Sandusky to downtown Fremont was designated under Ohio law a state scenic river. It's a stretch of water with well-forested shoreline, free-flowing water, and little anthropogenic impact on the water quality except for agricultural runoff. The Division of Natural Areas and Preserves, charged with administering scenic rivers, began acquiring

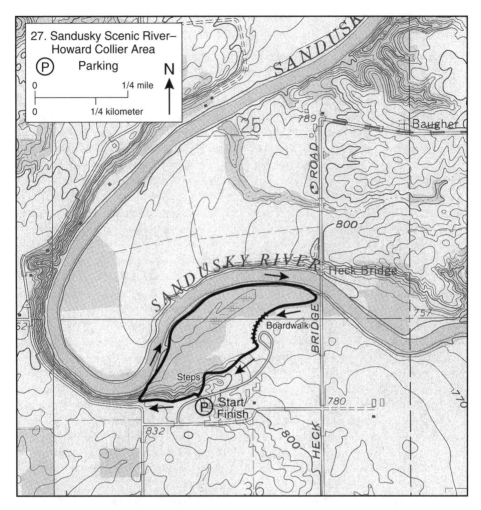

especially scenic properties along the river to provide further protection and access.

In Seneca township in southern Seneca County, where the river makes several wide, sweeping meanders as it cuts its way through the Defiance Moraine, the division purchased a 200-acre tract of bluff and river bottomland with an especially good stand of old timber. The holdings now include 301 acres on both sides of the river, as well as a river access area at Heck's Bridge near the east boundary. That the property included swamp with skunk cabbage and marsh marigold in profusion was a bonus. From the looks of the woods and the steepness of the bluff, I would judge that it has not been used as pasture, and the excellent vernal flora seems to bear that out. As a sizable piece of unfragmented riparian woods, both resident birds and the neotropical migrants find it attractive. In December 1970 it was dedicated as Howard L. Collier Area, in honor of the man who served as director of the Ohio Department of Finance from 1960 to 1971. It is one of the better-kept secrets in the division's portfolio.

How to Get There

The Sandusky State Scenic River—Howard Collier Area is located approximately 3 miles northeast of McCutchenville near the southwestern edge of Seneca County. From McCutchenville, proceed 3 miles east on CR 58, then 0.5 mile north on TR 131, and finally 0.25 mile east on TR 38. The entrance is on the north side of the road.

The Trail

Access to the trails of the Howard Collier Area was solved though the carpentry skills of longtime north-central Ohio area manager Eddie Reed. The steps that he built made it possible to make the 50-foot descent from the level of the surrounding countryside and the parking area to the river bottom with ease. Begin walking at the sign indicating the entrance to the beech woods trails just to the left of the bulletin board by the first parking lot inside the preserve. It was May 15 with thunderstorms threatening when I last explored this verdant trail.

Outside the woods, the phlox-like alien dame's rocket was just beginning to bloom, but once in the woods I found the beautiful native wild blue phlox there to greet me. I turned left among the beech and maple trees and headed for the staircase about 100 feet down the rim trail. Thirty-one steps carried me to the first platform where, as I pulled out my trusty Rollei 35 to take a picture, the sky opened up. At almost the same time, a chorus of tree frogs began calling loudly. I bathed momentarily in the beauty of the sensory assault of sound, smell, color, and warm rain but then beat a hasty retreat to my vehicle to wait out the storm.

Moments later, poncho back in my fanny pack, I made a second "beech head" attack on the preserve, but for diversion I turned instead to the north. I suggest that you follow only if you are prepared to drop straight down the hillside to the riparian paradise below. Not far from turning into the woods, the trail meets the preserve boundary, and to continue it required falling off the land. With my trusty Leki hiking pole propping me up, leg braces and all, I made it to the streambed without incident. The steps would be a better option . . . but then I would have missed the first big patch of skunk cabbage and scouring rush on the valley floor.

Turning right—upstream and, believe it or not, north—at an elevation about 20 feet above the water, the trail parallels the river through a forest of beech, maple, tulip poplar, basswood, buckeye, oak, and other hardwoods. A occasional fisherman's trail allows taking a peek and a picture close to the river. As I type this narrative, a very loud lightning strike on my tape-recorded trail notes brings back the memory of a cracking, booming trek through the wet woods on that turn-of-the-century May afternoon.

The trail crosses a side stream but, since this is a "wild trail," not the one at the bottom of the steps, there is no bridge. This is a wide river bottom forest and at this point, the trail follows higher ground between the present streambed and an earlier channel to the right.

Presently the trail joins a trail coming from the hillside off to the right—the official trail that carries hikers to the bottom via the staircase. Walking on a nice wide trail about 50 feet back from the water's edge, I met a nice shiny 5-foot-long black rat snake moving along the trail in the rain. Off to the right, the swamp that occupies the old river channel is clearly visible; it's the home of more skunk cabbage and a lot of marsh marigold.

The trail reaches a junction with a sign pointing right to the Little Fork Run Trail and straight ahead to continue on the Beech Ridge Trail. I opted for the latter to continue

A set of masterfully built steps lead to the riparian forest at Howard Collier access.

near the river, but I could see that the Little Fork Run Trail very shortly used a boardwalk to cross the old river channel swamp.

Both large-flowered trillium (the state's official wildflower, with a white flower held above its leaves) and drooping trillium (with a slightly smaller and paler white flower hung between two leaves) bloom along this trail. Still quite a distance back from the river's edge, the trail passes among huge forest-grown trees. I see no stumpage indicating even a selective harvest in recent years. A trail as lovely as this must have a distraction or two—in the case of my May sojourn, mosquitoes and nettles, but not to the point of being a real annoyance.

About 50 feet short of reaching Heck Ridge Road, the trail makes a 120-degree turn to the right rear to head across more wooded floodplain. It was in this area that I passed a tree alongside the trail to which a purple bra and a pair of very scanty women's panties had been nailed, one above the other. I blush at the thought of what kind of a shrine this might be. Traveling just inside the older woods, with young trees off to the right, the trail soon meets the other end of the Fork Run Trail.

This is a swamp forest area with red maple, silver maple, ash, cottonwood, and other wet-woods species. Here the trail climbs onto several hundred yards of boardwalk.

At the end of the walk you can go left to exit to a turnaround at the end of the access road. To the right, a trail heads past some tall maple trees and begins its low ascent to the valley rim. Old railroad tie steps are of little use, as the trail stays in the woods to soon arrive at the top of the staircase. A true work of art, this stairway—with its landing looking out into the trunks of tall trees—presents a different aspect of the vastness of the river bottom forest.

Once you're on the valley rim, it's just over 100 feet to the exit left where the hike began. Though the boardwalk was slippery underfoot on the rainy day I made my trip, I think the rain added a great deal to the scintillating sensation of a spring walk in the woods. And constant choral accompaniment of the advertising calls of *Hyla versicolor,* the tiny tree frog with suction-cup toes and the ability to shift its color ever so slightly to blend into its surrounding, made it an especially memorable day.

28

Sears Woods
State Nature Preserve

Total distance: 1.5 miles (2.4 km)

Hiking time: 1 hour

Maximum elevation: 980 feet

Vertical rise: 20 feet

Maps: USGS 7½' Series Oceola

Sears Woods State Nature Preserve is named in honor of nationally renowned Yale professor, Paul B. Sears, from whose family the woods were purchased in 1986. It is an old-growth beech–maple woods located in Crawford County on Wisconsinan-age central Ohio clayey till plain. The 99-acre tract is on the east side of the Sandusky River, where the river is following the front of the Wabash Moraine. Though it has been selectively cut during the years since settlement, it appears never to have been clear-cut and, at least in the last half of the 20th century, not used for grazing livestock.

Crawford County lies north of Greeneville Treaty line, in the congressional lands of 1819. It was a part of the "new purchase," the last part of the state under Native American domination, ceded to the United States in accordance with a treaty made at the foot of the Maumee Rapids in 1817. The county was created in 1820 but attached to Delaware County. In 1826 it was organized as county. The first settlers were largely from New England. In 1832 a federal land office opened in Bucyrus, and there was heavy immigration directly from Germany. The land office was closed in 1842–probably all the land had been claimed–but, due to political unrest in Germany, another wave of German settlers arrived around 1848. The farms of this part of Ohio have helped feed the nation for 150 years, shipping much of their bounty to market on the railroads that cross the country.

May, when the spring wildflowers are at their peak, is an especially good time to walk the trail at Sears Woods. Begin at the parking

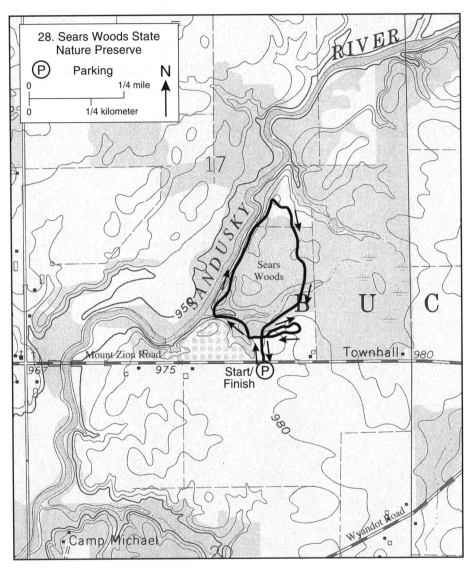

28. Sears Woods State Nature Preserve

Ⓟ Parking

N

0   1/4 mile

0   1/4 kilometer

lot along Mount Zion Road. The open field area where the lot is found was formerly a small orchard but serves now as habitat for grassland plants and animals. Nesting boxes have been erected to encourage bluebirds and other cavity-nesting birds.

How to Get There

Sears Woods Preserve is located on Mount Zion Road 2 miles west of SR 4 about 5 miles southwest of Bucyrus. From central Ohio, travel US 23 north to the Marion area, then follow SR 4 to Mount Zion Road.

The Trail

At the trailhead, there is a bulletin board where there may be a trail map available. Because it is locally based, the Crawford County Park District manages the area for the Division of Natural Areas and Preserves.

The late evening sun reflects off a small vernal pool deep within Sears Woods–probably a breeding site for woodland amphibians.

To start hiking, head west on the mowed trail to make a circuit around the end of the field. This is unimproved trail and can be a bit soggy after a rain; wear appropriate footwear. The trail loops back to an intersection where turning left takes you into the woods and turning right allows you to continue to the east along the edge of the field.

Entering the woods, the trail again turns west to begin descending on a winding trail among the oaks and maples. When it reaches the floodplain, it heads downstream among the tall trees and crosses an often dry streambed on a bridge before heading to high ground on the north side of the ravine. Soon it again drops into the valley to another stream crossing before following the ravine to within sight of the Sandusky River. Here the path turns uphill to the right to the bank above the river. A sign points right to the hiking trail. A "wild trail," probably made by bank fishermen, goes to the left toward the river.

From the bluff-edge trail that heads north along the river, you can see glacial boulders lying in the riverbed below. There remain close to the trail a few huge stumps that give you an idea of the size of trees removed at the last timber harvest.

Like most forest trails that are earthen surfaced, this one occasionally reveals its use by white-tailed deer. A great horned owl called as I moved up the trail on an early-March evening. At that time of the year, its nest should house a young brood. There are larger black walnut, wild black cherry, and other hardwoods species along the trail on this high ground.

The trail next turns away from the river heading east, and the large trees are replaced by much younger ones. Soon it passes through an opening rapidly being closed in by brush and young trees. Turning south now, the trail heads through the woods. As I passed through this area, I paused to photograph the reflection of the setting sun on a vernal pool and to listen to two barred owls calling in response to a call by me. At one point, there were three different birds responding to my call.

The trail winds through the woods, staying on dry ground and soon reaching the upper end of the ravine that had earlier carried it to the river. A bridge spans the creek, after which the trail rises and heads right, along the bluff of the ravine. When leaves are off the trees, you can see through the woods to the meadow. A left turn leads out of the woods into the meadow. At an intersection, the trail offers an optional loop to the left to facilitate exploration of the eastern part of the meadow. Straight ahead, the trail leads to the parking lot.

As a state nature preserve, this area offers no rest rooms, drinking water, or picnic facilities, and there are no parks close by. Likely, however, you will have a pleasant undisturbed walk. The 39-acre Carmean Woods State Nature Preserve lies directly to the east of Sears Woods, but there is no developed trail there and no connection between the two tracts.

29

Seymour Woods State Nature Preserve

Total distance: 1.5 miles (2.4 km)

Hiking time: 1 hour

Maximum elevation: 930 feet

Vertical rise: 60 feet

Maps: USGS 7½' Series Powell

When some look upon an unfamiliar piece of land, their first thoughts turn to how they could reshape it, landscape it, build upon it, or otherwise change it to serve one purpose or another. I am not of that ilk. Instead, my thoughts go immediately to what it must have looked like before affected by the hand of humanity, and to trying to discern what has occurred on the land since the time of that first encounter.

Upon first stepping into Seymour Woods State Nature Preserve, I began this process. Obviously, the area had felt the effect of the plow, cow, and ax of our European forebears, but long before that—located as it is facing a steady-flowing river—it must have heard the shouts of Native Americans traveling the watercourse, catching fish and mussels from the stream, and hunting game in its forest. Located in the area considered the homeland of the Adena and Hopewell culture prehistoric peoples of the Ohio Valley, not many miles from well-known sites of earthworks, visitation from humans must have followed closely behind the melting of the great Wisconsinan ice sheet. But my untrained mind can see no evidence of this.

Walk the trails of the 100-acre preserve and you can read the hopes and dreams of our kin who conquered Buckeye Country less than a quarter millennium ago. The plowman's furrows and gullies of soil erosion are still visible on the land surface beneath the new generation of hardwood forest. The stone-lined cellar hole visible high up the hillside above any potential

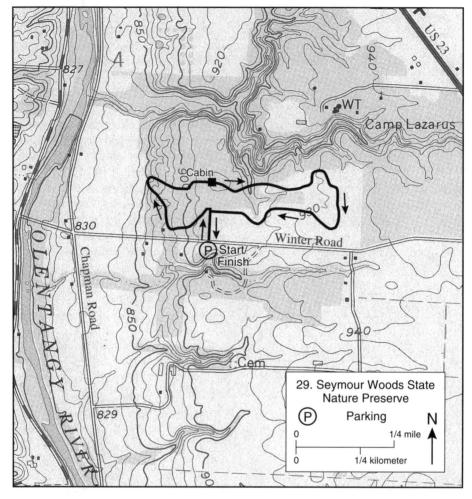

29. Seymour Woods State Nature Preserve

Ⓟ　　Parking

N

0 — 1/4 mile

0 — 1/4 kilometer

flood reflects the presence of a home once overlooking farm and field. In all likelihood it was wooden structure, since nothing but the foundation is visible today. Farther east, a stone cottage with slate roof probably reflects the longing of some city dweller to have a place in the country where he could retain or, perhaps, regain his connection with the land and nature. Plants and trees from other continents give away the hopes and desires of the occupants of former times. I find it fascinating to "read the landscape" as I explore the forests and fields

looking for all things natural that grow, creep, crawl, walk, and fly.

Located on the central Ohio till plain on the east bank of the Olentangy River, the Seymour Woods tract was most likely totally forested with the mixture of native hardwoods ecologists refer to as beech forest at the time of settlement. Since it lay south of the Greeneville Treaty line and within the lands designated in 1796 to be used to satisfy some of the claims of certain Revolutionary War officers and soldiers and on the banks of a stream with great potential for waterpower, it was probably claimed and cleared early in the 18th century. There was a land office up the river at Delaware where a land patent could be filed beginning in 1820. Limestone that broke into easily handled building stones was close by. There was good timber for building material and once cleared, the soils were fertile. For more than a century, it provided sum and sustenence to one family after another.

Today the victim of the less simple wants, it is in the process of reverting to nature, but still showing the effect of human occupancy. Not a virgin forest, nor even a stand of old-growth forest, it nevertheless is an oasis of peace and quiet in an ever-widening urban area. Abandoned fields are filling with native trees, and the forest is regaining a natural character. It was a gift to the Division of Natural Areas and Preserves from the late Columbus attorney James O. Seymour in 1972.

How to Get There

Seymour Woods is easily reached from US 23 north of Columbus. Turn west onto Winter Road. The entrance is on the north side of the road about a mile west of US 23. There are no facilities of any kind.

The Trail

Begin walking at the gate on Winter Road where a sign identifies the area and a bulletin board provides a map and useful information. There is no parking lot, but you will find adequate space for several cars along the road. Start walking by heading north along what was once a driveway to the abandoned cottage but is now a wood-chipped path. About 500 feet from the entrance, you will reach an intersection where trails go left, right, and straight ahead. Even though you can see a building through the woods in front of you, take the trail to the left and head gently

downhill into the woods. Wildflowers bloom along this trail in April and May. Soon the trail heads toward the northwest. Unfortunately, birds have carried in from somewhere the seeds of multiflora rose, so much of the natural shrub layer of the woods has been displaced by this alien species.

The trail soon nears the edge of the woods but, before doing so, it turns north, crosses two washes on short bridges, and passes the cellar hole for a structure of another era. There are some large trees in this area. Next, it goes uphill then—following the contour of the land—makes a loop on the high ground to the west before turning to the east, away from the river. The trail crosses another small bridge as it heads uphill to the cottage area. There are a large number of pin oak trees here, indicating the poorly drained nature of this clayey loam soil. The white pines seen here are, of course, not native but probably planted by the last private landowner.

Across the deep ravine to the left lies property owned by the local Boy Scout Council. I spent many a week there as a young Boy Scout and later as the leader of Troop 417 of nearby Upper Arlington. Two particular events stand out. It was at Camp Lazarus, as the area was known at the time, that in 1946 I passed my Eagle Scout board of review and a week later received the award. Many years later I was at Camp Lazarus when the United States landed a space vehicle and astronauts on the moon.

Ahead is the cottage of native limestone with its roof of non-native slate and windows blocked with steel plate. Since the slate looks to be from at least two different sources, it was probably salvaged from other structures being raised or having their roofs replaced. If the building could talk, it could likely tell some wild stories, both joyful and sad, about events that took place

This long abandoned cottage stands close to the trail deep in Seymour Woods.

under its heavy roof. There is nothing in the building, so there is no reason to try to look inside. Some beautiful beeches and red oaks grow nearby. While I was photographing the cottage on an early-March afternoon, a couple of mourning cloak butterflies went flitting by, assuring me that spring was just around the corner.

There is a choice of trails at this point. One goes to the east and will carry you to the entry trail and main gate. The other continues to the east through the woods. A concrete-block structure to the left looks like a barbecue pit or incinerator. In spring daffodils push through the leaves under the hickories and oaks.

There are more large trees along this trail that traverses the high ground of the preserve. Cross a stream on a bridge below which you can see outcropping shale. Just after this the trail climbs, passing on the left a tree with a hole in it that is obviously being used by wildlife. Even more interesting is that the tree has both old woven fence and even older barbed-wire fence embedded in the trunk.

In this area I heard a barred owl calling, so I answered back. Instead of pulling in the barred owl, I attracted a flock of crows that came to check me out and harass me as if I was a real owl. The Camp Lazarus lake where I spent many an hour swimming and boating and improving my lifesaving skills is visible to the left. This poorly drained area of the preserve has lots of beech and pin oak trees.

As the trail curves to head south, it opens into an old field that is fast becoming thicket and young woods—good goldfinch and sparrow country. Now following a mowed trail past planted pines and oaks, and through an occasional meadow that looks be a good place to spot a woodcock, the trail heads west with woods to the right and young saplings to the left and too much multiflora rose. It takes a left/right jog to avoid the end of the ravine that it had earlier crossed on a bridge. Glacial erratics protrude through the surface here and there, leading me to believe that this area may have been pastured rather than cultivated.

At the four-way intersection in the middle of the preserve, turn left to head back on the wood-chipped path to the entrance area. Again there is older woodland on the right and a stand of young saplings on the left— the old-growth forest of another century yet to be born.

30

Slate Run Metro Park

Total distance: 3.5 miles (5.6 km)

Hiking time: 2½ hours

Maximum elevation: 910 feet

Vertical rise: 110 feet

Maps: USGS 7½' Series Canal Winchester; CMPD Slate Run Metro Park brochure

From the northwestern edge of Slate Run Metro Park you can see the skyline of downtown Columbus, 16 miles away as the crow flies. Slate Run sits on the western slope of an end moraine that straddles the Pickaway-Fairfield county line, an area where elevations can reach more than 1,100 feet. The elevation at the corner of Broad and High Streets in the capital city is 768 feet. In between lies the Wisconsinan-age till plain called the Columbus Lowland, a relatively flat area with streams draining and the land sloping to the Scioto River basin.

The 1,708 acres mirror most of Ohio's variety of habitats, from wooded rolling hills with deep ravines and steep ridges to former farm fields, a 14-acre lake, and a recently established wetland. The original oak–sugar maple forest was cleared in the 1880s, and much of the land has been farmed since. Lower Mississippian shale lies beneath the drift and is exposed in the deeply cut ravine, giving the name Slate Run to the creek. The park district began acquiring the land in the 1960s, planting trees and removing it from agriculture in preparation for a future park. A special feature is the Slate Run Living Historical Farm, located on the south edge of the park. For the hiker, there are more than 5 miles of trails, including some where pets on leashes are permitted.

The main park entrance is on SR 674, 5 miles south of Canal Winchester. Once inside the park and past the ranger station, turn left where the sign points to a program

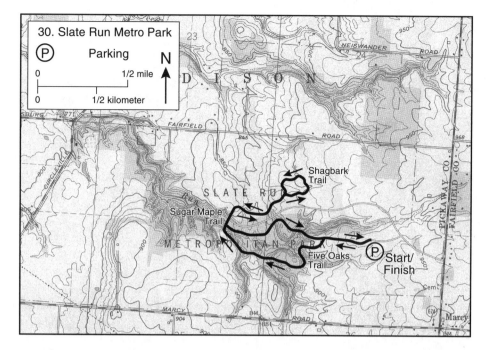

Shagbark
Trail

Sugar Maple
Trail

Five Oaks
Trail

Ⓟ Start/
Finish

area. Park at the far end of the lot to begin hiking on the Five Oaks Trail. The trailhead is to the right; the trail goes nearly due west from there. There are rest rooms to the left of the trailhead.

How to Get There

To reach Slate Run from I-270 on the south side of Columbus, take US 3 east toward Lancaster to the Canal Winchester SR 674 exit. Turn right onto Gender Road/SR 674. Follow SR 674 south to the park entrance. From US 23 south of Columbus, travel east on Duvall Road to Winchester Road, south on Winchester Road to Marcy Road, east on Marcy Road to SR 674, then north on SR 674 to the park entrance.

The Trail

The trail begins on tarmac but as soon as it leaves the mowed area, it changes to a fine gravel surface and is wide enough to hike side by side. A split-rail reminder fence

soon runs out. There is a sign with a map and some reminders about trail behavior. The winding trail begins dropping gently downhill, paralleling a deep ravine to the right. Soon there is an overlook on the right where you can look through the tall trees toward the creek below. This is the junction where the Five Oaks Trail splits to make a loop.

To continue hiking, turn left, heading downhill. Here there is a combination of pine plantings and native hardwoods. An occasional pileated woodpecker gives you the feeling that you are really away from the urban environment. The trail continues to drop into the narrow valley that the creek has cut though the deep glacial drift of this moraine country.

By the pieces of shale in the creekbed, you can tell that not far to the east, the stream has cut through the bedrock. Slate and shale are closely related and often confused. I suspect that the presence of the shale explains why the stream was named Slate Run.

A wood thrush was singing on the early-May morning when I crossed the bridge and began the steep climb beyond. There are some lovely large trees in the open woods along this section of the trail. Dropping once again, the trail reaches what is now called the family tree. This is a multitrunked red oak, doubtless the result of sprouts growing from the stump of a tree that had been very much alive when cut. This particular specimen was formerly referred to as the Five-Oak Tree—hence the name of the trail. A nicely done interpretive sign tells of the interrelationship of this tree with other living things of the forest.

The trail next drops to the spot where a side trail to the left connects to the Sugar Maple Trail. The Five Oaks Trail, which you have been following, continues ahead and to the right to return to the parking lot, making a 1.5-mile loop. To continue a longer hike, make the sharp left turn, travel downhill, and cross the main stem of Slate Run to meet the Sugar Maple Trail, which runs from the Living Historical Farm parking lot to the Buzzard's Roost picnic area lot. Many of the violets that bloom beneath the sycamores in this stream bottom are white, not violet, but the wild blue phlox are blue and beautiful.

If you wish to explore the farm or use the rest room located there, turn left. Otherwise, turn right onto the Sugar Maple Trail as it heads generally northwest, rising and falling among the many gullies leading to Slate Run. The trees in a small papaw patch in this area were absolutely loaded with deep mahogany flowers when I passed by. Since I seldom see fruit in that kind of abundance, I wonder if pollination doesn't occur, and if not, why not; or perhaps lots of fruit does occur and I am too late to see it. There is also a grove of sassafras along the trail here. Since sassafras has been suggested as a possible cancer-causing substance, I no longer snag the young shoots and chew on the bark of their roots.

After traveling a considerable distance in the valley of Slate Run, the Sugar Maple Trail climbs the left bank onto higher ground to move among young hardwoods. The creek valley is still visible downhill to the right. Just before the trail makes a sharp turn to the north, a new trail, the Bobolink Grassland Trail, exits to the left. This is a 3-mile-long unimproved trail that leads through mostly old field habitat to connect with the 1.5-mile Kokomo Wetland Trail in a newly established wetland. The latter includes a sizable length of boardwalk. This trail can also be accessed from a parking lot near the northwestern corner of the park off Circleville-Winchester Road. Sections of this natural-surface trail can be a bit muddy during rainy periods.

After a bench and trash barrel at a wide spot, the trail descends to again cross Slate Run. My May morning walk turned up a box turtle using the same trail as I; several first-hatch zebra swallowtail butterflies also found it easier flying along the trail corridor. A gentle climb leads to the edge of the woods and a road crossing, then to the Buzzard's Roost picnic area parking lot. At the far end of the lot are rest rooms, and drinking water is available nearby. There is a barnlike shelter and trails leading to Buzzard's Roost Lake.

In the metro parks, trails in mowed areas are generally paved, even though they are continuations of nature trails. South and east of the barn/shelter parking lot is a trail intersection where signs point two directions to nature trails. To begin a return trip to where you started, head south back across the road to reenter the woods. To add nearly a mile more to your hike, turn left onto

Moved from a nearby rural road where it could no longer support farm vehicles and trucks, this covered bridge now serves hikers on the Slate Run Metro Park trail system.

the Covered Bridge Trail. Be aware that hikers may have pets on leashes on this trail, as well as on the Shagbark Trail to which it connects. Canada geese also frequently use this trail. Need I say more?

The improved Covered Bridge Trail leads through old field and thicket to a covered wooden bridge of Queen-post-type construction that was moved to the site from elsewhere in the county. Beyond the bridge the trail climbs through young open woods, where it soon comes to another junction. Here the unimproved Shagbark Trail exits right to travel in a counterclockwise fashion for 0.5 mile, rising and falling through young woods and thicket. For most of the trek, you may wonder why the trail is called Shagbark. Suddenly you will be in the midst of a nearly pure stand of this species, and you will understand. The Shagbark Trail will shortly wind its way back to the Covered

Bridge Trail. There is lots of multiflora rose in the understory along this trail.

Go straight ahead to follow the Covered Bridge Trail in a counterclockwise manner as its return leg carries you back onto blacktop to the nature trail intersection encountered earlier. On a bright day, this is a good area in which to observe many of the smaller species of butterflies of the open field. When you reach the trail intersection, turn left onto the Sugar Maple Trail and head across the road to begin your inbound trek.

At a T in the trail just inside the woods, turn left (the opposite direction whence you earlier came) to follow a trail that will connect with the return leg of the Five Oaks Trail. The trail runs 15 to 25 feet inside the woods as it heads generally in an easterly direction. There are many glacial erratics lying on the hillside just inside the woods, having been dragged there from nearby

---

more level land more than a century ago so that the land could be plowed and crops planted. Buckeye trees grow along this trail, and the maroon-blossomed sessile trillium or toad trillium blooms on the forest floor.

Now reaching the intersection with the Five Oaks Trail, turn left and continue on the high ground parallel to the park road. The trail emerges from the woods to a managed grassland area where, in the warm months, you will be entertained by butterflies and dragonflies. As I left this opening to reenter the woods, a flock of crows was making a racket terrible racket overhead. I suspect they were badgering an owl somewhere nearby, but I was not able to spot it.

A switchback carries the trail to the creek and a crossing. Turning upstream, the trail follows the stream for a short distance. For the first time on the trail, bedrock is visible in the creekbed. Look also for shale in the bottom of the streambed and blocks of sandstone on the hillside. From here the trail makes a long, steady climb through a beautiful forested ravine to close the loop at the overlook. It's but a short walk to the parking lot and the end of a good day's hike.

While you are in the area, take time to visit the Slate Run Living Historical Farm. A brochure giving information about the farm and its hours of operation can be picked up outside the ranger station.

31

Stonelick State Park

Total distance: 2 miles (3.2 km)

Hiking time: 1 hour

Maximum elevation: 910 feet

Vertical rise: 25 feet

Maps USGS 7½' Series Newtonsville; ODNR Stonelick State Park brochure

The poorly drained flatwoods country of northeast Clermont County has sometimes been called the White Swamp region of Ohio. It's a region of high-lime, deeply leached, Illinoian-age silt loam soils with a cap of loess (fine-grained yellowish brown wind-deposited soil). Beneath the surface are 500-million-year-old Ordovician-age carbonate rocks and calcareous shales. Beech–maple forests that included the southern species, sweet gum, occurred in the area when settlers began arriving at the beginning of the 19th century. Many of those pioneer families were from nearby Kentucky, and others from Maryland and Virginia. During the mid–19th century, anti-slavery sentiment ran high, and help for slaves escaping from the South was provided by an active Underground Railroad movement in the county. The Civil War general, U.S. statesman, and 18th president of the United States, Hiram Ulysses Simpson Grant, was born in Clermont County.

Stonelick Creek carries the runoff from these lands south to the East Fork of the Little Miami. In a program to provide state-wide fishing opportunities, the former Division of Conservation and Natural Resources began buying land along Stonelick Creek in Wayne Township in 1948; in 1950 a dam was completed, creating the 200-acre lake. With the creation at about that time of the new Department of Natural Resources and its Division of Parks and Recreation, it was decided to assign the 1,058-acre area to the new Division of Parks and Recreation. Picnic areas, a beach, and

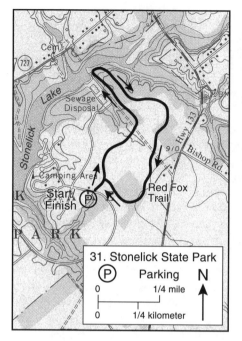

31. Stonelick State Park

(P) Parking   N

0   1/4 mile

0   1/4 kilometer

them unpicked so that others may also take pleasure in discovering them for, perhaps, the first time.

Several of the trails such as the Beech-Tree and Lakeview Trails are one way, requiring that you either walk them two directions or return on a road. I have no problems with that, but some do.

How to Get There

Stonelick State Park is reached by taking I-275 east of Cincinnati to Milford and SR 131, and SR 727 east to Lake Drive and the park entrance.

The Trail

The 2-mile Red Fox Trail is a loop that originates near the campground check-in station and nearly all woodland. You can park in the campground visitors lot and walk out the road away from the checking station and camp store to the trailhead on the northeast (left) side of the road. The park brochure shows it to be opposite the entrance to the Beechwood Trail on the other side of the road, but it is actually about 60 yards beyond.

That these woods resulted from secondary succession on abandoned former farmland is immediately revealed by the presence throughout of old red cedar trees barely hanging on among the hardwoods. These junipers were early invaders in the old fields that followed the abandonment of grazing and row-crop production. Red cedars play the role of early invader in this part of Ohio where calcareous bedrock is not too far beneath the surface—the same role some species of sumac play in the abandoned fields on the acid soils of southeastern Ohio and hawthorns in other parts of the state. Alas, once the cedars begin growing, hardwood seeds that blow in begin to sprout in the damp mulch in their

campgrounds were developed, and it became a poplar vacation area for southwestern Ohio outdoor enthusiasts. It was one of the early parks to offer a summer nature interpretive program for park visitors.

Seven miles of hiking trails offer travel through old fields, forests, and along the lakeshore. With the terrain quite flat, none has difficult walking. Because of the poorly draining soils, they can be wet and muddy so hikers should give attention to the water repellence of their footwear. Wet woods are the home to mosquitoes and other biting insects during the warm months, so be prepared when walking at Stonelick at that time of year. There are many beautiful woodland spring wildflowers at Stonelick, but even more special are several of the summer flowers of the wet meadows such as dense blazing-star and purple fringeless orchid, which can be found here in midsummer. If you happen upon them, photograph them and otherwise enjoy them but leave

Till Plains

Less conspicuous than the state wildflower (large-flowered trillium) is the deep mahogany-flowered sessile trillium, which blooms in late April and early May.

shadows and, being faster growing, in half a century or so overtop the cedars, causing them to die.

This is a packed-dirt trail through the damp woods. Roots of trees growing in this poorly drained environment are often near or on the surface, so mind your step. Notice the pin oak trees among the beeches and hard maples, and be sure to look for the sweet gum trees with their star-shaped leaves. Not far into the woods the trail splits into outbound and inbound segments; you make the choice. The trail is blazed with red paint marks on trees, but they are not always visible, and they're farther apart than you might wish. Nevertheless, I had no difficulty distinguishing the path.

The red cedars have disappeared, and this appears to be an area that may not have been cleared. There are large bur and swamp white oaks and an occasional old stump from earlier selective timber harvests.

The rustle of oak leaves underfoot on a clear October day is enjoyable. A check of the topographic map reveals that, sure enough, this appears to have been a woodcut at least as far back as when the map was made.

Soon, just as my map indicates, the old trees disappear and the red cedars among the young trees return—the result of the cessation of farming when the state purchased the area in the 1940s. The trail drifts to the left toward the lake and soon comes to an old road, where it makes an abrupt turn to the left and heads directly to the lake. The topographic map shows that at one time this road crossed Stonelick Creek and joined SR 727 at the cemetery south of Edenton.

As the trail slowly descends toward the lake, it passes old sewage disposal ponds. They appear to no longer be in use and are not offensive. At this point, watch for an opening in the woods on the right side of the road where the trail turns northeast. From here the trail winds its way through the woods, turning ever more to the right so that soon it is heading in a southeasterly direction. There are old trees on the left in the valley of a small stream that flows into the lake; the trail will pass through other areas of large timber as it winds its way back to the original junction, but it also passes through successional woods. At the farthest point from the trailhead there is a junction with a trail to the right that cuts some distance off the hike if you wish. Keep your eyes open for the many creatures that make their home in the woods. Listen for the scream of a red-tailed hawk or the chip of a chipmunk. The eastern wood frog is found in this part of Ohio, and though they are usually only seen when they converge on vernal ponds to mate in February, I saw one along the trail one summer, just moving through the woods. After a summer shower is a good time to keep your eyes open for a box turtle on the move along a trail. And I seldom walk a woodland trail in April or May without seeing the metallic green six-spotted or green forest tiger beetle.

You will likely hear traffic off to your left as the trail nears the junction where you turn left to complete your hike. If you want to extend your hike, cross the road and head through the woods on the 0.8-mile Southwoods Trail. It crosses several small streams that flow to the lake before joining the mile-long Lakeview Trail to end up at a picnic area overlooking the lake. There are other trails that will extend your hike farther, but some pass through areas that are open to hunting at some times of year. You can check with the park office as to when those time are.

32

Sycamore State Park

Total distance: 7 miles (11.2 km)

Hiking time: 4 hours

Maximum elevation: 950 feet

Vertical rise: 95 feet

Maps: USGS 7½' Series Trotwood; ODNR Sycamore State Park brochure

Wolf Creek drains a relatively small area of the rolling Wisconsinan-age ground moraine in the northwestern corner of Montgomery County, carrying the runoff to the Great Miami River in downtown Dayton. The upper end of the watershed, where Sycamore State Park is located, is the kind of land where farming as a livelihood is passing from the picture. Silurian-age limestone lies beneath the loamy high-lime soil, and in some places buried preglacial channels hold rich deposits of gravel from glacial outwash. When settlers moved into the area at the end of the 18th century, they had to clear forests dominated by beech and sugar maple, along with oaks, hickories, chestnuts, and other hardwoods. The land had already seen the Indians pass this way, and before them, earlier Native peoples had been here long enough to leave their mark in the way of a few small earthworks.

By the middle of the 20th century, dairy farming was waning and row-crop farming was succumbing to those who could exercise the economies of scale by amassing large holdings of continuous fields and using large, expensive equipment. Land that had a little character to it and was close to a city was fair game for the developer who could turn it into a "new town." In the 1970s a development corporation that had successfully created communities outside Columbus and elsewhere in the Dayton area began acquiring the land that is now Sycamore State Park. For one reason or another, plans did not materialize and the land was acquired by the Department of Natural Resources. In 1979 what was to be a

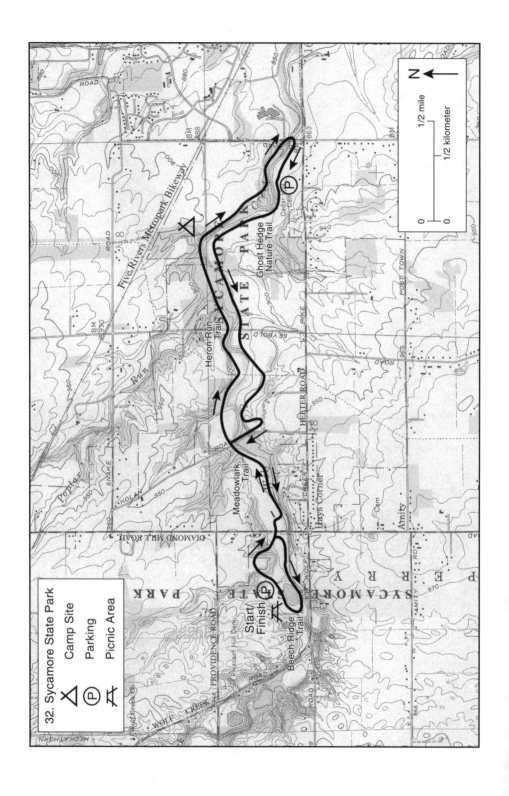

32. Sycamore State Park

△ Camp Site

Ⓟ Parking

🔱 Picnic Area

N

1/2 mile

1/2 kilometer

community of "all brick homes" was dedicated as Sycamore State Park. Since there was already another park with the name wolf in the system, and since the sycamores stand tall and beautiful against the sky along the lower reaches of Wolf Creek, the name seemed a good choice.

How to Get There

To reach Sycamore State Park, travel west from the Dayton/Springfield area on I-70 to Brookfield-Salem Road. Turn south and go into Brookfield. There, turn left onto Wolf Creek Pike and travel east to Providence Road. The park entrance is less than 0.5 mile east of Wolf Creek Pike on the south side of Providence Road.

The Trail

The best place to access the park's 8 miles of hiking trails is the Sycamore Spring Picnic Area on the south side of Providence Road at the west end of the park. From there you can hit the trail and explore the picturesque Wolf Creek Valley in short or increasingly longer bits and pieces. There are picnic, rest room, and playground facilities and drinking water near the parking lot.

This is all land that has been lived on and worked by families for around two centuries—cleared, cultivated, drained, quarried, sprayed, and all the other things humans have done to support themselves from the resource base. Through it all, most of the other living things that used the land have remained. True, the charismatic megafauna—elk, bison, mountain lions, wolves, bobcats, and the like—are gone, but most of the other creatures remain. Species may have shifted from those that abide in the woods to those of the thicket and grassland, but from soil microbes to soaring vultures, most are still here. The challenge when walking this kind of trail is twofold: to figure out what uses the land was put to by

our ancestors, including the sequence of various uses and practices; and to discover how all things natural have coped with or adapted to these uses, and how they might be reclaiming the land as it returns to its natural state. Enjoy the exercise of muscles but stretch the mind along the way.

Park in the easternmost of the two parking lots at this area and begin hiking by walking to the trailhead located to the left of the shelter beyond the playground equipment. If you don't already have one, pick up a park map at the bulletin board on your way. The 6-foot-wide mowed trail heads downhill into old field habitat where, in fall, monarch butterflies nectar on goldenrod and New England aster, garnering fuel for their flight toward Mexico. Crab apples and red cedars are invading the old fields, a first step in the return of the area to hardwood forest.

Bush honeysuckle, the ubiquitous alien shrub that has been planted for years as a good food source for wildlife but has now become a nuisance in natural areas, is certainly present here. It is beautiful and fragrant in spring, and its pulpy fruit is used by all kinds of birds. What those who once touted it failed to realize, however, was that the birds eat the fruit whole, swallowing but not digesting the seeds. Then they fly into a woods, or a neighbor's yard, or almost anywhere and leave their droppings, including the undigested seeds complete with a bit of fertilizer. Honeysuckle thrives marvelously on the sweet (lime-rich) soils of western Ohio. Thus in places like Charleston Falls Preserve, Glen Helen Preserve, and Mount Airy Forest, it outcompetes native shrubs like spicebush; since it leafs out early, it also shades out native wildflowers that depend upon the sunlight falling in the forest before native trees leaf out for the energy to survive. The solution to one perceived problem, in this case the desire to have fragrant shrubs that feed birds, created a new problem. I shall try to not get on that soapbox again.

Along the trail there is a sign that I have been seeing along park trails for more than 50 years. It is the "Prayer of the Woods," and as true today as it was when first written.

I am the heat of your hearth on a cold
   winter's night, the friendly shade
screening you from the summer sun, my
   fruits are refreshing grout quenching
your thirst as you journey on; I am the beam
   of your house, the bed on which
you lie, the timbers that built your boat; I am
   the handle on your hoe, the door
of your homestead, the wood of your cradle,
   the shell of your coffin; I am the
bread of kindness and the flower of beauty.
   He who pass by listen to my prayer.
Harm me not.

Donated by Troop 44

A fitting tribute to trees that we take so much for granted. Now, as the park map indicates, the trail heads downhill toward the creek. Before reaching the streambank, the old field and thicket come to an end and the trail makes an abrupt left turn into an opening in the woods. As it enters the woods, it passes a pair of signs—one with a backpacker symbol and the other, a cross-country ski symbol. Stick with the backpacker sign along this entire walk. A 20-foot bridge carries the trail across a small glacial cobble-filled stream that runs to the right and into Wolf Creek.

The Beach Ridge Trail continues east on the north side of Wolf Creek, going in and out of the streamside woods and the successional fields back from the stream. Bridges wide enough to carry mowing equipment span side streams that head toward the creek. At Diamond Mill Road are duplicates of the earlier signs indicating that hikers and skiers are welcome but vehicles are not. At this point, either follow the trail uphill and loop back to the parking lot to complete a 1.5-mile hike or cross the road and head east on an old blacktop drive.

You are now on the Meadowlark Trail that goes between Diamond Mill and Nolan Roads. Shortly after entering, turn right on the old road then left, leaving the decaying blacktop to stay close to the stream. Tall arborvitae trees were probably foundation plantings around a building of some sort long ago torn down. In autumn tall lobelias grow along the trail in the bottomland; there are large areas of milkweed and beautiful New England asters, both ambrosia to monarch and other species of butterflies. The trail passes a small pond as it continues east. A shelter on private property can be seen beyond the creek. The walk to Nolan Road is about 0.5 mile and takes less than half an hour.

At Nolan Road, you have the option of turning around and returning to the trailhead or crossing the road and entering upon the Heron Run Trail. If you choose to cut your trip short and head back to the Sycamore Spring parking area, try the alternate trails to those you came on. On the Beech Ridge Trail, stick close to the creek and arrive back at the parking lot by going downhill and west of the pond.

On the Heron Run Trail, there is a climb to the left into old fields, two bridle trail crossings, and a drop into a ravine to cross another tributary of Wolf Creek. From there to Seybold Road, the trail remains in the stream bottom with tall trees along the creek and old field and young trees to the left. It crosses a grassy utility right-of-way en route. When it reaches Seybold, it is a grass trail in scruffy woods close to the creek. It emerges onto a small parking lot where there is one picnic table but no other facilities. Again, you

For a short ways, the trail passes through a tunnel formed by the overhanging branches of osage orange trees along an old road.

can use this as your turnaround point: Cross the bridge to the south and head back upstream to the trailhead.

If you want to continue east on the Ghost Hedge Nature Trail to complete the full 8-mile loop, cross Seybold Road and turn right where the trail enters the woods just north of the bridge on railroad tie steps. To return to the trailhead, either turn around and return via the route you have just followed or turn right onto the road, cross the bridge over Wolf Creek, then turn right on the other leg of the Heron Run Trail. It stays close to the creek, once again crossing the utility easement and a bridle trail before exiting onto Nolan Road. At Nolan, you must turn right and follow the road across the bridge to meet the Meadowlark Trail on the west side of the road. On your way back upstream, take the left branch of the Meadowlark Trail farther from the creek. It connects back to the creekside trail in the

area of the tall arborvitae trees just before you reach Diamond Mill Road.

On the return trip on the Beech Ridge Trail, I chose to stay to the left closer to the creek. That brought me out on the lower side of the pond, and I returned to the parking lot climbing the hill at the west end of the pond. It was late on a September day, and I stopped alongside the pond to rest and take a few late-afternoon photos of trees in their fall foliage reflected in the water.

If you have chosen to continue the 8-mile trek by following the Ghost Hedge Trail east to Snyder Road, you will enjoy the walk through the woods. Bridges carry you across to side streams; there are benches where you can look out across Wolf Creek. The trail passes within sight of the group camp area. At one point you will need to walk a short distance on paved park road and, in another area, share the trail with horses for 100 or so feet. Eventually the trail

---

emerges onto Snyder Road directly opposite the entrance to the Trotwood-Madison Middle School.

Turn right and cross the bridge, staying close to the guardrail and watching for vehicular traffic. At the far end of the bridge, turn right and begin your return trip on the other leg of the Ghost Hedge Trail. Through the woods and thickets to the left there is a staging area for the bridle trails that are also found in this part of the park. The foot trail crosses a bridle trail coming from the creek and heading to this staging area. Don't take it. Shortly, the mowed trail reaches a junction where you'll see a short path to the right to the creek, a path directly ahead that heads downhill to a wet crossing of a small tributary, a path at an angle to the right ahead that leads to a bridge over that tributary, and a path to the right rear that travels on an old road between a double row of Osage orange trees. This hedge-apple-lined trail leads to a trailhead for hikers with a parking lot and rest room. It is, of course, from this piece of the trail that the Ghost Hedge name originates.

After using the facilities, return to the trail alongside the creek and begin your inbound trip. Use the spur to the bridge or ford the tributary, then walk the wide trail beside more hedge apple trees and beneath tall sycamores to return to Seybold Road. The trail is in woods the entire reach, at times close to the creek and at other times back a way on higher ground. The wild blue phlox was in full glory on the April afternoon when I completed this section of the trail—but walking the trail when there are no wildflowers in bloom or leaves on the trees can be equally rewarding. There are some lovely old sycamores along this part of the trail that are especially beautiful in winter against the deep blue north sky. The holes you see 20 feet or so up in sycamore trees are often used in late winter by nesting great horned owls; they're created when a heavy branch falls. In the past, barn owls also used sycamores for nesting (they must have used something before there were any barns), but these raptors are now quite uncommon in Ohio. The reason seems to be the loss of meadows where they can catch voles, their favored food. Barred owls are cavity nesters, too, and river bottoms are a favored habitat. During their late-winter breeding season, keep your ears open for the familiar *Who cooks for you? Who cooks for you'all?* advertising call of a male barred owl. If you hear or see a flock of crows in the top of a tree scolding loudly, look to see if an owl of any sort is the object of their contempt.

When the Ghost Hedge Trail reaches Seybold Road, look directly across the road for the entrance to the south leg of the Heron Run Trail. Follow it until you reach Nolan Road, then turn right and cross the road to enter the Meadowlark Trail headed upstream. Where the trail splits, try the left fork for a little different habitat. When you cross Diamond Mill Road, take the trail closest to the river so that you finish your hike as I described above, on the downhill side of the pond. You will enjoy the different view, and the hillside overlooking the pond is a good place to rest and reflect upon the day's adventure on this series of connecting trails.

If you enjoy bicycling, the 13-mile long Wolf Creek Rail Trail runs from Trotwood to Verona very near the park along what was originally the route of the Dayton & Greenville Railroad. Brochures are available at kiosks and the park office.

Another park in the area with a trail of about the same length as Sycamore's is Germantown Reserve of the Five Rivers Metro Park System in the southwestern part of Montgomery County west of Germantown. There is a description of that trail in my first hiking book, *50 Hikes in Ohio*.

IV

Huron-Erie Lake Plains

33

Augusta-Anne Olsen State Nature Preserve

Total distance: 2.5 miles (4 km)

Hiking time: 1½ hours

Maximum elevation: 860 feet

Vertical rise: 110 feet

Maps: USGS 7½' Series Berlin Heights

The Vermilion River drains 272 square miles of late-Wisconsinan till plain north of the Defiance Moraine along the eastern edges of Erie and Huron Counties, dropping more than 500 feet to the level of Lake Erie in a distance of about 35 miles. As it does so, it cuts through the Berea Escarpment, creating steep bluffs along its meandering watercourse. One of the loveliest sections of this relatively short, young stream lies just north of Wakeman in the northeast corner of Huron County.

Here, in the early 1970s, Mr. and Mrs. William Olsen purchased a 140-acre farm on the west side of the river. The land reminded Gussie Olsen of the family farm she knew in southern Maryland where she'd grown up. It even had dense patches of club moss—or crowfoot as they called it—like the farm the family had owned before the Second World War. The land she knew and loved in Maryland had been destroyed and been used for housing for a nearby naval installation.

In 1985, never forgetting the loss of her family farm and its subsequent destruction, Mrs. Olsen donated 83 acres of the Vermilion River property to the Division of Natural Areas and Preserves to become the Vermilion River Preserve. In 1997 the division purchased an additional 47 acres of the farm, and in 2000 it was dedicated as the Augusta-Anne Olsen State Nature Preserve honoring the Olsens' efforts in preserving the land in its natural state. More than 3 miles of trails lead through deep woods and along almost a mile of the beautiful Vermilion River.

How to Get There

This lovely riverside preserve lies on the east side of West River Road approximately 2 miles north of Wakeman. To reach it, take US 20 east from Norwalk or west from the Oberlin area to where it makes a right-angle bend just west of the center of Wakeman. West River Road runs north from that point.

The Trail

The names given to the trails in most nature preserves are pretty descriptive of what, in a broad sense, you are likely to see. Yet no trail is likely to be named for the beautiful great spangled fritillary butterflies that were seeking nectar on the milkweed flowers blooming near the parking lot when I began walking the Old Field Trail into Olsen Preserve. The trail moves along the north edge of a small pond near the lot, then skirts what could be no better described at this phase of succession than an old field. To the left of the trail is deep woods, remnant of the vast beech and mixed-hardwood forest that occupied this land at the time explorers and settlers entered the area.

The land in that forest to the left slopes steeply toward the river. After choosing the left fork at a split in the trail, I made a hard left to enter the Spring Trail to explore the woods on that slope. After passing a planting of pines, the path enters deep woods and makes a large loop among the maples and oaks. This damp woods is an excellent place to see wildflowers in April and May. Returning now to where the trail began, make a left to follow the River Trail downhill to the banks of the Vermilion. Just as you reach the river, a short side trail heads downstream in a short loop to explore the riparian woods.

Next, follow the meandering river upstream through the woods. You will pass a trail to the right that will take you back to the

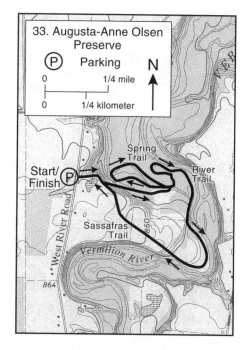

33. Augusta-Anne Olsen Preserve

Ⓟ Parking N

0 ————————— 1/4 mile

0 ————————— 1/4 kilometer

Spring Trail

Start/Finish Ⓟ

River Trail

Sassafras Trail

Vermilion River

864

parking lot if you want to shorten your hike. Otherwise, continue upriver on the Sassafras Trail. There is a long section of boardwalk to keep the trail above soft ground. Along the way you will pass one of Ohio's largest specimens of sassafras. Ohio's species and two Asiatic species are the last survivors of a long line of sassafras species that date back to the close of the lower Cretaceous, or almost to the beginning of the record of dicotyledonous trees. The sassafras tree, a member of the laurel family, is best known for its aroma, once the source of the flavoring of root beer but now replaced by artificial flavoring. Some scientists have implicated the bark of the root, the source of the flavoring, as a carcinogen. Sassafras trees are usually relatively small understory trees but can occasionally be found as large as 6 feet in diameter. A 4-foot tree such as the one that grows along the trail here is a large specimen. They are usually found on noncalcareous

The Vermilion River flows toward Lake Erie along the eastern boundary of the Augusta-Anne State Nature Preserve.

soils like those that have developed here over the Mississippian-age Berea sandstone and Bedford shale.

After a tight meander in the river the trail turns toward the west, beginning the climb away from the river and out of the woods. There is only a short section where the climb is very steep. Berea sandstone is exposed in some places on this hillside, but not nearly like it is on the east side of the river.

The trail soon returns to the old field habitat after emerging from the woods, then winds its way northwest to rejoin the outbound trail near the pond. Your vehicle is only moments beyond this intersection. It was along here that on one cool morning that I encountered a beautiful large black rat snake warming itself in the sun while stretched out on the trail. I am not sure which of us was more surprised.

There are no picnic or rest room facilities at Olsen Preserve, but Wakeman is less than 3 miles to the south. Wakeman is on US 20 about halfway between Norwalk and Oberlin in Huron County.

34

French Creek Reservation

Total distance: 2.5 miles (4 km)

Hiking time: 1½ hours

Maximum elevation: 623 feet

Vertical rise: 43 feet

Maps: USGS 7½' Series Avon;
LCMP French Creek Reservation Trail Guide

French traders were probably the first whites to visit the area near the mouth of the Black River in Lorain County, likely in the 17th century. They were here to explore and trade with the Native Americans of the area. Moravian missionaries came into the area in 1786, hoping to move on south to the Moravian missions in the Tuscarawas Valley that had been burned out in 1782. After a warning of danger from local Delaware Indians, they moved south to near the site of the present-day Milan then, after five or six years, continued on to near the River Thames in Canada.

In 1795 agents for the Connecticut Land Company bought the land for a few dollars an acre, and the area became known as the Western Reserve. Settlement by folks from Connecticut and other New England states began in earnest.

As one of the best harbors on Lake Erie, the mouth of the Black River became the center of industrialization. Shipbuilding and steel making reached their peak with the all-out war effort in the middle of the 20th century. French Creek, the meandering stream that passes through French Creek Reservation and joins the Black River about a mile to the west, became known as "the Ruhr of the West Side of Cleveland." Air and water pollution plagued the area for decades. The nature center at French River Reservation sits adjacent to an abandoned railbed, and a huge steel plant lies not more than a mile to the south, but the 428-acre wooded tract is a real gem in an otherwise urban/industrial area.

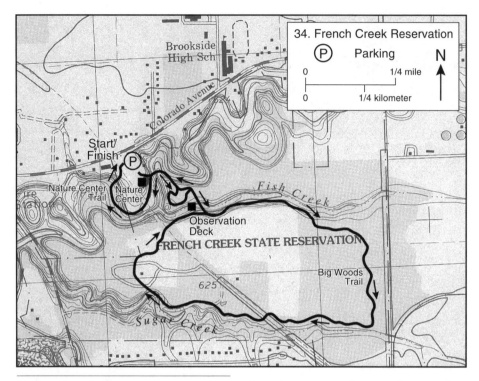

How to Get There

Reach the park by taking SR 611 northwest from I-90, the Sheffield exit. Travel west approximately 2 miles to the park entrance on the south (left) side of the road. The nature center and trail entrances are at the far end of the lot. Begin your visit to French Creek Reservation with a visit to the center.

The Trail

The hike begins when you step out the back door of the center, turn left, go down a set of steps, and cross French Creek. (There is an alternate route with a tarmac surface down the hill to the creek should you be in a wheelchair or using a walker.)

The blacktop ends and the improved Nature Center Trail—with a limestone-screening surface and marked with blue Carsonite posts—begins beyond the bridge. From the bridge, you can see exposed Devonian-age shale (perhaps Ohio shale) in one bank. In the streambed look for the granite boulders so characteristic of land that has been glaciated in not-too-recent millennia—glacial erratics, we call them.

The trail cuts across a meander so that almost immediately you can see French Creek, which you just crossed, below on the left. There is now elevation to be gained to return to the level of the old lake bottom that this creek is cutting its way through. The soil on top of the bedrock in the park is lacustrine (lake-deposited) sand, silt, and clay and easily eroded. Through nice woods, the trail ascends with a wide sweep to the right. A shorter, steeper route goes left up a ridge, but save this for the way back.

Surprisingly, once you're back to the elevation of the center, the trail again descends to cross Fish Creek, an east–west tributary that empties into French Creek just

Well designed signs with maps provide directions to hikers at French Creek Reservation.

behind the center. As you approach the bridge over Fish Creek, you can see an observation platform that overlooks the creek from the Big Woods Trail. If you need to rest, nice benches are provided along the trail. At the intersection of the Nature Center Trail and Big Woods Trail, I suggest that after a rest on another bench you turn left and follow the yellow posts as you walk east along the high ground south of Fish Creek. Early records suggest that the valley of French Creek along the northern edge of the park (where the trail system does not take you) was originally swamp forest but that the higher land where the Big Woods Trail travels was mixed-mesophytic forest. My observations of the current blend of hardwoods agrees—nice oaks, hickories, maples, and beech. The forest on the right is not very old, but the woods to the left along Fish Creek, which include some nice sycamores, are much more mature.

Soon, just beyond another bench, the trail enters an area of larger trees with bur oaks, pin oaks, and red maples now in the mix, indicating a more poorly drained woods. Now, 150 feet into the "big woods," the improved trail makes a turn to the right and an umimproved but quite passable forest trail heads straight ahead. If you need the smooth surface, go right. Otherwise, take the trail straight ahead. It's the place to see more spring wildflowers. Orange markers identify this trail. Don't be alarmed if you find deadfall; you will be able to get around it. After a couple of hundred feet, the trail leaves Fish Creek and swings left to head south. There are more beech trees here and consequently some roots to step over. A football field's distance to the left is the railroad right-of-way that marks the east border of the reservation. Speaking of football fields, on the autumn day that I walked the trail, along here I could hear a marching

---

French Creek Reservation

band rehearsing out-of-doors, doubtless for the following Friday night's gridiron battle.

In this corner of the woods is a large stand of nearly solid pin oak trees, causing me to think that this flat area probably has a clayey soil that drains poorly—an area to which I would surely come armed with insect repellent during the warmer months. The trail next makes another sweeping 90-degree turn, this time into the valley of Sugar Creek, another French Creek tributary. The stream has not cut as deeply as Fish Creek.

Heading west now through nice woods following orange blazes, the trail soon travels close to the creek, where it makes a wide meander. Farther away from the creek again, the trail rises and, where the big trees run out, intersects with the Big Tree Trail and its yellow blazes.

Continue your hike on this improved yellow-blazed trail. It shortly jogs right and crosses the park road that leads to the Pine Tree Picnic Area. According to the topographic map, this park road is a recycled former railroad right-of-way. During the winter you can see the U.S. Cobey steel plant to the south of the park. Among many young maple trees, both red and sugar, the trail continues west, winding its way more or less parallel to Sugar Creek. There is a drainage ditch alongside the trail here. The trail moves briefly closer to the creek, now rapidly cutting more deeply through the till to a spot where shale cliffs line both banks; there are still scattered glacial erratics in the streambed. At another area of old woods, a former road that descends into the stream valley is blocked by a rail fence.

The trail now turns northwest, leaving the woods to enter the Pine Tree Picnic Area. There is a rest room, some playground equipment, some picnic tables, and a water fountain. At the west end of the picnic area is the 0.55-mile improved Sugar Creek Trail, marked with red. It leads to an overlook above the now quite deep valley of Sugar Creek before looping right to return to the picnic area loop road. Sugar Creek turns to the northwest and enters French Creek just beyond the trail overlook.

Return to the blacktop Big Tree Trail as it crosses a picnic area and the parking lot loop to pass a trailhead sign and return to the woods, again on a stone surface. The woods are younger here, with crab apple trees left over from the thicket stage of succession still visible alongside the trail. After the leaves have fallen, you can see another picnic area through the trees to the right. This is just off the old railroad right-of-way. If you look carefully, you can see where the Big Woods Trail you are walking crosses the old railbed.

Fish Creek is now down the hill through the woods to the left of the trail. A boardwalk comes in from the right connecting the Big Woods Trail to the orphaned picnic area. Just before the boardwalk, steps leave to the left to the overlook above Fish Creek. In moments, the trail returns to the bench and an intersection with the Nature Center Trail. Turn left to follow the blue markers back to the bridge below the nature center. Or as an alternative, after you cross Fish Creek and start up the hill, catch the shortcut side trail to the right to climb back to the Nature Center Trail on the ridge between Fish and French Creeks, enjoying another overlook on the way.

Once across French Creek on the bridge, turn left. Note the high banks of shale across the stream and the old foundation where the train came through here. The trail arcs widely to the left and climbs to the west end of the nature center, where it splits into a walk going to the center and one to the parking lot, using the old roadbed for part of the way.

35

Magee Marsh
State Wildlife Area

Total distance: 2 miles (3.2 km)

Hiking time: 2 hours

Maximum elevation: 575 feet

Vertical rise: 4 feet

*Maps: USGS 7½' Series Oak Harbor;
ODNR Magee Marsh Wildlife Area map*

Many midwestern birders know Magee Marsh as one of the region's premier birding hot spots—the place to go in spring when the birds that last autumn left the northern temperate zone to winter in warmer climates are now rushing back to ancestral breeding grounds to help perpetuate their kind. Given the optimum meteorological conditions, what ornithologists refer to as a fallout may occur, and the trees and shrubs along the Bird Trail at Magee can be dripping with neotropical migrants. Even on a "poor day" in April and May, dozens of species of birds can be observed at closer-than-normal range along the Boardwalk Trail. Mostly, they are feeding in preparation for the next leg of their journey north, across Lake Erie. This is the place to go to add birds to your life list, or just to enjoy a great variety of species close at hand. I have spent many an hour hanging out on the Bird Trail boardwalk looking for rarities such as the Kirtland's warbler or just waiting to get my first look of the year at beautiful creatures such as the scarlet tanager or rose-breasted grosbeak.

Birding aside, I find that Magee Marsh is also a refreshing and inspiring place to walk when the migration is over, the birders have packed up their field guides and binoculars and gone home, and the swimmers have deserted the beach. It's a place to feel the elements, to experience the sound of a howling wind or of cracking ice; a place to pick up a shell or a piece of sand-ground old glass from the beach. And you never know what fellow creature may fly, run,

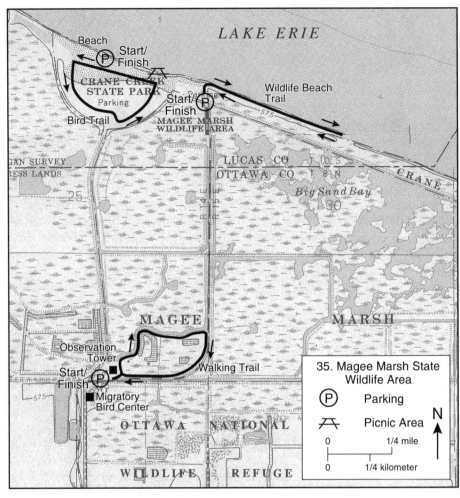

LAKE ERIE

Beach
Start/Finish

CRANE CREEK
STATE PARK
Parking

Start/Finish

MAGEE MARSH
WILDLIFE AREA

Wildlife Beach
Trail

Bird Trail

GAN SURVEY
RESS LANDS

LUCAS CO T 10 S
OTTAWA CO T 8 N

CRANE

Big Sand Bay

MAGEE   MARSH

Observation
Tower

Walking Trail

Start/Finish

Migratory
Bird Center

OTTAWA   NATIONAL

W[]LDLIFE   REFUGE

35. Magee Marsh State
Wildlife Area

P   Parking

Picnic Area

N

| 0 | 1/4 mile |
| 0 | 1/4 kilometer |

creep, crawl, or swim your way. I've been eyeball to eyeball with saw-whet owls, watched fox snakes basking in the sun, and enjoyed the beauty of the wildflowers of spring, summer, and fall. In all, 309 species of birds have been seen at Magee, and 143 of those have been recorded as nesting there.

The wildlife area offers three designated area for walking. They are the 0.6-mile-plus, totally accessible Boardwalk Trail; about 0.75 mile of Lake Erie beach; and the Walking Trail, just under 0.5 mile long, located near the Migratory Bird Center. The area is open during daylight hours year-round except mid-October through November, when the Beach and Boardwalk Trails are closed for safety reasons during waterfowl hunting season.

When the earliest explorers reached the southern shore of the western basin of Lake Erie in the 17th century, they found a vast area of marsh and swamp. Early records show that from what is now Vermilion, Ohio, to the mouth of the Detroit River in Michigan, western Lake Erie was rimmed with 300,000 acres of wetland. In Ohio the marsh averaged about 2 miles wide and in places extended farther from the lake into what we know as the Great Black Swamp, an enormous swamp forest that covered former beds of the lakes that followed the receding Wisconsinan glacier. In higher portions there were wet prairie areas dotted with small groves of trees, probably bur oaks.

In the area of Magee Marsh, French hunters and trappers were followed by German settlers who cleared and drained the land for agriculture. Market hunting took place and, by the middle of the 19th century, the first duck hunting club had been established. By 1900 most of the swamp forest of the area had been cleared and drained and the area was farmed to the edge of the marshes. Attempts were made to dike and drain the marshes for farming, but fickle weather and fluctuating water levels made that a risky business. In the period following the Civil War, wealthy city dwellers began acquiring large tracts of marsh for duck hunting. From 1830 until 1903, the area near the mouth of Crane Creek now known as Magee Marsh was a natural deep marsh of about 4,000 acres and was called the Crane Creek Shooting Club. Artificial management was begun with a system of dikes and pumps being used to manipulate water levels to produce optimum habitat for waterfowl. Muskrat trapping helped offset the high cost of marsh maintenance. In 1951 increased maintenance costs due to damage from higher lake levels and the demand from creditors for mortgage payments made it possible for the Department of Natural Resources to purchase this once private club. The Division of Parks and Recreation manages about a mile of land 400 feet wide along the beach for swimming and picnicking, and the Division of Wildlife manages the remaining area—about 2,000 acres—for

Rose-mallow blooms along the trail near the migratory bird center.

public hunting and fishing and wildlife diversity. The division also maintains a wildlife research station on the property.

How to Get There

Magee Marsh Wildlife Area is located 25 miles east of Toledo off SR 2. It is 130 miles from Columbus and is reached from there by US 23, SR 53, and SR 19, which dead-ends into SR 2 at a spot 2 miles east of the combined Magee Marsh/Crane Creek entrance. Good hiking and good birding.

The Trails

Where you start hiking is dependent upon your interests. If you want to see a great variety of birds during spring or fall migration, then head for the Boardwalk Trail as early in the day as you can. Most people begin at the west entrance near the far end of the Crane Creek State Park lot. The total length of the trail one way if you simply walk from one entrance to the other is 0.6 mile, but two loops and a short spur add to that distance. During peak birding periods there will be birders from near and far milling on or moving along the trail observing birds; generally they are more than willing to share their finds with anyone interested. If you simply want to hike through, they will give room, but respect the concerns of the birders for minimum disturbance.

Magee Marsh State Wildlife Area

During many months of the year, traffic on the boardwalk will be very sparse and you can walk as you wish. You can, of course, return to your car via the boardwalk. The road is another alternative, as is the beach. After your exploration of the Boardwalk Trail, try the wildlife beach. The trailhead is at the east end of Crane Creek beach, to the left of the park road where it makes a sharp right turn to the south. There is ample space for parking, as well as a nice beach to stroll on unimpeded by bathers. Hiking is permitted for about 0.75 mile along the beach at this point.

Don't leave the area without visiting the Migratory Bird Center, the observation tower, and the Magee Marsh Walking Trail. You can start the wood-chipped trail at either the tower or the back door of the center. As I walked the trail alongside and between the ponds near the center, I stopped to listen to a bullfrog, photographed a crayfish chimney, unsuccessfully stalked a couple of dragonflies with my camera, and sat on a bench for a few moments admiring a family of geese swimming in a straight line across a pond. During hawk migration season in spring and fall there is often a volunteer hawk-watcher on the tower who will be happy to point out the birds of prey moving across the sky.

Directly to the west of Magee Marsh Wildlife Area lies the federally operated Ottawa National Wildlife Refuge. There are several miles of dikes open for hiking there. For a number of years one or more pairs of bald eagles have nested nearby, affording the opportunity to see one of our national symbols hunting in the area.

36

Secor Metropark

Total distance: 2 miles (3.2 km)

Hiking time: 1½ hours

Maximum elevation: 660 feet

Vertical rise: 10 feet

*Maps: USGS 7½' Series Berkey;
MPDTA Secor Metropark brochure*

West of Toledo, a broad ridge of fine yellow quartz sand extends from Liberty Center, near the Maumee River, northeast to Detroit. This is the region known as the Oak Openings. The sand came from the area we now call Michigan over thousands of years, carried by longshore currents along the several lakes that preceded Lake Erie as the Wisconsinan glacier was in recession. The sand does not replace the clayey soil of this area but lies on top of it, where it may be anywhere from 15 to 50 feet deep. When these sand beaches were originally formed, they were fairly flat, but as the water level dropped and they dried out, they began to shift and drift, forming ridges and dunes.

Part of a larger area referred to as the Black Swamp, the Oak Openings feature water very close to the surface. When this area was being settled, it was vegetated with a mixture of swamp forest, wet prairie, and "openings," or stands of widely spaced black oak trees. It is difficult land to drain, so farming has been marginal at best. It is an area of high natural diversity, rich in rare and endangered plant species.

Artifacts discovered on the dunes indicate that people lived there as early as 12,000 years ago. Early explorers used the sand ridges as a route between Detroit and the Maumee River rapids. French and English explorers dominated in the area during different eras, but by the early years of Ohio's statehood, as the port of Toledo expanded rapidly, people began moving to the fringes of the Oak Openings. There the land was cheap but somewhat easier to drain with ditches and tile.

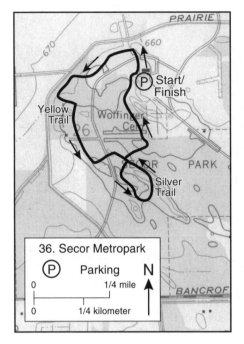

The area has always been rich in wildlife, the woodlands serving birds migrating around the western end of Lake Erie and the wetlands providing habitat for waterfowl, shorebirds, and wading birds. Greater prairie chickens were found in the openings as late as the 1880s.

Secor Woods Metropark preserves a 600-acre tract of the Oak Openings to protect the natural diversity of the region and provide recreational opportunities for the people of northwestern Ohio. It owes its existence to a small paved lot in downtown Toledo, at the corner of Jefferson and Erie. That real estate was bequeathed to the Metropark District in 1941 by Arthur J. Secor in memory of his parents, Joseph K. and Elizabeth Secor. Income from the lot was used to purchase the park's land in the late 1940s and early 1950s. In September 1953 Secor opened as the seventh metro park. The parking lot was sold in 1985 and the proceeds used to fund most of the

improvements at the park's Nature Discovery Center. Other facilities include shelters and picnic areas, rest rooms, play equipment, and nearly 10 miles of trails that provide an opportunity for visitors to explore this rich part of Ohio's natural heritage.

How to Get There

Secor Metropark is easily reached by driving 5 miles west on US 20 from I-475 (US 23) on the west side of Toledo.

The Trail

Begin hiking at the trailhead located near the southwest corner of the Nature Discovery Center. That building is open from 1 to 5 pm Wednesday through Sunday. There are rest rooms attached to the building that are accessible at all hours when the park is open. Ample parking is provided on the south side of the center, and a paved walk leads to the trailhead. My preference is for the trails designated walking-only, but there are many fine all-purpose trails throughout the park shared by walkers and cyclists.

For my day at Secor Woods, I chose a morning during the first week of May, when wildflowers were near their peak of bloom and the trees were likely to be full of birds in spring migration. Still, there is something new and different to see every day of the year. When snow covers the floor of the forest, visitors are invited to use their cross-country skis to travel the trails.

The trailhead kiosk provides a thorough description of the routes and the labeling of all the park's trails. A color-coding system makes it easy to follow the trail of your choice. I suggest starting on the Trillium Trail, choosing the 1.3-mile-long loop option. Start hiking north from the trailhead past the lilac bushes at the west end of the center and across the park service road through a lawn area. Beyond the road the

Information about distances and trail blazes is provided at the trailhead sign.

trail soon reaches a post where color markers indicate that the all-purpose trail continues straight ahead toward a large glacial erratic, a bridge over Prairie Creek, and lots of flowering crab apple trees. The yellow trail, which goes into the woods, goes to the left; the Prairie Trail, to the right.

In summer and early autumn, I suggest adding a walk to the prairie and back on the 0.5-mile Prairie Trail to your hike.

Turning right on the mowed bluegrass, the trail passes through some ornamental plantings of flowering trees and shrubs and tall spruce trees before finally reaching the forest.

A shelter off to the left between the trail and the road is the location of a memorial to the late Max Shepherst, the director of the Toledo Park District during its early years. As a young man just beginning in the park business in the 1960s, I was privileged to have met him at several professional gatherings, and to have benefited by some of his

professional advice. Before I continued on my hike, I stopped at the memorial to reflect upon the changes in the natural area preservation movement that have occurred in the intervening years.

As I entered the woods, a large flock of crows overhead had a great horned owl cornered and were giving it a scolding as only crows can do. All the familiar woodland wildflowers were in bloom on the forest floor. A thrill for me was to see a tiger swallowtail butterfly drinking nectar from a large-flowered trillium. The trail now has a sandy surface. The red and white oaks in this part of the park are spectacular.

After passing a junction—a cutoff to the left here will reduce your hike's distance by 0.4 mile—the yellow trail turns left and moves closer to Prairie Creek. It is obvious from its straightness and from the presence of dredge spoil on which the trail is moving that the stream was man-made to drain what was probably once an abysmal swamp. Occasionally you can see the decaying stump of one of the huge trees that at one time stood here. The all-purpose trail on the far side of Prairie Creek can be seen from the Trillium Trail.

Tall jack-in-the pulpits grow close to the trail. Just before you turn away from the stream, pass a large walnut tree and an equally big bitternut hickory. Now the trail travels on a boardwalk for about 80 feet, passing papaw and spicebush in the well-developed shrub layer and many more familiar wildflowers close to the ground. The other common white-flowered trillium of western Ohio, drooping trillium, is present along the trail here. The trail has come 0.5 mile when it reaches a T where the short loop exits left and the yellow-blazed long loop turns and continues to the right.

Soon you can see a shelter to the right through the woods. The trail then crosses a service road that leads from the main park road, Tupelo Way, to the Meadowview Area. When I walked the trail it appeared that a prescribed burn of forest litter might have taken place recently. At another T in the trail, the 1.2-mile Swamp Forest Trail heads right and the Trillium Trail turns left. If you have the time, leave the Trillium Trail and follow the red markers through the swamp forest in the park's southwest corner. It will return you to the same point on the Trillium Trail, sharing the tread with the all-purpose trail for part of the way.

Now heading east, the Trillium Trail crosses Tupelo Way and shortly intersects with the Forested Dune Trail. From this point back to the trailhead, the Trillium and Forested Dune Trails share the same tread. There is a loop of the silver-labeled Forested Dune Trail off to the right that is well worth adding to your hike before returning to the trailhead on the combined trail. Instead of being almost flat, like the earlier trail, this trail rises and falls several feet on the tree-covered dunes.

The combined trails now head northeast then north on slightly higher ground where beech and maple trees enter the mix of forest hardwoods. To the right are much-younger trees that have begun growing since the establishment of the park. Where the trail crosses a service road, you can see the Wolfinger Cemetery off to the right through the woods.

At another intersection, the 0.3-mile Woodland Pond Trail leads to a pond where chorus frogs were calling on the day I was walking. Continue north on the blue trail past the outdoor exhibit that interprets pond life. The trailhead kiosk and the walk to the parking lot are just beyond.

While you are in this area, you will want to visit Irwin Prairie State Nature Preserve located on the south side of Bancroft Street directly south of Secor Park. There you can walk through pin oak woods, sedge meadow, and wet prairie on a boardwalk about 0.25 mile long. It is especially lovely when the spiked blazing-star is blooming in July.

Elsewhere in the Toledo metropark system, the trail at Oak Openings Park offers an 8-mile hike through a variety of Black Swamp habitats. A description of that hike can be found in *50 Hikes in Ohio.*

37

White Star Park

Total distance: 2.25 miles (3.6 km)

Hiking time: 1½ hours

Maximum elevation: 692 feet

Vertical rise: 10 feet

Maps: USGS 7½' Series Helena; SCPD White Star Park map

In the excruciatingly flat lake plain area near the western Sandusky community of Gibsonburg, the limestone bedrock lies so close to the surface that sometimes you can stub your toe on it. The topsoil is only a few inches thick. Here 420,000-year-old Silurian dolomite of the Niagaran Series lies on the crest of the Cincinnati Arch. About 65 feet thick, this light gray rock known as the Guelph formation is considered to be of high purity and it has been commercially quarried for the better part of a century.

The White Star Stone Company (probably so named because of the very light color of coarsely crystalline rock) operated a quarry here in the 1920s. Later, for a few years during the middle of the Great Depression, it was operated by the Gibsonville Lime Association. By 1938 the quarry was closed and the pit, about 10 acres in size, was full of water.

When the Sandusky County Park District was founded in 1975, this park was its first major acquisition. The presence of a lake made the property attractive for outdoor recreation activities, and the district has done a fine job of providing for fishing, swimming, boating, scuba diving, picnicking, and camping. But it is the unusual "walk about" area that I find most attractive, an area of former agricultural fields adjacent to the quarry property where a trail system has been developed in an area planted in native tallgrass prairie.

This is Black Swamp country, land that was, for the most part, elm–ash–maple–oak swamp before it was tiled, ditched, and

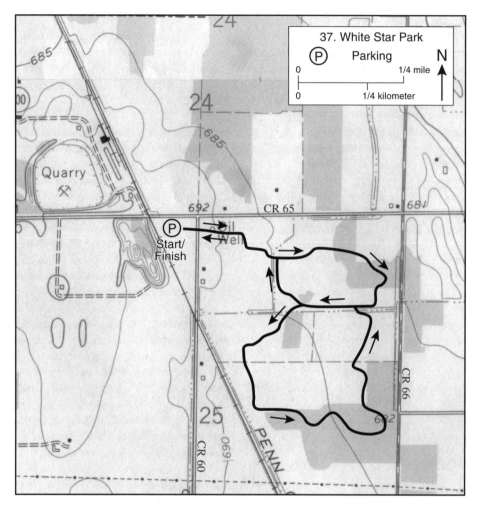

drained. But prairie was not a foreigner to the county. Where there were areas of former postglacial beach, as there were here, there were areas of tallgrass prairie. With financial assistance from Pheasants Forever, the park district has created an outstanding prairie area that does a good job of conveying the feeling you get when you are exploring wild prairie preserves in Kansas and Missouri.

So while others are crowded around the quarry-turned-watering-hole, pass by the park entrance and turn east from SR 300 onto CR 65 and travel 0.4 mile to the "walk about" area parking lot. It's on the south side of the road just east of the railroad right-of-way.

How to Get There

White Star Park is in Madison township in Sandusky County just south of the small community of Gibsonburg, about a dozen miles west of Fremont. Travel US 6 west from the Fremont area or east from the Bowling Green area to SR 300. Go 2 miles north to CR 65 (Shade Road) and turn east 0.5 mile to the trailhead.

The Trail

At the "walk about" lot, park, lock, and prepare for any unkindnesses such as ticks, sun, and mosquitoes that Mother Nature might throw at you during your visit. Check the bulletin board, and begin walking by heading east. The trail is well marked with good interpretive signs. My only comment about the signs is that I would have preferred to read about prairie chickens, upland sandpipers, badgers, and bison—native animals that were part of the original prairie ecosystem at the time of settlement—rather than, or perhaps along with, those that are in place, which describe the non-native ring-necked pheasant and managed-for-the-hunters white-tailed deer. But I understand, knowing the difficulty in raising funds for restorations and considering where the help came from to recreate this prairie. Bond money raised by the State NatureWorks Program was also used to develop this area, and public hunting is permitted during certain seasons. Be aware of times such as opening day and weekends during upland game season. It might be wise to at least wear hunter orange clothing at these times, if not refrain from hiking entirely.

Almost immediately the trail crosses CR 60; then very soon it makes a right turn through old field being invaded with shrubs and trees such as prickly ash, gray dogwood, and cottonwood. The prickly ash is a pleasant surprise, since it is one of the food plants of the giant swallowtail larva. At this point the trail is wide with a gravel surface, but soon it emerges from the woody area, crosses over a ditch, passes a bench, and splits. One branch goes to the right and the other, which I chose to walk, goes straight ahead, now on a mowed grass surface with tallgrass prairie on both sides. The trail veers slightly to the north then continues east, where it soon enters a woods of white oak, hickory, cottonwood, and sycamore, reminding me of the Great Black Swamp that at one time occupied most of this part of Ohio. Mind the poison ivy on the edge of the woods as the broad trail turns slightly to the south on a stone surface.

Emerging from the woods, the gravel trail passes what can best be described as meadow or old field—not a restoration of native tallgrass but the Eurasian grass and weedy herb species that have grown on the land since its last use as farm fields. Grasshoppers were plentiful on the late-summer day when I last hiked the trail. Still on limestone screenings (an abundant supply is available on the property), the trail reenters wet woods, where it passes bur and swamp white oak trees and a large granite boulder as it winds its way to the east then south. Red and white oak, good acorn producers, stand by the trail along here. At the spot where the trail leaves the woods to return tallgrass prairie, there is another resting area. The trail again has a mowed grass surface. A hundred feet into the prairie, an interpretive sign discusses open fields, meadows, and prairies.

Now headed west, the trail reaches another wooded area where it splits, with a track straight ahead and one to the left. I suggest continuing into the woods and eventually circling left to travel this way again in a figure-eight hike. Here again, this is not an old woods but an area of field turning to thickets turning to woods. Many species that appear and disappear at different stages of plant succession can be seen. Red cedar, the evergreen that often invades old fields with thin soil over dolomite, such as this one, grows here among hardwoods that are slowly overtopping it. The presence of a sizable deer population is revealed by the red cedars: They all have that browsed-as-high-as-a-deer-can-reach look. As you

In August, monarch butterflies seek nectar from New England asters en route to their overwintering sites in Mexico.

approach the far side of the woods, alongside the trail are some sizable glacial erratics, granite boulders transported by the glacier from the Canadian Shield country to the north 10,000 to 15,000 years ago.

Beyond the woods, another bench beckons you to rest and contemplate the world around you. On grass and glacial gravel surface, the trail heads southwest through more prairie. A service road joins the prairie path. On the day I walked the trail, it appeared that some prairie hay had been harvested here, perhaps for use in an interpretive program at the nature preserve barn 0.5 mile to the west. The trail comes close to the railroad right-of-way here. A ditch comes under the track from the west, passes beneath the trail, and runs east toward the woods. Just after the trail crosses the ditch, it turns left, headed for the woods in the southeast corner of the park.

At the forest edge is another bench; the trail again is gravel. You pass among young trees, most less than a foot in diameter—no red cedars here.

At the far corner of the preserve beech and maple trees fill an area that looks as if it might stand in water a good bit of the year and swarm with mosquitoes in season. This also looks like an area where vernal flora is at its best in April and May. The trail turns north here and parallels a ditch that has also turned to the north. Across the ditch more tallgrass prairie occurs. At the end of the trees, a trail splits off to the right and goes out to CR 66 where there is a small parking lot, probably for use by hunters.

Where the gravel surface runs out at the end of the woods, a mowed grass trail heads northwest across the ditch and winds its way through the prairie to return to the successional woods you passed through earlier. A three-leafleted shrub, fragrant sumac, grows here in the thin soil above the dolomite—just as it does, for example, near the Trailside Museum at Glen

Helen in Greene County. It is easily distinguished from poison ivy (which was once considered to be in the same genus, *Rhus,* as the sumac) by its smaller stemless leaflets and its bright red long hairy fruit in small irregular clusters. Poison ivy has whitish berrylike drupes. Crush a sumac leaflet to catch the scent whence its specific epithet, *aromatica,* comes. Noticeably absent here is bush honeysuckle that has become such a nuisance in the limy soils in the southwestern part of the state. The presence of a young hackberry tree comes as no surprise, as it is another species that does especially well on soils over calcareous bedrock. Hackberry is the food plant of the larvae of several species of native butterflies of the brushfoot family: the question mark, tawny emperor, and, of course, hackberry butterfly. With prickly ash, the larval food plant of the giant swallowtail, also present here, this is a good place to observe the summer butterflies.

Upon again emerging from the young woods, this time follow the trail to the right through more tallgrass prairie. Soon the trail turns right to run alongside a ditch headed north to intersect the entrance trail. The prairie is not as well developed along here. There are bluebird boxes, and I saw a male eastern bluebird perched on the top of one as I brought my hike to a close. Although the park map showed the area west of the ditch to be forest, for part of the way it is old field. Here this trail makes a T, turns left (west) to cross CR 60, and returns to the parking lot.

Very few trails in the state travel through as much tallgrass prairie as this one. The time to see and enjoy the prairie is July through frost—a time of year when it can be very hot in Ohio, so pace yourself, carry adequate drinking water, and be prepared to fend off ticks and mosquitoes. I also look at this trail as a good place to use the 100-millimeter macro lens on a single-lens reflex or one of the new close focusing-zoom point-and-shoot cameras to capture good images of butterflies, dragonflies, mantises, spiders, and the like. Enjoy, as I did.

V

Glaciated Allegheny Plateau

38

Charles F. Alley Park

Total distance: 2.5 miles (4 km)

Hiking time: 2 hours

Maximum elevation: 1,035 feet

Vertical rise: 155 feet

Maps: USGS 7½' Series Lancaster

Charles F. Alley Park, located in Fairfield County 3 miles south of downtown Lancaster, came to the Lancaster Park and Recreation Board in 1978 through a gift and sale of a 300-acre tract from Charles and Loretta Alley. Situated on the west flank of the valley of the Hocking River, it is not far from the point of the glacial ice sheets' farthest advance into this part of Ohio. Near the entrance to the park along Old Logan Road are hillside deposits of sand and gravel. Farther back from the highway, the parkland is dissected Illinoian ground moraine with weathered bedrock exposed on the hillsides. The Black Hand sandstone that is so well known from the nearby Hocking Hills region and Rising Park on the northern edge of Lancaster can be seen along the trails of Alley Park.

The Hocking (in earlier times, the Hockhocking) River Valley is really the valley of a preglacial river that, unlike the Hocking, flowed north. When the Illinoian glacier (and later the Wisconsinan glacier) advanced from the north, the course of the original river was blocked. Water rose in the valley, and eventually the river found a new route through the unglaciated hills to the south, its waters flowing to the Gulf of Mexico via the Ohio and Mississippi Rivers. When the Illinoian glacier (whose leading edge stopped just south of Alley Park) and, later, the Wisconsinan (which advanced to the area of downtown Lancaster) began to melt, a huge volume of water began flowing out into the Hocking Valley. It carried with it great quantities of glacial gravel, which filled

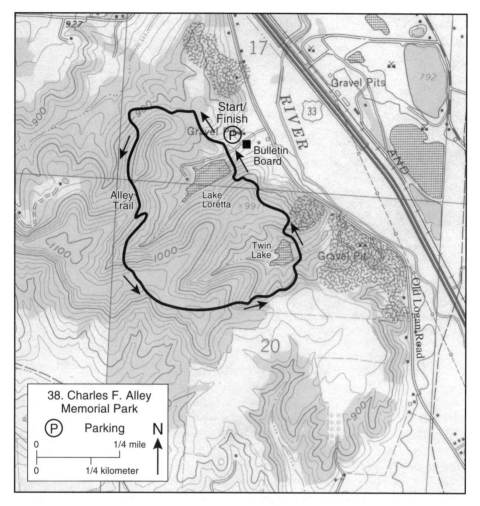

38. Charles F. Alley
Memorial Park

Ⓟ Parking   N

0 _____ 1/4 mile

0 _____ 1/4 kilometer

the valley and was deposited as benches and terraces along its edges. Sand and gravel extraction has long been a major industry in the Hocking Valley. It was also the route of the Hocking Canal, which was built to connect Athens to the Ohio & Erie Canal near Columbus during the prerailroad years of the 19th century. Central Ohio and railroads have made use of the level route to haul coal and other freight into the hill country. In my early days of visiting the Hocking Hills, what is now the Old Logan Road was Route 33, a narrow, winding brick road.

At Alley Park the center of activity is the Charles and Stella Gosling Nature Education Center on the shore of Lake Loretta. The late Charles Goslin was a renowned naturalist and historian from Lancaster who wrote for the local paper and was very active in the community. He served on the board of park commissioners and, with his son Jim, laid out most of the trails in Alley Park. Following his death, his family provided the major gift for construction of the education center. A monument at the entrance to the road to the center commemorates his life. It was my privilege

The author's long-time friend and fellow naturalist/historian, Charles Goslin of Lancaster, is memorialized with a bronze plaque on a glacial erratic at the entrance to Alley Park.

to have been his friend for half a century. On the beautiful May day when I walked the trail, I felt his presense at my side, beguiling me with tales about the wildflowers, trees, and birds I was seeing along the way.

How to Get There

Charles F. Alley Park is easily reached by traveling US 33 southeast from Lancaster to Stump Hollow Road. Turn right and immediately left onto Old Logan Road. The park entrance is less than half a mile down the road on the right. The park is open every day year-round.

The Trail

Upon arriving at the park, leave your vehicle in the main lot. Rest rooms and drinking water are available there. To begin hiking, head up the road past the monument toward the visitors center for a very short distance. When you reach an outdoor program area,

turn right and go toward the woods. There you will find a small post marking the entrance to the trail. Enter through the opening between the hardwoods on the left and the pines on the right, then turn left and hug the edge while making a fairly steep climb. Soon the trail will duck into the woods. From there on, nearly all of the trail will be in the mixed-mesophytic woods so typical of this region of Ohio. This is the 2.5-mile-long Alley Trail. It circumnavigates the park and should take a couple of hours to hike if you take time to admire the natural objects along the way.

Once the trail enters the woods, it continues to climb on what looks like an old road or logging trail. Hardwood forest is on the left, but the right side of the trail is a planting of white pines. Numbered posts along the trail indicate that a self-guided tour was available at one time but I was unable to locate a guidebook, and many of the posts lack numbers.

When the trail turns left, leaving the old road, it enters an area of large hardwoods. Unfortunately, the invasive alien garlic mustard has found its way to Alley Park and is now a part of the wildflower mix in May. The trail soon reaches a T where a short connecting trail goes uphill to the left to join the Buck Run Trail. Keep to the right to travel the outer edge of the woods.

At the northwest corner of the park, the trail drops down the side of the hill. As it turns south, it moves steeply uphill to meet the Buck Run Trail coming in from the left. Note the 15- to 20-foot Black Hand sandstone cliffs up the hillside. The shrub layer of the forest through here includes much mountain laurel, a real treat to see.

Beyond the mountain laurel, the trail rises to its junction with the Vultures Roost Trail. The latter goes left, drops through a cull, and connects to the Blackhand Trail below the cliffs in the hollow where Lake Loretta and the education center are located. If you want to shorten your walk, this is a good place to take the shortcut back to the parking lot.

Leaving this junction, the Alley Trail climbs to the top of the Black Hand sandstone with more mountain laurel all around, then drops down the hillside on a rugged path with exposed bedrock and several switchbacks before meeting the Trillium Trail coming in from the left.

Now on a narrow path, the trail climbs between Black Hand sandstone slump blocks to meet the Ridge Trail on the high ground. Staying right on the Alley Trail, you next walk through a beautiful section of open woods before reaching the Poplar Trail angling off to the left. Next, the trail falls very sharply with sandstone exposures and slump blocks and, in spring, gorgeous wildflowers. The Oak Trail veers off to the left, with the Alley Trail staying right. Soon a hole through the woods to the right with grassland visible in the distance marks the route of the Meadow Trail Loop. You can add 0.25 mile more hiking by taking this loop, but be warned that it does drop steeply at the other end.

Since both trails are headed for the same place, the Alley Trail must also lose altitude, and it does so shortly. You'll emerge from the woods onto a grassy trail on the east bank of Twin Lake. Straight-ahead travel will bring you to a short steep climb up a sometimes muddy section of the trail. Aound the corner, the steepest climb of the trail confronts you as you move up a wide trail to eventually take a well-worn path to the top of the sandstone bedrock, meeting the Ridge Loop Trail joining from and leaving to the left. Next, head downslope through the elevation of the cliffs to pass the Blackhand Trail on the left and a service road to the right. Traveling straight ahead downhill, the Alley Trail soon comes to the Muskrat Trail on the shore of Lake Loretta. A short walk leads to the road to the education center; a turn to the right will return you to the parking lot.

While in the area, consider hiking at Rockbridge State Nature Preserve, located only a few miles south off US 33 beyond the town of Rockbridge.

39

Charles Mill Park

Total distance: 2 miles (3.2 km)

Hiking time: 1 hour

Maximum elevation: 1,125 feet

Vertical rise: 100 feet

Maps: USGS 7½' Series Pavoni; MWCD Charles Mill Lake brochure

Charles Mill Lake area resident Jack Donaldson was looking for a place to walk his dog when, in 1998, he stumbled upon a little-used trail in an isolated corner of a property that the Muskingum Watershed Conservancy District owns at the upper end of Charles Mill Lake. On the park map, there was a dashed-line loop simply labeled "nature trail"—but when Donaldson took a look at the trail, he found it overgrown.

He approached Dan Mager, the park manager, about what he'd found. Together they devised a plan to renovate the trail.

After Donaldson offered to contribute money to pay for clearing the trail and placing some benches alongside, the project moved forward. In the summer of 2000, park officials dedicated the renovated trail with a ceremony at which they renamed this the Donaldson Family Trail.

How to Get There

The 2-mile path through an area the district has designated a nature preserve originates from a small parking lot at a 90-degree turn in Crider Road across from US 30. To reach it, take US 30 east from I-71 to SR 603. Turn north onto Crider Road, which goes left off SR 603 just before you reach the I-71 underpass. The parking lot is on the left at the corner of the road just over 1.5 miles south of SR 603.

The Trail

Begin walking by following the trail east from the parking lot on a fill that may have at one time carried a township road. A thousand

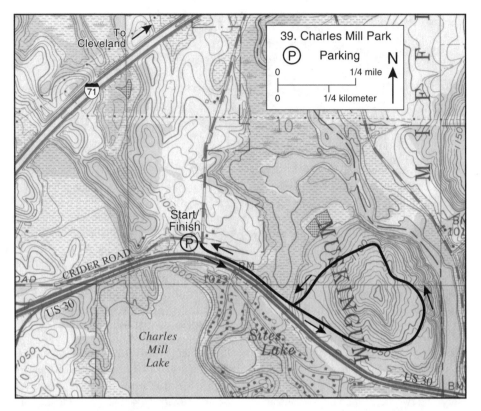

feet in, you will find a wetland north of the fill, full of frogs in the early spring. Near here you'll find extensive growth of an exotic Oriental bittersweet. It is not nearly as conspicuous in fruit as is the native American bittersweet, but it surely has acclimatized to this warm south-facing hillside environment, being almost like kudzu in the southern states.

Soon you will reach a mowed grass area with a bench. The trail splits here to make the loop. I chose the right-hand trail and found myself climbing slowly around a wooded hillside on a well-defined trail. The hill has the appearance of a kame, a pile of glacial gravel deposited under the ice sheet having washed through a hole in the glacier before it melted from the land. Mississippian-age bedrock lies below 1,000 feet in elevation

here. The preglacial valley of the river that preceded the Black Fork lies buried deep below glacial outwash just west of the parking lot. The current channel is just east of this hill. The top of this kame is at 1,200 feet in elevation.

Early records show that this was oak–sugar maple forest at the time of settlement. Today's secondary forest cover bears little resemblance to the extensive old-growth hardwood forests that greeted settlers when they arrived here in Ohio's early years. Delaware Indians lived in the area; the massacre of the Copus, Ruffner, and Simmer families in 1812 took place just up SR 603.

After about 0.5 mile of walking parallel to but uphill from US 30, you will find the trail turning north around the eastern side of the

In late August, beautiful tall bell flower with their blue blossoms bloom along many Ohio woodland trails.

hill, climbing steadily for many yards. There is an extensive planting of white pine on this hillside. Next, the trail crosses over a dry ridge and, on a switchback, turns toward the northwest to travel close to the bluffs overlooking the Black Fork of the Mohican River, the stream that was dammed in 1935 to create Charles Mill Reservoir as a part of the flood-control program on the Muskingum River watershed. There is a bench on the blufftop from which you can view the valley below. The abandoned bed of an earlier road through the valley is also visible below when the leaves are off the trees. Incidentally, the community of Charles Mill for which the dam is named is located at the south end of the lake. When the Army Corps of Engineers was building flood-control dams during the depression days of the 1930s, it was the custom to name the dam and reservoir (as they were then called) after the commune closest to the dam on the old 15' USGS topographic maps. Today authorization for such a project would never leave Congress without some politician's name already attached to it.

The trail leaves the bluffs and continues around the hillside toward its reunion with the inbound trail. In so doing, it passes through another stand of the alien bittersweet. At the intersection you have another chance to rest on the bench provided by Mr. Donaldson. The parking lot is about 0.25 mile to the west at the end of the old track.

40

Cuyahoga Valley National Park—Virginia Kendall Unit

Total distance: 2.5 miles (4 km)

Hiking time: 1½ hours

Maximum elevation: 1,050 feet

Vertical rise: 100 feet

Maps: USGS 7½' Series Peninsula; CVNP Trails of the Virginia Kendall Unit

Less than one month after the inauguration of Franklin Roosevelt as the nation's 32nd president in March 1933, Congress established the Civilian Conservation Corps. From the following summer until the corps disbanded at the beginning of World War II, more than 2.5 million young men and boys, mostly from America's cities, spent six-month tours of duty in the nation's forests. By the end of 1933 a camp had been established near Peninsula, probably along Truxell Road, where park district shops stood for many years. Over the course of its existence, the boys of the corps built shelters, rest rooms, stairways, and miles of trails in what was then known as Virginia Kendall Park. In 1937 they completed the Ledges Shelter. Two years later, they finished the building known as the Happy Days Camp, 2 miles east of Peninsula along US 303.

That structure was built to be operated as a day camp for children from the inner city. It replaced an old farmhouse near the same site that had previously served the same purpose.

The feature attraction of this area is the Ritchie Ledges, an outcrop of Sharon conglomerate dating back about 300 million years to the days when a large shallow sea covered this area. The conglomerate resulted from the fast movement of streams carrying sediment from the north. With time and pressure it was compacted into conglomerate rock made up of cemented sand and small quartz pebbles. Occurring here as caprock at about 1,000 feet above sea

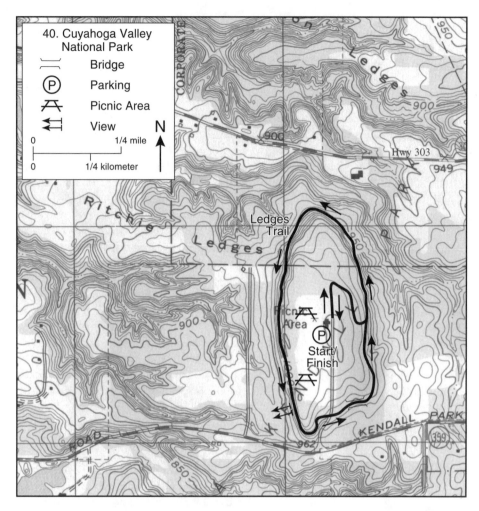

level, it is exposed in a similar way at Nelson and Kennedy Ledges, Thompson Ledges, Cuyahoga Falls in northeastern Ohio, and Lake Katharine in Jackson County in southeastern Ohio. Here, as at other places where it is exposed, Sharon conglomerate is usually closely associated with hemlock, yellow birch, ferns, and bryophytes in the microclimate that the ledges create. Look for hardwoods of the mixed-mesophytic forest on the hillside below.

The land around the Richie Ledges known as Virginia Kendall Park had been owned by Hayward Kendall, a Clevelander who called himself a "coal peddler" because he was in the coal and oil business. He had named the area after his mother and maintained a retreat home there in a parklike setting. When he died, he bequeathed it to the National Park Service, state of Ohio, city of Cleveland, or a trust at his bank, in that order. The federal government turned it down but the old Division of Forestry of the Ohio Agricultural Extension Service, part of the Ohio State University, accepted it and began operating it as a park. The state of

Ohio had no state park organization in those years and, even though there was an endowment to help pay for its operation, the area was a bit of a "stepchild." In 1933 Harold Wagner, director of the Akron Park District, is reported to have complained about what a poor job the state was doing in managing it as a park. In response, he was told, "If you can do a better job, you take it." Arrangements were made with the OSU Board of Trustees to transfer operation to the park district, along with an annual operating income, and the 1,600-acre tract was operated as Virginia Kendall Metro Park until the late 1970s. After the creation of the Cuyahoga National Recreation Area (now a national park) by Congress in 1974, 400 acres of the park, including the ledges, were turned over to the national park district.

The old day camp facility, where thousands of boys and girls had spent Friday nights on cots when the park district ran it, is now the Happy Days Visitor Center. Here you will find exhibits, program space, a sales area and offices, and, to the rear of the building, a historic cemetery. In 2000 a bronze statue of a corpsman was erected outside the entrance to the visitors center as a tribute to the work of the young men of the Civilian Conservation Corps, though the former Virginia Kendall CCC camp had not been at this site.

A 0.5-mile loop trail, the Haskell Trail, originates from and returns to the visitors center parking lot. From it, a spur connects to the other trails of the Virginia Kendall Unit, but the best way to reach the trails of the area is from the south.

How to Get There

To reach the 2.5-mile Ledges Trail that, as the name implies, circumnavigates the high land surrounded by the ledges, come in from the south by driving either west from

SR 8 on Kendall Park Road or east from Akron–Peninsula Road on Truxell Road. In either case, you must watch for a not-very-bold sign directing you to the Ledges Shelter. Drive as far north as you can, and park in the available spot.

The Trail

Begin hiking by walking north past the Ledges Shelter. Indoor and outdoor picnic facilities and rest rooms are located there. Just beyond the building there is a trailhead bulletin board. Continue walking north on the wide service road, which quickly changes from blacktop to gravel. Ignore the assorted picnic tables that are scattered here and about in the woods. Traveling through oak–hickory forest, you soon reach an intersection where a wayside interpretive sign illustrates the ledges area. Turn right on this trail as it leaves the oaks and hickories of the hilltop and enters a grove of hemlock. You have reached the top of the conglomerate in an area where tree roots both create and use the fissures in the rock. To prevent the accidental destruction of this spectacular area's vegetation, visitors are asked to remain on the trails. Rock climbing is strictly prohibited.

The trail drops cautiously over the ledges and soon reaches a level near the bottom of the conglomerate that it will use to carry you completely around the mesa-like formation. For no particular reason, I opted for the counterclockwise route. Begin hiking by turning left as you reach the bottom of the ledges. About 100 feet beyond the turn, the trail reaches Ice Box Cave. Not a true cave—it is not the result of solution of rock by water—Ice Box nevertheless reaches nearly 50 feet into the dark through this narrow slit in the rock. Just beyond the cave entrance there is a bridge over the flowage from a spring. Ferns grow vigorously in this cooler, moist environment.

The Ledges Trail follows the base of this sandstone cliff.

Beyond here, the trail crosses a bridge and climbs a set of steps. Several wild trails lead into a maze of ledges. Follow the trail along the cliff base. After about 0.25 mile, the trail reaches a set of stone steps to the left that lead to the picnic area and playing fields above. These steps were built by the boys of the Civilian Conservation Corps nearly 70 years ago. The Berea sandstone was quarried at Deep Lock Quarry alongside the Ohio & Erie Canal on the west side of the Cuyahoga River south of Peninsula. A trail in that area is described elsewhere in this book.

Follow the Ledges Trail straight ahead along the base of the ledges. Not far beyond the steps a trail to the right leads to the Happy Days Visitor Center. Can you imagine the voices of children of 60 years ago, here from the city for the day, running up the path to hike the trail or to go up to the play fields?

Continue around the north end of the exposed rock via boardwalk and steps. Another trail exits to the right to lead to the Ledges Shelter; shortly after, a trail leads downhill to the right to the Octagon Shelter in the valley to the west. To continue the Ledges Loop Trail, stay on the trail straight ahead at the base of the rock, along the towering rock face.

After about 0.5 mile of southerly travel, you will notice that the ledges are beginning to diminish. At the next trail intersection, turn to the right and follow the trail uphill at an oblique angle as it heads toward the play fields and picnic areas. (If you follow the trail to the left at this intersection, it will take you to the Lake Shelter nearly a mile to the southwest.) When you reach the top of the ledges, watch for one of several trails to the right along the edge of the woods on the west side of the play fields. One of these will lead you to an expansive area of exposed clifftop where you can enjoy a great view of the Cuyahoga Valley—a good photo point on a clear day. Don't get too close to the edge.

Back toward the play field from the overlook is a rest room. Look just beyond for a trail just inside the woods; it's heading east. It soon makes a road crossing and reenters the deciduous forest. Still circling counterclockwise, the trail crosses a wooden bridge then enters into a magical forest of hemlock trees as it turns north on the east-facing slope. Continue until you reach a trail to the left that returns you to the top of the trail you came out on. If you reach Ice Box Cave, you have gone too far; backtrack a short distance.

Once back on top, take advantage of one of the many picnic areas provided for a meal or a short break. It was a warm early-November day when I walked this trail the first time, kicking leaves ahead of me most of the way. I marked it on my list of parks to return to when I find myself in this Glaciated Allegheny Plateau area of northeastern Ohio in other seasons. It was hard for me to believe that this area—which looks so much like areas in unglaciated southeastern Ohio—had been under the Wisconsinan ice sheet not too many millennia ago.

While you are in the area, consider a 9.5-mile loop trail hike on the Ohio & Erie Canal towpath and Buckeye Trail, originating from the trailhead at Boston Mills or the park headquarters area at Jaite. A description of that trail is provided in *50 Hikes in Ohio.*

41

Deep Lock Quarry Metro Park

Total distance: 1.5 miles (2.4 km)

Hiking time: 1 hour

Maximum elevation: 805 feet

Vertical rise: 105 feet

Maps: USGS 7½' Series Peninsula;
AMPD Deep Lock Quarry Metro Park
brochure

With 17 feet of lift, Lock 28, located 0.6 mile south of Peninsula on the northern sector of the Ohio & Erie Canal, was the deepest lock in the entire system. Deep Lock, as it became known, was one of 44 locks built to create a set of steps on the canal that allowed canal boats to be lowered 395 feet from the Summit Lake in Akron to the level of Lake Erie at Cleveland. It was perhaps one of the most important sites along the canal.

The divide between watersheds flowing north to Erie and south to the Ohio River is the high ground at Akron. Though the Wisconsinan glacier pushed across this land, it did not flatten it as it had the western part of the state. The effect on the landscape where the glacier moved over the Mississippian and Pennsylvanian sandstones and shales of the Appalachian Plateau was not to level it but to leave ridges and flat uplands, covered with thin drift. In places these are dissected by steep valleys, some of which have narrow rockwalled reaches, while others are filled with drift. This higher country established the north-side watershed divide in central Summit County.

When surveyors were laying out the route of the Ohio & Erie Canal that was to carry boats from Lake Erie to the Ohio River by the most feasible route, they recognized what Native Americans had known for centuries: It was a relatively easy trek from the farthest point that the Cuyahoga River reached south before flowing north to the lake to the headwaters of a stream system

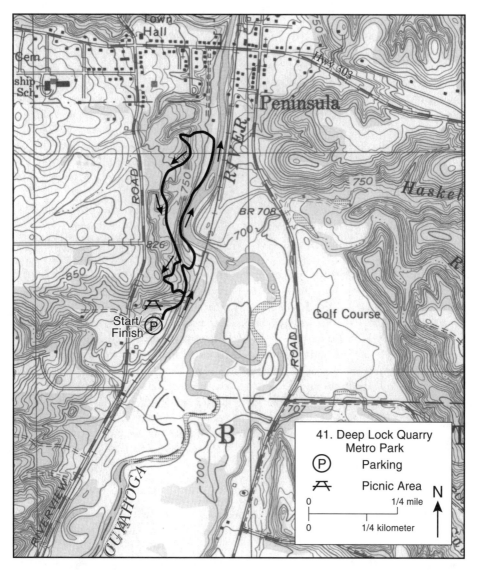

41. Deep Lock Quarry Metro Park

Ⓟ   Parking

⨬   Picnic Area

N

0   1/4 mile

0   1/4 kilometer

flowing south to the Ohio River. The "Portage Path" of the Natives was not far from the route chosen for the canal, and for a good reason—it worked.

The Cuyahoga River, often called a "crooked river," originates in an outwash-filled preglacial valley in central Geauga County, where it's blocked to the north by moraines, and runs southwest until it comes up against not easily eroded bedrock at a higher elevation. There the river swings around to flow north, cutting its way through Wabash and Defiance Moraines as it heads for Lake Erie.

In the area of Peninsula, the course of the meandering Cuyahoga brings it close to 100-foot bluffs where the Mississippian-age Berea sandstone outcrops. Canal engineers early on recognized the value of this massive bedrock as high-quality dimension stone that could be used for the construction of canal structures. Its location immediately adjacent to the river and the proposed route of the canal made it even more important, since it could be quarried, cut to size and shape, and loaded onto river or canal boats for transport to construction sites. Possibly it was this fortuitous juxtaposition more than anything else that allowed this massive public works project to move with deliberate speed in this part of the state. Even though work was being done largely by manual labor and domestic animal power, it progressed well.

Construction of the entire project had begun with the ceremonial turning of a shovel of dirt by New York Governor De Witt Clinton at Heath on July 4, 1825. Two years later, the 38-mile length of the canal between Cleveland and Akron was completed. Many of the stonemasons who got their start in this quarry went on to build major structures in Akron. Shortly after the establishment of Summit County (at the summit of the canal), Berea sandstone from the quarry at Lock 28 was used to build the courthouse (alas, replaced by a more "modern" one in the 20th century).

In later years, imperfect canal stones and rubble from the quarry were hauled north by canal boat to the mouth of the Cuyahoga River at Cleveland to be used in the construction of the breakwater.

In 1879 Ferdinand Schumacher purchased the property now known as Deep Lock Quarry. Schumacher was the person largely responsible for bringing oatmeal to the American kitchen table. He had found a way to remove the hulls from oats and supplied large quantities to Union troops during the Civil War. Grindstones made from the Berea sandstone quarried at Lock 28 made

excellent "haulstones" for use at his mill in Akron. They were turned at a water-driven mill hauled way up the hillside. In 1886 the Schumacher interests suffered a $1-million fire loss—a huge sum for the time—but by 1891 they had recovered by means of a merger, incorporated as American Cereal Company, absorbed other units including the Quaker Oats Mills in Ravenna, and adopted Quaker Oats as a trademark. This was soon a familiar name in every household.

At about the turn of the 20th century, the quarry was taken over by the Cleveland Stone Company. It was a busy, modern-by-the-times operation with a steam-powered channeling machine that for nearly 20 years made the vertical cuts in the quarry. There was also rail trackage and a steam-driven locomotive, perhaps a Lima Locomotive Works shay, and quarry cars to move stone by rail down the slope to first the canal, and later the mainline railroad. The canal ceased operation in this reach and most other places in Ohio following the devastating flood of 1913, but the railroad was busy for most of the 20th century.

In 1934, thanks to the good efforts of Peninsula author Fred Kelly, the stone company made a gift of the 41-acre quarry and lock property to the Akron Metropolitan Park Disrtict. During the heart of the Great Depression, stone was taken from the quarry by the men of the Civilian Conservation Corps for use at nearby Virginia Kendall Park. As you walk the trail, you will pass a stack of dressed stones. These were intended for use at the toboggan but were never delivered.

Cuyahoga Valley Trail, developed by the national park, passes through Deep Lock Quarry Metro Park on the canal towpath. Exercise caution as you walk through this area; cyclists sharing the trail are often

Unfinished millstones lie close to the trail.

moving right along. The Buckeye Trail, a mostly foot trail that touches all corners of the state, also passes through here.

How to Get There

The entry to the park is just short of a mile south of SR 303 on the east side of Riverview Road south of the village of Peninsula. Reliable reports tell of the area being completely devoid of trees when it was in operation as quarry, but not so today. You will be in woods during your entire visit. It was a gorgeous mid-September day when I hiked the trail.

The Trail

There is a trailhead sign at the northeast corner of the parking lot closest to the river, the place to begin your walk. Entering between white pines, the wide gravel trail immediately begins to drop downhill toward the railroad track and canal bed at a gentle angle. The original vegetation of the area is said to have been mixed-mesophytic forest; today it has returned to that mixture of native hardwoods, with the addition of pines, hemlocks, and some ornamental trees and shrubs around the parking area.

The trails are well signed with symbols distinguishing which trail you are on. There are also excellent interpretive signs that relate the past to the present. To the right of the combined trails you'll find several large-diameter, thick millstones and lots of quarry rubble.

At a trail intersection, make a hard right to go downhill on a switchbacked trail to cross a stream on fill. You'll then reach Lock 28, Deep Lock. Take time to read the plaques and interpretive signs on this very deep, single-chambered lock. Now, moving upstream from the lock alongside the swampy old canal beds, the trail is surfaced with limestone screenings and is shared by bicyclists. The edge of the river to the right has been armored with rock-filled gabions to keep the river from washing away the bank and cutting into the canal. There is a good view of the river from here. At a bend in the river, the trail shifts left to travel where the canal once flowed, the river having eroded the towpath completely away. When the river swings once again to the right, the trail returns to the historic towpath.

At a sign indicating that the Buckeye and Cuyahoga Trails continue straight ahead and the Cuyahoga Trail also goes to the left—along with an interpretive sign describing the Cleveland Stone Company's quarry 15 at Peninsula—turn left. A 3-foot-wide, 35-foot-long wooden bridge carries the trail across the canal bed. Off the bridge, the trail heads right then circles left before climbing the hillside toward the quarry. It can be a bit muddy here on a rainy day, but there is enough gravel for good friction. Winding back and forth, the trail passes some sandstone blocks as it climbs past Christmas fern and lots of rubble to eventually ascend a set of about 20 well-worn sandstone steps circling to the left. A trail to the right leads to the quarry rim. From that trail, you can look down into the quarry. There are lots of trees growing from the quarry bed. Following the main trail around the left side of the quarry pit, at certain places you can see through the trees to the vertical back wall. After shuffling carefully up and down the gravel trail and wood-and-stone steps, the trail reaches the rock floor of the quarry. Imagine the collection of mechanical human- and steam-powered devices that were needed to cut and remove the stone during the years of the quarry's operation! It's fun to stand here and wonder how the operation functioned—especially when the trees that have overgrown the quarry are without leaves. I've been told that the stack of cut stone slabs that still stands in the pit was destined for construction that was never completed in Virginia Kendall Park.

The trail leaves the quarry on what was once the roadbed of the railroad that carried stone from the quarry to the mill where millstones were turned. There is a trail junction where the Towpath and Quarry Trails go right and the Cuyahoga Trail head down the hill ahead. If you continue straight, you very quickly reach the trail that you came out on; a turn to the right will lead you back toward the parking lot.

Instead, take the trail that turns right up the hill, climbing some wooden steps, crossing the stream, and dropping past lots of sandstone rubble from the millstone-making operation. It soon drops down the hillside to lead you to the parking lot.

I spent an hour and a half hiking, exploring, reading interpretive signs, and taking photographs in a light rain on the day I visited Deep Lock Quarry. I hope that you find your visit as interesting as did I.

42

Girdled Road Reservation

Total distance: 3.75–6.25 miles (6–10 km)

Hiking time: 2½–4 hours

Maximum elevation: 1,070 feet

Vertical rise: 210 feet

Maps: USGS 7½' Series Painesville; LCPD Girdled Road Reservation trail map

French explorers and trappers were probably the first Europeans to set foot in the beautiful valley of Lake County's Big Creek. They had entered the region before 1700, and by 1750 had established a trading post at the mouth of the Chagrin River. But it was enterprising New Englanders who, following the Revolutionary War, established farms, villages, and commercial and industrial ventures along this stream that flows from Chardon north to the Grand River. In 1795 the Connecticut Land Company was formed to survey and sell land in the northeastern corner of Ohio, known as the Western Reserve.

By 1797 it was proposed that a road be built from the Pennsylvania line to the new city of Cleveland at the mouth of the Cuyahoga River. General Simeon Perkins was hired to cut the 100-mile road, "the small stuff to be cut out 25 feet wide and the timber to be girdled 33 feet wide and sufficient bridges to be thrown over streams as are not fordable . . . ." This method made eventual clearing easier by cutting off the flow of nutrients, causing the trees to die and dry out, to be felled in another season. That first road in the Western Reserve, the Girdled Road, is found along the north edge of the metro park with the same name along the east bank of Big Creek. The stream arises south of the Defiance near Chardon, cutting through the moraine and the lake escarpment to join the Grand River at Painesville. The Cascade Valley of Big Creek (so named because of the falls where East Creek drops 85 feet into Big Creek),

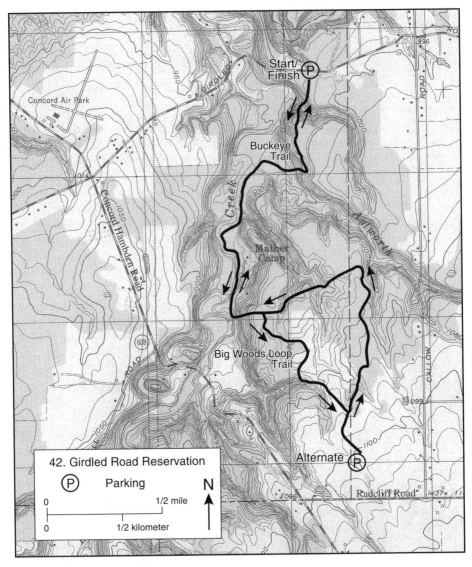

42. Girdled Road Reservation

P Parking   N

0   1/2 mile

0   1/2 kilometer

just north of Girdled Road, was the site of many 19th-century factories that depended on waterpower: flour and feed mills, wood-turning mills, and iron furnaces that smelted locally abundant bog iron ore. Though no record can be found as to whether they were ever built, at one time a series of 30 locks was planned between Big Creek's headwaters and the Grand River, 6 of which would have been in the area that is now the park.

Because of the rolling terrain of this Glaciated Allegheny Plateau country, the vegetation that greeted the settlers was far from uniform, though the land was largely forested. Beech and sugar maple were found on the uplands, mixed mesophytes on the slopes and in the valleys, with yellow birch and hemlock in the cooler locations. By the end of the 19th century, the industry was all but gone. So, too, were the forests. The upland was being used for pasture and, later, row-crop farming. Not suitable for farming and the trees no longer needed for fuel for now-silent iron furnaces, the creek bottom and steep-walled valleys began to revert to forest. By the middle of the 20th century, the Cleveland Boy Scout Council had established a small wilderness-type camp in Big Creek Valley south of Girdled Road. It was known as Mather Camp after the family that provided the site.

In the mid-1960s the Lake County Metropolitan Park District purchased the land for Girdled Road Park. These purchases were a part of a long-range master plan to purchase nearly all the land along Big Creek from Huntoon Road to Radcliff Road at the county line. Some development began in the mid-1980s, including the establishment of the route of the Buckeye Trail from Girdled Road to Radcliff Road roughly following the east bank of the creek. In 2001 the park boasted 6.25 miles of trails with good surfaces and well-built and -maintained stairs and bridges.

Guided by a carefully considered natural resource management plan and a good resource inventory, the park district is both allowing land to revert to original plant communities through natural succession and managing other areas to provide a diversity of habitat. At 642 acres, Girdled Road Reservation is the largest element in the park system. Inventory has shown it to have a modest number of rare and endangered plant and animal species. Though not confirmed to den in the area, black bears have even been observed very close by. I found the day I spent exploring the reservation to be most enjoyable and I know you will, too.

How to Get There
Reach SR 44 from I-90 on the north or US 6 on the south and take it to Girdled Road, which is located about 2 miles south of I-90. Turn east and travel just over 3 miles to the park entrance on the south side of the road.

The Trail
I suggest that you begin hiking at the lot on the south side of Girdled Road at the north end of the park. Two trails leave the parking lot there. The first is the 1.3-mile Pioneer Loop, named in honor of General Perkins and his survey crew, who laid out the Girdled Road more than 200 years ago. This improved-surface trail makes a loop on relatively flat forested upland in the northeast corner of the park. I walked counterclockwise in order to start my exploring on the valley rim, but either way works. The woods closest to the lot include some nice tuliptrees and sugar and red maples. Farther east, as you near the edge of the park, you'll find mostly younger red maple. At the point where the trail turns to head back toward the lot, there is a wetland area; there are also wetlands when you get closer to the lot. This is a good place to listen for male eastern wood frogs making their quacklike advertising call in late winter, just as the ice is leaving the ponds. This species of "true frog" with its face mask is found all across North America clear to Alaska. After the breeding season they seem to disappear from sight, but occasionally as I walk alone in the woods in summer I will hear something shuffle in the leaves and find a solitary wood frog in the dry woods.

Back in the lot, head out on the Buckeye Trail. It has a natural surface except where making it passable required the addition of some gravel. A set of neatly crafted wooden stairs will carry you into the valley of a Big Creek tributary, which you then cross on a

A female monarch butterfly clings to the bird's-nest-like, unopened flower on a Queen Ann's lace plant.

bridge. From there the trail returns to high ground to follow the valley rim closely before making a switchback to drop into bottomland where Aylworth Creek empties into Big Creek. This is an especially rich area for spring wildflowers. The trail crosses the mouth of Aylworth Creek on a bridge that remains in the bottomland for close to 0.75 mile, sometimes close to the creek, other times not. Here you will see rich woodland that includes an occasional yellow birch and some hemlock.

Near the site of the former Boy Scout Camp Mather the trail splits, with one fork continuing along the stream and the other going left to begin a slow rise away from the creek. If you look to the left of the trail you may be able to see where several buildings once stood. The Buckeye Trail follows the former entrance road to the camp downstream to SR 608.

Leave the Buckeye Trail and take the left fork to connect with the 2.1-mile-long gravel-surface Big Trail Loop. A fairly steep climb carries the trail at an angle up the valley wall to the upland and an intersection. I suggest that you bear right and enter the Big Woods Trail in a counterclockwise direction. The trail winds its way through younger successional hardwoods, across the end of an old field, and through more young hardwoods before passing a fishing pond and arriving at the lawn that surrounds the south entrance to the parking lot.

Across the lawn to the west are rest rooms, a play area, and a picnic shelter. When I visited the area on a late-summer evening, goldfinches were feasting on the freshly ripened seeds of giant sunflowers in a large planting to the west of the entrance.

Before you continue on the Big Woods Loop, if you want to add some more mileage to your hike, the 0.75-mile gravel-surface Big Pond Trail circumnavigates the pond. Walk if you wish but in either case, hit the outbound Big Woods on the same spur you arrived on, turning right to continue in a counterclockwise manner. The trail is again back in young woods. Aerial photos taken around 1950 reveal that this area of young hardwoods was then under row-crop cultivation. About 0.75 mile north of Big Pond, where the trail is in beech–maple forest on level ground, it stops paralleling the east park boundary and turns west. In deep woods it dips as it passes through the upper end of a ravine that heads northwest toward Big Creek. Back on high ground and still in the woods, the trail soon reaches the junction with the spur to the Buckeye Trail. Turn right and follow this now-familiar trail to the Mather Camp area, then turn right to return to the Girdled Road entrance parking lot via the same route you used on your outbound journey.

Girdled Road Reservation's trails are the kind you want to return to often. Pick and choose how much you want to do. Catch the cacophony of a chorus of wood frogs in early March; revel in the soft green, pinks, and violets of spring wildflowers; search for butterflies, the wildflowers of the winds, on the thistles and milkweeds of summer; or pretend you're a kid again and kick the leaves along in front of you on a crisp autumn day. And when the snow is deep, see if you are really the only creature in the woods as you search out tracks in the snow beneath the shadow of tall hemlocks. Go often and stay as long as you can. Your life will be better for every moment you spend in the out-of-doors.

As you depart from Girdled Road Reservation, I suggest that you turn west onto Girdled Road then, almost immediately, turn north onto Cascade Road. Try to picture in your mind's eye what this small valley must have been like on a hot summer afternoon 175 years ago, before motor vehicles and steam power. Two iron furnaces might have been in full blast, with smoke bellowing from the chimneys as well as from charcoal production, at least two water-powered turning mills, a water-powered flour mill, a water-powered gristmill, and, likely, a water-powered sawmill and perhaps a tanning mill. An incredibly busy place with mule-, horse-, and ox-drawn wagons and lots of hardworking mill workers and farmers.

43

Great Seal State Park

Total distance: 4.75 miles (7.2 km)

Hiking time: 3 hours

Maximum elevation: 900 feet

Vertical rise: 170 feet

Maps: USGS 7½' Series Kingston; ODNR Great Seal State Park brochure

Only a few of the many trails that I have walked in Ohio have the aura that I felt when walking paths at Great Seal State Park. The magic of being on the land depicted on the Great Seal of the State of Ohio is in and of itself exciting to me. The story has been written many times. Here it is as told in Michael O'Bryant's *Ohio Almanac:* "It is said that when 21-year-old William Creighton (who later became Ohio's first Secretary of State) was charged with designing the state seal, he rode from the temporary capital at Chillicothe to the nearby country estate Adena, where he consulted with the owner, Thomas Worthington, a future U.S. Senator and one of Ohio's founding fathers. Creighton and some other guests enjoyed an all-night game of cards, and when the dawn broke, he stepped outside and was immediately taken with how the sun rising behind Mt. Logan cast a rosy glow upon the surrounding wheat fields. 'Gentlemen' Creighton proclaimed, 'there is our seal!'" Though the design has been modified in the interval since then, the low gap between Sugarloaf Mountain on the left and Bald Hill on the right is still central to the seal as it remains in the 21st century.

The feeling of the significance of walking on that hillside and in that gap has its origin much earlier than the first days of Ohio's statehood, however. There is credible evidence that long before white European settlers came into the Scioto Valley, prehistoric Indians, probably the culture of 2,200 years ago that we call Hopewell, passed through this low gap en route from their villages in the valleys of the Scioto and Paint Creeks

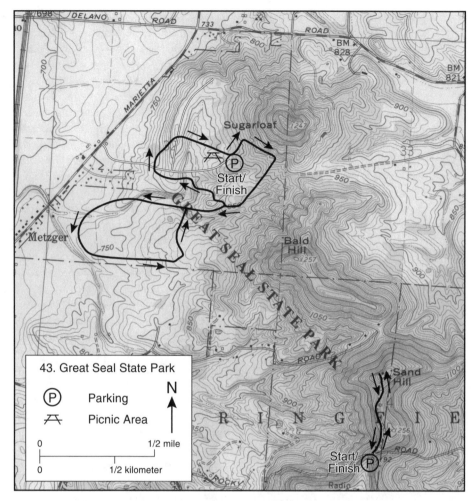

to the major Hopewell center at the confluence of the Muskingum and Ohio Rivers.
More than that, recent studies by Dr.
Bradley T. Lepper, curator of archaeology at
the Ohio Historical Society, suggest that a
"Great Hopewell Road" traversed the gap
en route to the third great Ohio Hopewell
culture center–the Octagon mound and
other earthworks in the valley of Licking
River and its tributaries in Licking County.

There is no doubt that one of the major
foot trails of historic Native Americans
heading east from Chillicothe followed this

route. (Another probably followed close to
present-day US 35 to reach the salt springs
at Jackson.) And when Marietta, Cincinnati,
and Chillicothe were in hot contention to
serve as the capital of a still-undefined state
to be carved from the Northwest Territory,
the Marietta Road left the Chillicothe area
on the old road you can still travel in Great
Seal State Park. Retired forester Emmett A.
Conway of Chillicothe has spent many
years tracing the old road on the land.

Marietta was settled in 1787, Chillicothe
in 1796. Chillicothe was the headquarters

for the Northwest Territory before statehood and was the first capital of Ohio, in 1803. A political map known as the Bourne map of 1820 and a government survey map of that period referred to as the Hough map both show that during the first 20 or 30 years of the 19th century, the Marietta Road stayed true to the ancient route. And why not? It was dry, level, and direct, serving travel on foot, horseback, and coach very well.

Also exciting is the setting of Great Seal Park as it relates to Pleistocene glaciers that made their way across much of Ohio. Great Seal is located in one of the places where the last ice advance, the Wisconsinan of 20,000 to 25,000 years ago, did not reach as far as its immediate predecessor, the Illinoian of 125,000 years back. It is a place at which the advancing glacier ran into the edge of the Appalachian Plateau, land that was considerably higher in elevation than western Ohio, bringing further southeastwardly movement to a slow halt. At Great Seal you will find glacial moraine of Illinoian origin at the base of hills, glacial erratics brought to the area by the Illinoian glacier on the surface and in the creek beds, and on the ridge, outcrops of Mississippian-age sandstone. The Illinoian glacier overran the tops of the hills here in its final advance reaching almost to the Vinton County line, but more than 100,000 years later little evidence remains on the ridges and high hillsides.

When early settlers from Virginia and other Middle Atlantic coastal states began arriving in this part of Ohio, oak–sugar maple forests thrived on the rolling hills. In the broad valley of the Scioto River—really the valley of the preglacial northward-flowing Teays River—hardwood forests on that rich bottomland soil sometimes grew to huge proportions. According to early reports, many hollow sycamores were used for sheds or barns, and pioneers would occasionally live in them. One tree near Waverly, not many miles south of Great Seal Park, had a cavity more than 10 feet wide and was used as a blacksmith shop for a time. The river bottoms seen to the west of Great Seal soon yielded to the ax and plow to become great "corn bottoms," helping to feed—and incidentally quench the thirst of—a growing population in middle America. When, in the early 19th century, the Ohio & Erie Canal opened the Scioto Valley to the exporting of agricultural products, shipping corn liquor in barrels offered a real advantage over shipping grain, subject to spoilage, in the hold of a canal boat.

Great Seal offers 5 miles of exclusively foot trails and another 17 miles of trails that hikers share with equestrians and mountain bikers. The hiking trails are on moderately hilly terrain on the lower slopes of the park. The multiuse trails traverse rugged, steep terrain and are a challenge to hike, but they do afford access to the high terrain of the park. The multiuse trails are color blazed and easy to follow; still, you might want to pick up a park map as you enter the area if you are going to strike out on the Sugarloaf Mountain, Shawnee Ridge, or Mount Ives Trails.

How to Get There

To reach Great Seal State Park, take US 23 south from Circleville to SR 159. Turn right onto SR 159 and take it to Delano Road. Go east on Delano Road to Marietta Road and turn right. The park entrance is on the east side of the road less than a mile after the turn.

The Trail

Begin your hike from the main parking lot off Marietta Road (not the original, but a straightened-out latter-day version). I suggest you begin hiking at the upper end of the picnic area near the volleyball and horseshoe-pitching areas, where you will find the entrance to the multiuse trails. The Sugarloaf Mountain Trail, blazed with yellow, 2.1 miles in length; the Shawnee Ridge Trail, blazed with blue, 7.8 miles long; and the Mount Ives Trail, orange blazed, 6.4 miles beyond the Shawnee Ridge Trail, are all accessible from here. So too are the Picnic Loop and Spring Run Trail via a short walk on the multiuse trail that includes the ancient footpath-turned-road.

The trail begins climbing at once and after 100 yards reaches a junction where the yellow-blazed Sugarloaf Trail goes left or more or less straight. The Sugarloaf Trail is a very strenuous trek, climbing 350 feet in less than 0.25 mile through dense maple-dominated forest to reach the crest of Sugarloaf Mountain. The trail returns to this parking lot or, via a spur, to the park campground, so you can hike it by going either direction at this junction and following the yellow blazes.

For a shorter hike using the footpaths, follow the yellow blazes straight as the trail winds its way through the woods to the right toward the gap. You will know when you reach the Marietta Road. At a Carsonite post marked B the yellow trail continues ahead and the Shawnee Ridge Trail, blazed blue, goes right to follow the ancient footpath downhill toward Chillicothe. If the rocks and the trees could talk, what tales they might tell about those who passed this way in earlier centuries. Old culverts are still visible.

A pileated woodpecker called as I walked through here on an early-November day, kicking oak leaves before me like I was a kid. Note here that granite boulders, those intrepid travelers of eons ago, are plentiful in the creek bed.

At another trail junction, the blue and orange trails go left and, following a sign that points to PARK, leave the multiuse trails to connect to the Picnic Loop and Spring Run Trail. Hanging on the left side of the hill, the trail passes among red cedar and mound-building ant hills. Shortly you are confronted with another choice. Now traveling on wide mowed trails suitable for cross-country skiing, turn left onto the Spring Run Trail to make a loop walk of a little over 2 miles. The trail winds its way slowly downhill among young trees, fields, and thickets, soon splitting to make a loop. It loses around 100 feet in elevation. After making a wide swing to the south, it regains the elevation as it travels parallel to the park boundary before heading north to close the loop.

Back at the junction with the trail coming off the hill, turn left to drop into the valley of the stream you followed on the Spring Run Loop. Beyond the bridge, a 100-foot climb brings you to a T where the trail splits once more. A sign identifies it as the hiking trail and tells you that traveling to the right will return you directly to the parking lot. Turn left to enjoy the Picnic Loop as it winds among the red cedars and old field on a mostly quite wide trail among very young trees. The red cedars show evidence of deer browsing. The trail drops to a bridge across a chasm where sandstone bedrock is visible below the deep glacial drift. A straight-up-the-hill climb brings you via a winding path through thicket to a crossing of the park entrance road. Carsonite posts on each side of the road identify this as a hiking trail.

Beyond the road, the trail passes through a white pine planting as it circles right and climbs among young sassafras and Virginia pine to soon reach the road to the campground. There is a good view of Sugarloaf Mountain from this crossing.

Beyond the crossing, the trail drops down the hill and crosses the ravine on a bridge

The famous skyline of Ohio's Great Seal is visible from an overlook at Adena State Memorial, the ancestral home of Thomas Worthington across the Scioto River Valley to the west.

wide enough to carry a mower. After winding its way to the right and uphill, when the road come into view ahead, the trail makes an abrupt left turn to climb to the parking lot.

If you want to assault Bald Knob, the hill on the south side of the gap, opt for the blue-and orange-labeled trail instead of the cutoff to the hiking trails as you descend from the gap on the old road. Along with the supplies you normally carry, tuck a park map in your pocket and plan your hike so you can get back well before nightfall. Know your limitations. Bald Knob is at 1,257 feet, more than 300 feet above the old road, and there are several very steep sections on the trail.

The blue-blazed Shawnee Ridge Trail also includes trail on the south side of Rocky Road on Rocky Knob. As an alternative to approaching this area from main parking lot, you may prefer to drive to the ridge by leaving the park and turning left to follow the

Marietta Road to Rocky Road, where you can turn left and drive to the ridge. There is room to park one or two cars there. The hike to the north to Sand Hill and the rock outcrops is a nice, fairly level walk along the ridge of about a mile round trip. To the south are the somewhat more strenuous trails of Rocky Knob and the connection to the many miles of the Mount Ives Trail Loop with its several scenic vistas–also a strenuous trail.

Great Seal State Park has a small camping area located to the north off the main park entrance road. There are also two picnic shelters for day use as well as rest rooms and drinking water. The park includes 1,864 acres and was established in the mid-1970s. There are 900 acres of public hunting land east of the park.

Sugarloaf Mountain Amphitheater borders the northeast corner of the park off Delano Road. The famous outdoor historical drama *Tecumseh* is presented there from late June through September.

The Chillicothe area is resplendent with historical and archaeological sites to visit. While in the area, be sure to stop at Adena, the historic home of Thomas Worthington, Ohio's first senator and sixth governor, considered the Father of Ohio Statehood.

The National Park Service operates the Hopewell Culture National Historical Park, which includes a prehistoric Indian complex with 23 burial mounds just north of Chillicothe on SR 104, well worth the visit. The Ross County Historical Society at 45 West Fifth Street in Chillicothe features exhibits and programs during most of the year.

44

Johnson Woods State Nature Preserve

Total distance: 1.5-mile (2.4 km) accessible boardwalk

Hiking time: 1 hour

Maximum elevation: 1,110 feet

Vertical rise: 18 feet

Maps: USGS 7½' Series Doylestown; ODNR Johnson Woods Nature Preserve brochure

At 206 acres, Johnson Woods is one of the largest tracts of old-growth timber remaining in the Glaciated Appalachian Plateau country of northeastern Ohio. How it survived the pioneers' ax and the modern timber buyers' chain saw is a complicated story that involves the nature of the land and the love of the woods by several generations of owners. I first became acquainted with it in the late 1960s when I was assigned to assist a joint Ohio legislative committee that was studying the possible need to establish a system of natural area protection. The woods showed up as "Graber Woods" on a list of natural areas that Dr. Arthur Herrick of Kent State University had earlier identified as being worth saving. I was so impressed by its description that on my travels about the state, I hunted it out and walked as much as my street shoes and tolerance for mosquitoes could stand. It was a fine woods. I wasn't the only one who admired it. The late renowned ecologist, E. Lucy Braun of Cincinnati, had described Graber Woods in her 1950 book, *Deciduous Forests of Eastern North America.*

When the Division of Natural Areas and Preserves came into being, Graber Woods went into the data bank as a place that ought to be saved—but because it was not on the market, and because the state did not normally use the power of eminent domain to acquire nature preserves, it remained in private hands.

In 1994, at the urging of service foresters from the Division of Forestry, the owner of the land, Mrs. Clela Johnson, and

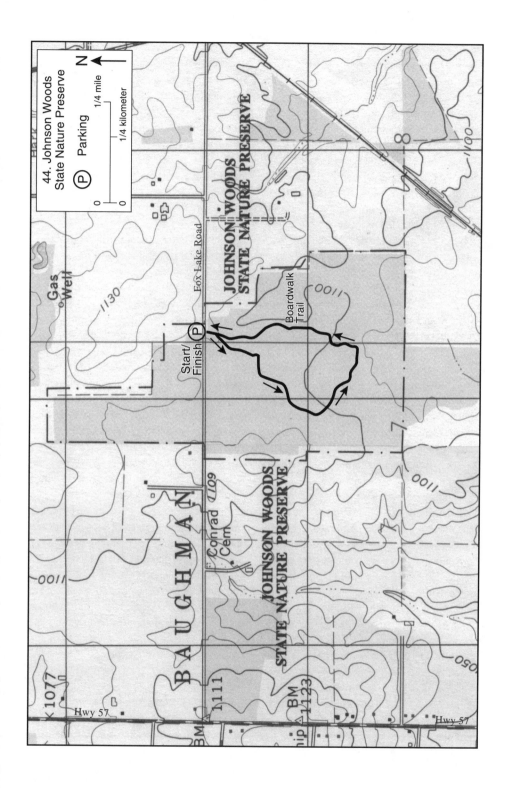

44. Johnson Woods
State Nature Preserve

Ⓟ Parking

N

0   1/4 mile

0   1/4 kilometer

JOHNSON WOODS
STATE NATURE PRESERVE

JOHNSON WOODS
STATE NATURE PRESERVE

Boardwalk
Trail

Start/
Finish Ⓟ

Fox Lake Road

Gas
Well

1130

1100

1100

1100

1100

1050

B A U G H M A N

Conrad
Cem

1109

1111

BM
1123

BM

×1077

Hwy 57

Hwy 57

8

her family donated the 155 acres that lay south of Fox Lake Road to the Division of Natural Areas and Preserves in memory of her late husband, Andrew C. Johnson. It was Mr. Johnson's great-grandfather, Jacob Conrad, who had come to America from France in 1823 and purchased land in Baughman township in Wayne County that included this woods. A part of the congressional lands of 1799–1804, this part of Ohio had only been organized as a county since 1812. Like 90 percent of Ohio at the time of settlement, it had been covered with tall timber and needed to be cleared before it could be farmed. Located on almost flat Wisconsinan-age ground moraine, the woods likely consisted of oak and mixed-mesophytic forest on the swells and humus-filled flats and swamp forest in the depressions. When Conrad cleared his land to farm, he probably skipped this area of woods because it was so wet. In 1884 Fanny Graber, Andrew C. Johnson's grandmother, inherited the woods from Anna and Martin Conrad, and she left them alone. Later, during the Great Depression of the 1930s, it was the influence of Anna Graber Johnson, Andrew C. Johnson's mother, that kept the woodsman's ax and saw away. In 1950 Andrew, for whom the woods are now named, came into ownership. He and his wife lived near the woods, and their children grew up playing, hunting, and sometimes even getting lost in the "Big Woods," as they were often called.

In addition to the 155-acre gift, Mrs. Clela Johnson sold the 51 acres of old-growth woods north of Fox Lake Road to the state. In 1995 the entire tract was dedicated as Johnson Woods State Nature Preserve. Because it is a wet area, with standing water much of the year, a 1.5-mile-long trail system was built of Trex, a recycled plastic–wood composite.

The woods include some huge oak white trees that stand near the trail. Many of them are reaching the end of their life span and are dying. Often they are replaced by shade-tolerant species such as sugar maple and American beech, trees that have been growing in the shade of shadow of the behemoths that will fill the hole in the canopy made by the falling of an old tree. Several buttonbush swamps are also found in the depression areas in the woods. Standing water serves as breeding ponds for amphibians, including the eastern wood frog whose quacklike calls can be heard in Johnson Woods in late February or early March.

From the time skunk cabbage blooms in February until frost, something is always in bloom alongside the trails. Huge patches of spotted jewelweed will greet you when you visit the woods in summer; deep within the woods cardinal flowers bloom just in time to provide nectar for a brood of newly fledged ruby-throated hummingbirds. Needless to say, wet woods everywhere swarm with mosquitoes during certain times of year— come prepared to cope.

In springtime neotropical birds—the warblers, orioles, thrushes, vireos, and other perching birds that spend the winter far to the south—drift through Johnson Woods, pausing to feed on insect larvae that are busily champing tender green tree leaves. Surely at least one pair of red-tailed hawks must nest in Johnson Woods—and I would bet on a family of Cooper's hawks, too. Barred owls as well as lots of the smaller cavity-nesting nonmigratory birds like woodpeckers, chickadees, and titmice must share the woods with cardinals, blue jays, crows, and more.

How to Get There

Johnson Woods is easily reached by traveling SR 585 northeast from Wooster or

A plastic lumber boardwalk makes it possible to enjoy low-lying Johnson Woods even in the wettest of seasons.

southwest from Norton to Fox Lake Road in Wayne County, then going east about 4 miles to the preserve. The parking lot is on the north side of the road.

The Trail

The entrance to the trail is directly across the road from the parking lot. Its surface to the beginning of the boardwalk is black-topped to provide easy accessibility for those using wheelchairs or walkers. A number of planks in the boardwalk honor people who have contributed to the pre-servation of Ohio's natural heritage though their hard work or financial support. In sum-mer there are nettles, the food plant for a number of angle-wing butterfly species, close to the trail but not close enough to be a problem.

The trail is a large loop with a cutoff al-lowing you to reduce the length of your walk if you wish. I suggest that you begin walking by taking the right fork at the first split in the trail. When you reach the cutoff to the left, go straight ahead on the boardwalk as it loops around to eventually pass the other end of the cutoff and return to the lot. An occasional large granite boulder near the trail in the woods reminds you that this land was once covered with ice.

On an early-August late afternoon when I last walked the Johnson Woods trail, I came to an area where a small stream ran alongside the boardwalk. There, growing among beds of spotted jewelweed, were a dozen or so plants of cardinal flower in full bloom They were absolutely spectacular, backlit as they were by the warm, late-after-noon sun. Their beauty almost took my breath away. The flowers of spring are al-ways a joy to behold, a sign that life is re-turning to the forest floor after the long deep winter, but to me there is something extra special abut the flowers of summer, be they cardinal flowers of the woods or cone-flowers of the prairies. I suppose the same could be said about the gentian of October and the skunk cabbage of February. Each has its own time and its own place. The forests and fields of Ohio are truly beautiful in all seasons. Johnson Woods, with its magnificent old trees, is one of the best. Be sure to return often to enjoy it in its cloaks of many colors.

45

Punderson State Park

Total distance: 3.25 miles (6 km);
up to 14 miles available

Hiking time: 2½ hours

Maximum elevation: 1,230 feet

Vertical rise: 70 feet

Maps: USGS 7½' Series Burton;
ODNR Punderson State Park brochure

In the center of northeastern Ohio's Geauga County is an area of hummocky landscape where, as the Wisconsinan glacier was melting from the land, over a period of many years the leading edge melted, then readvanced, leaving glacial till spread thinly over earlier-deposited kames and eskers. In some places massive blocks of ice may have been trapped in the till, which upon melting left depressions in the landscape. With no outlet, they quickly filled with water, creating what geologists call kettle lakes. Smaller kettles often filled with sphagnum moss and a host of acid-tolerant plants, forming classic bogs.

The smallest of these bog-filled kettles are no longer visible; they have completely grown in and are now appear only as round areas of dark soil in plowed fields. Others, such as Fern Lake Bog owned by the Cleveland Museum of Natural Science in this same area of Geauga County, are treasured as pristine natural areas.

A number of the larger of these kettle lakes still had sizable areas of open water when settlers began moving into the Western Reserve country of Ohio in the early 19th century. Though the surrounding land was not an ideal place to engage in agriculture, early settlers found them attractive places to build. As prosperity came to the urban areas of northeastern Ohio, the lakes became choice places to build country cottages and retreats.

There is a cluster of kettle lakes in the northeast corner of Newbury township that includes Punderson Lake. It is said that an

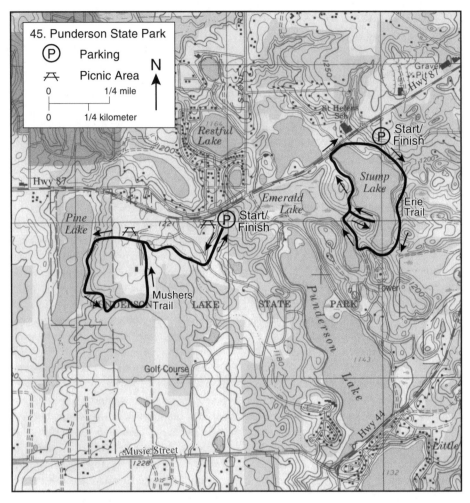

enterprising young land agent by the name of Lemuel Punderson, who became the township's first settler in 1807, recognized the worth of the lake that now bears his name. On the south side of what he called the "big pond" he constructed a small dam to stabilize the water level, then used the outflowing water to power a gristmill. The Punderson family developed a small estate on the edge of the sparkling blue lake; their home is said to have become a popular gathering place for family and friends. It doesn't take much to imagine folks gathered

from near and far for a wonderful weekend of skating on the lake and tobogganing on the hills. You can almost smell the smoke from the shoreline bonfire where weary revelers warmed themselves and feasted on roasted venison or wild duck.

Over the years the area around Punderson Lake developed into a quiet resort community providing a getaway from nearby Cleveland. Cottages and even a small hotel were built on the hills surrounding the lake. In 1929 construction was started on an English Tudor manor house, but it was not

---

completed until 1948. That year, the Division of Wildlife purchased the land for hunting and fishing. In 1951, shortly after the establishment of the Ohio Department of Natural Resources, the land was transferred to the newly created Division of Parks and Recreation to eventually become Punderson State Park. The manor house was completely remodeled and opened to the public in 1956. In the mid-1960s it was further remodeled; vacation cabins were built along with other modern outdoor recreation facilities. Land purchased expanded the park so that it now encompasses 846 acres of land and 150 acres of water in four named lakes. Fourteen miles of trails entice hikers to the area. And because this is in Ohio's "snow belt," cross-country skiers find it a good mid-winter destination.

The original beech and maple forests that covered the land have been gone since the 19th century but are being allowed to slowly return in the undeveloped areas of the park. Hundreds of acres of pine plantings now half a century old provide green even on the deepest of winter days. Beavers have found their way to the edges of the lakes, and the ubiquitous white-tailed deer make their appearance during the crepuscular hours.

How to Get There

To reach Punderson State Park, travel I-76 or I-90 east to SR 44, then SR 44 north or south to SR 87. The park entrance is about 3 miles west of SR 44 on the south side of SR 87. It is a multifaceted outdoor recreation area with campground, lodge, vacation cottages, beach, boating, golf course, nature center, and winter sports facilities that you will find enjoyable to visit at any time of year.

The Trails

With a park map in hand, you can find a trail that will take you to just about any corner of the park. Among them are two that I enjoy hiking when I am in the area. One is most easily reached by parking in the lot at the Sports Chalet by the sledding hill. The other is accessed either from within the campground or from a parking lot off SR 87 at the northeast corner of the park.

If you are camped in the park, you can reach the 2.25-mile-long Erie Trail from a trailhead to the left of the rest room that is just north and west of the amphitheater. If you have come to the park only to hike, I suggest that you enter from the parking lot on the south side of SR 87 just west of Stump Lake at the park's northeast corner, almost exactly 1 mile east of the main park entrance. It's not well marked and easy to miss, so begin signaling a turn, slow down, and watch the traffic behind you as you approach. Park and lock and begin walking by taking a short connecting trail off the corner of the lot.

At the Erie Trail, turn left and head south, clockwise, as it begins to circle Stump Lake. In the warm late-afternoon sunlight on the mid-September day when I last hiked this trail, I was blown away by the regal beauty of the Canada goldenrod and New England aster that greeted me at the entrance to the trail. A late-summer monarch was sipping sugar water from the aster blossoms but, as luck would have it, I was carrying a small Rollei 35 camera with no telephoto or close-up capabilities. Thus that perfect picture is stored in the carbon-based computer in my head rather the silver-halide-based film in a slide tray. Ah well. I probably have more photos of monarchs on asters than I can ever use, but you photographers understand that there is always a better one yet to be taken.

A metal sign directs you toward the campground, the way you are going. Side trails lead to the lake where fishermen have

The trail at Punderson State Park circumnavigates Stump Lake, shown here from the north end leaking south.

headed with high hopes for a full stringer. From the gravelly loam under your feet you can tell that you are on glacial drift. It is not hard to pick up a small rounded rock that on close examination appears to be granite. Hundreds of miles from its point of bedrock origin, it was a traveler with the ice that 12,000 or so years ago covered this land.

Soon the trail leaves the open field near the lakeshore and heads uphill into the woods. There are granite cobbles in the roadbed and a good mixture of native hardwoods overhead. Young pines were recently planted where a pipeline project had displaced the natives, but nature will have its way and the hardwoods will win out. Still traveling through the woods, the trail rises from perhaps 8 to 10 feet above lake level to 25 to 30 feet up. The beautiful tall lobelia—the species that was once thought to cure syphilis, hence the specific epithet, *siphilitica*—blooms in the shade at the side of the trail. As expected, American beech and sugar maple dominate the forest on the high ground overlooking Stump Lake.

From this point it is possible to see the upper end of the lake. Indeed, it is full of stumps. Once a swamp, apparently this area's trees were harvested in winter from the frozen lake, leaving the stumps to stand long after the timber was used for lumber or consumed as fuel. Out of the woods now, the trail goes through a grassy area before reentering the woods and beginning to curve right around the end of the lake. A huge fallen beech tilted its 10-foot-wide rootball in the air above the hole that it had occupied.

At a trail junction, where there are benches upon which you can rest your weary body, a sign points up the hill ahead to the campground. To continue hiking, turn right and begin moving east around the end of the lake. Soon the woodland trail moves out of the low wet area at the end of the lake. There is a hill now to the right, between the trail and Stump Lake. Shortly you arrive at a four-way junction where there is a small pond and another bench. The trail uphill to the left is the Erie Trail connection to the campground. The trail straight ahead leads to the camp road near the boat concession. The trail to the right, also the Erie Trail, is the one to follow to continue around the lake and return to your vehicle.

Heading downhill toward the shore of Stump Lake, in 100 yards the trail reaches a T intersection. Turn right to follow the trail through the woods to a bench on Magnolia Point overlooking the lake.

Back on the main trail, head north to follow the trail along the shoreline toward SR 87. A parallel road off to the left appears to be for service vehicles and snowmobiles. When the shoreline trail reaches SR 87, turn right and follow close, then take the trail as it leaves the highway. Soon it reaches the connector to return you to the parking lot.

A second hike that I recommend at Punderson is a combination of the Huron and Mushers Trails. This makes a loop trail of about 2.5 miles in length in an essentially level area of pine woods and old fields between the entrance road and Pine Lake. The park service building sits in the center of the loop.

To begin this hike, park in the lot at the Sports Chalet and follow a mowed path southwest away from the chalet and across the park entrance road. There the trail splits, with the Huron Trail heading left, parallel to the road. In less than 0.25 mile it moves farther from the road, heading due south. Take the first trail leaving to the right. After a very short distance it reaches a T intersection. Turn right again and follow this trail to the west-northwest. After about 0.5 mile the Huron Trail reaches a T with the Mushers Trail. Turn left to follow the Mushers Trail as it make a more or less rectangular loop to eventually head due east back to the park road and, across the road, to the parking lot. This trail is used for cross-country skiing in winter and occasionally for scheduled special events, so if you are planning to walk it when snow is on the ground, check with the park office to see that it is open to the public. I walked it by myself on a midweek day in fall when no one else was around and I found it a nice hike to exercise my body and my mind. I believe you will find it the same.

The other trails in the park include one designed to give distance to Nordic skiers or to allow the park visitor to move from one place to another on foot, such as the trail from the lodge to the beach and on to the boat concession area. For greater hiking distance, you can join them together in a hiking route of your own.

46

Pymatuning State Park

Total distance: 1 mile (1.6 km)

Hiking time: ¾ hour

Maximum elevation: 1,030 feet

Vertical rise: 20 feet

Maps: USGS 7½' Series Andover;
ODNR Pymatuning State Park brochure;
Beaver Dam Trail brochure

In the Glaciated Allegheny Plateau country of northeastern Ohio and northwestern Pennsylvania are two major river systems that have been called "crooked rivers" because of the nearly 180-degree turns they both take. Ohio's Cuyahoga River, which rises in the wetlands of Geauga County and flows south to the northern edge of Akron, where it turns north to Lake Erie—on its way passing through a magnificent deep valley—has been described in another chapter. In contrast, Pennsylvania's Shenango River originates with a collection of mountain streams and flows north into what was once a huge wetland, then turns west, then south to wind its way to the Beaver, Ohio, and Mississippi Rivers on its way to the Gulf of Mexico. They called that wetland the Pymatuning Swamp. The name is said to be derived from the Iroquois, probably from the Seneca tribe of that great American confederacy, and means "the crooked-mouth man's dwelling place," with the "crooked-mouth" referring to deceit rather than facial disfigurement. Previous to the occupation of the area by the Iroquois, it was the home of the Erie tribe said to have then been ruled by a queen noted for her cunning strategy and crooked dealings.

In 1784 the second Treaty of Fort Stanwix secured for Pennsylvania from the Iroquois and Wyandott Indians the area north of the Ohio River. Many settlers from Connecticut and New York began moving into the area. These farmers found the swamp to be a harsh neighbor because it swallowed stray cattle, housed "dangerous" animals like bears and mountain lions, and was home to

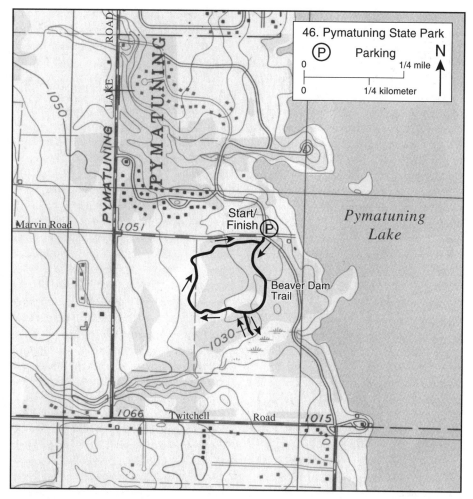

millions of mosquitoes. As the demand for more farmland grew, so too did the demand to do something about the swamp. In 1868, just as thousands of young men who had fought in the War Between the States returned to the land to build farms and families, the Pennsylvania General Assembly provided for a survey and an estimate of the cost to drain the Pymatuning Swamp to create farmland. But the swamp was not drained because many thought it would cripple the industry that had sprung up downstream in the Shenango and Beaver Valleys.

In 1913 a severe flood hit much of this part of the country, spurring the legislature back into action. The Pymatuning Act was signed that same year, appropriating $100,000 to initiate building a dam on the Shenango below the swamp. The purpose of the act was to conserve the waters entering the Pymatuning Swamp and regulate the flow of water in the Shenango and Beaver Rivers. A secondary purpose was to impound floodwater during periods of excessive runoff from the 158 square miles of the watershed above the dam.

The First World War and the start of the Great Depression would pass before this dam would be built. Over a period of 18 years, public and private organizations raised the $3,717,739 needed to build the dam. In 1933, 7,000 men began work, turning the dream into reality, and three years later Governor Gifford Pinchot dedicated the 17,088-acre Pymatuning Reservoir with these stirring words as a part of his address: "All human accomplishments begin with a dream."

In 1935 the state of Ohio acquired land within its borders on the western shore of the lake, to be administered by the then-existing Division of Conservation, forerunner to the present Division of Wildlife. With the 1950 creation of the Division of Parks and Recreation, development began on Ohio's Pymatuning State Park, the counterpart to Pennsylvania's park of the same name.

Today Pymatuning Park includes a modern campground, 59 vacation cottages, swimming beaches, picnic areas, several boat-handling facilities, and a nature center on close to 3,500 acres of land. While the major focus is on water-based recreation, there are two developed trails in the recreation area near the park office and cottages.

Prior to settlement, the low-lime Wisconsin-age till of this area of relatively low relief supported beech forest with the usual assemblage of other hardwoods, including sugar maple and white oak on the better-drained sites. Where water stood on the land, it was swamp forest, with hardwoods that included red and silver maple, ash, American elm, pin oak, and bur oak. None of the original forest remains intact, but there are some grand old trees scattered about in the forested area.

How to Get There

Pymatuning State Park, on the eastern edge of Ohio's largest county, can be reached from the Cleveland area by driving east on US 6 to Andover then continuing east on SR 85 to Pymatuning Lake Road. There, turn south to the major recreation areas, including the campground and trails. From central Ohio, travel I-71 north to I-76, then go east on I-76 to I-80, then east on I-80 to SR 7. Take SR 7 north to Andover and SR 85 east to Pymatuning Lake Road.

The Trails

The Beaver Dam Trail passes through terrain representative of what the Pymatuning Swamp might have looked like 200 years ago. This mile-long trail originates at the corner of Marvin Road and the main park road, just west of the beach and boat-launch parking lot south of the vacation cottage area. Park on the west edge of the lot and walk across the road to the trailhead. This is a self-guided trail with numbered posts keyed to the text in a small leaflet. If you want a copy, pick one up at the nature center or park office. They are not provided at the trailhead.

Since this is a loop trail, you will find the beginning and end of the trail just inside the trail entrance. Except for an open-water area at an observation shelter, this is a woodland trail. For the most part, it has a natural surface, so wear appropriate footwear. As a wet woods it will at times have a good mosquito population. Begin walking by turning left at the split in the trail to travel clockwise. For the first couple of hundred feet, the trail is defined by logs alongside.

At post 1 the authors of the leaflet answer a question often posed by youngsters: "If this is a nature trail, where are the animals?" Most of Ohio's quadrupeds are nocturnal (active at night) or crepuscular (active at dawn or dusk); the exceptions are tree squirrels and ground squirrels, including chipmunks. All are secretive. If you want to know where the mammals are, you can look and listen for the squirrels, but you must look for wildlife signs to detect the presence of others. Look for tracks in the earth. Deer often use the same trails that we walk. Look for signs that show where animals may have rested, such as the forms made in the grass by a rabbit or a larger area of grass laid down that looks like a deer may have rested there. Look for denning holes such as those used by woodchucks and foxes, and look for holes in trees where the surrounding bark is well worn from creatures entering and leaving. On several occasions I have sighted a small hole 15 or 20 feet up a tree, whacked the side of the tree with a walking stick, and had a flying squirrel sticks its head out to see what the disturbance was. On a sunny but still nippy spring day, you might see a raccoon lying half in and half out of a larger hole 25 feet up a tree such as an old sycamore.

Massasaugas, of the Delaware Indian family, according to the text for post 2, were the most numerous Native Americans of the area. (That is the same name as given to a small rattlesnake sometimes called the swamp rattler or black snapper, a species found in fens, wet prairies, and marshes, not swamps. I could find no historic record of them being in this area.) The Indians came to this area to gather cranberries in the bogs and to make maple sugar. They did this by boiling the sap of sugar and red maples in bark troughs by putting fire-heated rocks in the troughs to evaporate the water, leaving only the rich maple sugar.

By the time you reach post 3, you have encountered depressions, perhaps water filled, in the trail and at places like the bases of trees. In early spring salamanders, toads, and frogs utilize these to lay their eggs. As amphibians, they must lay their gelatinous eggs in water, where they then develop from embryos into adults. You can probably think of other species, including six-legged creatures, that use these woodland pools. If they only have standing water in spring, they are called vernal pools. There are some bur oak trees growing along here. At one place, the trail had at one time a corduroy surface—small branches laid crosswise atop, looking like the wale of the fabric of that name. How I used to be embarrassed by the whistle my new corduroy "knickers" (short for knickerbockers) made when I walked during the first few weeks of school each fall. After a few sessions at Mom's washboard, they lost their tune.

Continuing the theme of water at post 4, think about how close the water table is to the surface in these woods. The upper level of underground water is called the water table. When the water table is high, water may appear above the surface of the ground, hence those vernal and year-round woodland pools. Unless there is a prolonged drought, the water table here does not fluctuate very much. Plants including the trees that grow with a high water table are especially adapted to do so. Not all can survive with their feet that wet, so to speak.

Plant protection is the subject at post 5—not the kind we humans give endangered species but the kind plants afford to other living things. Many birds find hawthorn trees, such as those growing here, good places to nest. Dense branching, thorniness, and heavy foliage help protect the nest and nestlings. Indians, early settlers, and desperate hikers have used the thorns on this tree to sew clothing.

As you approach post 6, look for teeth marks on tree stumps along the trail. The sharp incisors of the beaver are tools for cutting and felling trees. They gnaw the trunk to an hourglass shape; when enough wood is removed, the tree will drop. Beavers often choose aspen, willow, and poplar to construct their dams and dens. Gaps in the dam are filled with small twigs or other small material and covered with mud to make the structure watertight.

The trees are younger here. A gravel trail to the right leads to a very nice observation platform overlooking a beaver pond. Half a dozen steps up give you a splendid view of what the bucktoothed engineers can do.

Back on the main trail, crab apples, seen growing near post number 7, provide food for a variety of wildlife. Among the many species that use this species for food, white-tailed deer browse on the foliage and twigs during fall and winter, and ruffed grouse feed upon the fruit, seeds, and buds. Can you think of other species that use a crab apple tree?

The trail travels along the ecotone between brush and deep woods. Some species of songbirds and other wildlife utilize such habitat, as it gives them simultaneous access to different kinds of food. On the other hand, many of the neotropical species avoid such edge situations because such nest predators as blue jays and black rat snakes are found there.

Between the trail and the beaver pond is a large stand of scouring rush or equisetum. Yes, a handful of it will help get the burned food out of the bottom of the pan you left too long on the fire. The presence of a glacial erratic in the surface of or alongside the trail reminds you that about 15,000 years ago, the ice sheet had spread over much of Ohio, pushing and shoving these granite boulders from the Canadian Shield country hundreds of miles to the north. The text for posts 9 and 10 relates that ice as much as a mile thick covered parts of Ohio in the millennia when the amount of winter snowfall in the northern part of Canada exceeded

the rate of summer melting, the excess oozing its way south as a glacier that eventually covered about half of the Buckeye State.

The area around post 11 was still being farmed in the early 1900s. The Pymatuning Swamp that lies just to the east had yet to be drained. Many changes have taken place in the area since the Pymatuning Lake was impounded 65 years ago. Can you identify some of those changes?

Every species of bird has a particular habitat in which it is found. Birds are found in a specific area because of particular food and nest site requirements. Pileated woodpeckers are especially fond of carpenter ants and often make their characteristic rectangular excavations near the bottom of an ant-infested tree to get at them. Great horned owls will eat rabbits and mice found in nearby fields. Tree swallows, chickadees, bluebirds, woodpeckers, and other species are tree cavity nesters, so it is important that dead and dying trees be left standing in the woods rather than "cleaned out."

Bur oaks, seen growing near station 13, are one of the largest and most majestic of America's oaks. The wood is often used for furniture, interior trim, and flooring. They can grow in an area of high water table and are a component of northwest Ohio's Black Swamp forests, as well as of the oak savanna of wet prairies such as those that originally existed on the Darby Plain west of Columbus. They could withstand the periodic fires that were typical of the tallgrass prairies of the Midwest.

Some of the largest pin oak trees I have ever seen grow in the area of post 12 in what could best be described as a pin oak flat. Unlike most of the oak species, the pin oak does not "self-prune," retaining the lower branches of its youth and leaving the trunk sadly bedecked with dead limbs. They grow in poorly drained areas such as the edges of swamps and are not generally used for lumber because of the knots. Difficult to split but good firewood when it makes it to the hearth.

At a dead tree stands post 15 and, appropriately, the leaflet talks about decomposers, those living things such as fungi, millipedes, centipedes, and insects that help move the nutrients stored in dead plant tissue back into the cycle of life. Beyond here, the trail heads due east as it completes the circle. On just slightly higher ground grow some large American beech trees with the usual companion sugar maple trees. Shortly the trail reaches the road; your vehicle is just beyond.

A second hiking trail of about the same length originates on the north side of the park entrance road just east of the park office. It passes through slightly drier habitat with beech and maple forest and pine plantings as it winds its way east to the lake. It is not a loop trail but in fall, when traffic was no problem in the park, I walked it by returning to my car, which was parked at the park office, on the grass strip alongside the road. You could, of course, walk it by returning via the same route.

An interesting aside is that the Pymatuning area was the location of a magnitude-5 earthquake on September 25, 1998. In a region not particularly known for earthquakes, that was a fairly substantial tremble. The event, which occurred at 3:52:52 pm, shook a multistate area from Wisconsin to New York and was recorded on seismographs as far away as Mongolia. It appears to have occurred along a northwest–southeast fault. Three small earthquakes (in 1873, 1936, and 1985) are previously known from the general epicenter but they were considered minor and did not suggest that this area of northwestern Pennsylvania was capable of generating a magnitude-5 earthquake. The damage from the 1998 event was light, consisting of broken dishes and a few damaged chimneys near the epicenter, which was at the southern end of the reservoir.

47

Ramser Arboretum

Total distance: 3.25 miles (5.2 km)

Hiking time: 2½ hours

Maximum elevation: 1,220 feet

Vertical rise: 170 feet

Maps: USGS 7½' Series Jelloway

In the not-so-hurried days before interstate highways and jet airplanes, the way to travel between Cincinnati, Columbus, and Cleveland was on the "3C Highway," a two-lane road that wound its way diagonally across the state. A drive from Columbus to Cleveland was pretty much an all-day trip, with stops along the way for food and fuel. The road passed through many small cities and towns along the way, touching county seats as it did so. That road still exists as SR 3 (though here and there the route has been adjusted), and I still travel it as I "shunpike" my way around the state exploring natural areas and parks. It's really quite interesting terrain: Not long after leaving Franklin County, the old road leaves behind the nearly flat till plains and enters upon the narrow strip of Glaciated Allegheny Plateau that lies between the till plains and the unglaciated hill country of eastern Ohio. Most of the way the land was last scraped and shaped by the Wisconsinan glacier 10,000 to 12,000 years ago. But when you get past Mount Vernon in Knox County, the road travels through hill country where the till was deposited by the Illinoian glacier that invaded Ohio about 125,000 years ago.

The sleepy village of Jelloway lies close in the Illinoian drift country, not very far from the easternmost edge of the advance of ice onto the plateau of that part of the state. Jelloway was laid out in 1840 by Freeman Pipher and originally called Brownsville. The current name memorializes Tom Jelloway, a Native American chief whose tribe is said to have often camped near this site on the

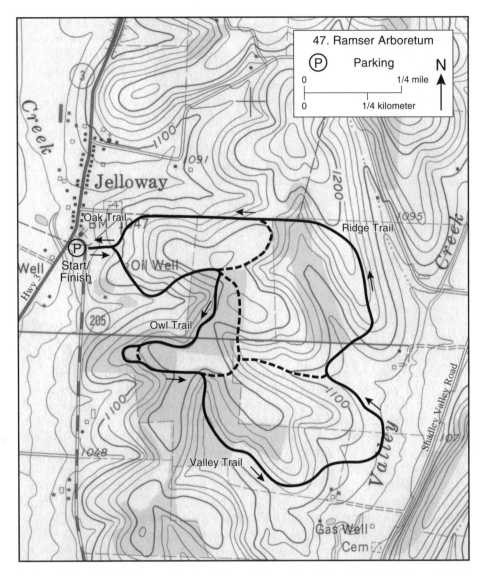

banks of Big or Little Jelloway Creeks, tributaries of the Kokosing River.

It was on the south edge of Jelloway that, in 1989, the late Russell E. Ramser Jr., local farmer and businessman, decided to turn from raising beef cattle to hardwood trees on the pasture and hay ground of his farms in the area. During the next five years, he and his family and friends, with advice from Howard Bower, the state service forester, planted more than 70,000 trees, including ash, red oak, and white oak. By the time Mr. Ramser passed away in 1996, he had planted more than 152,000 trees, including 10 different species of native trees, on 140 acres and had purchased adjacent farmland in order to further his plan to reforest the land between Jelloway Creek and Shadley Valley Creek.

In 1996 his family founded the Ramser Arboretum to carry on Russ Ramser's dream. Now nearly 600 acres in size, the arboretum is becoming an educational and outdoor recreation resource for individuals and groups interested in native Ohio hardwoods and other plant species. In addition to the planted fields, there are areas of old-growth forest and of old pasture and cultivated fields in different stages of natural succession. More than 5 miles of trails have been created with the help of local Boy Scouts. In the future, the arboretum hopes to rehabilitate a nearby 1880s church building and open it to the public as a visitors center. It will house a botanical library, lecture space, gift shop, and public rest rooms. In the meantime, the grounds of the arboretum are open to the public without charge during daylight hours.

How to Get There

The entrance and parking lot for Ramser Arboretum are located about 0.1 mile east of SR 3 on the north side of SR 205 on the south edge of Jelloway, in Knox County. There you will find a bulletin board with information about the area. Mark Ling of Loudonville Boy Scout Troop 537 built the bulletin board as partial fulfillment of his Eagle Scout award requirements. Nearby is a cluster of granite boulders, a reminder that this hilly Allegheny Plateau country was long ago deep under flowing ice. The trails of the arboretum are clearly marked by posts with identifying symbols.

The Trail

Cross the old field area uphill from the right end of the parking lot to find an opening in the tree plantation. Begin hiking here with the highest climb in elevation of the day. Slowly, the trail climbs just about 160 feet in 0.3 mile. At the beginning, the trail passes between some of the first trees Ramser and his crew planted in 1989: red and white oaks and white ash. On the September afternoon of my exploration, joe-pye weed and Canada goldenrod were in bloom among the trees, belying the plantation's old field heritage.

Soon the trail reaches a T. With a turn to the right, the trail follows the contour of the land to resume its climb to the east. Pines soon appear on the right, with white snakeroot blooming on the forest floor along the edge of the trail. This is a part of the Oak Trail, a 0.9-mile loop that circles the field to the left on the slope above the parking lot. A routed white oak leaf identifies it on the trail marker posts. As the trail nears the summit, pines on the right are replaced by a natural stand of hardwood forest. At a trail junction under a large red maple tree, a post identifies the Owl Trail going to the right. Take that trail.

Once inside the woods, there is another trail junction. The Owl Trail is a 1.1-mile loop through this woods mostly on high ground. I suggest turning right to continue your trek using part of this trail. Notice the gravel in the trail with an occasional piece of granite, more indication of the glacial past. As I passed through a nice stand of ferns, a wood pewee was serenading me in September. Along here, I picked up a turkey tail feather to stick through the brim of my cap. At a trail intersection, a trail turns right into a old pine plantation partway down the hillside. I would like to believe that those who named the trail did so because they saw owls here.

Circling to the left, the trail rejoins the original Owl Trail and heads east through more hardwoods, soon arriving at a 3- or 4-acre hilltop meadow. The trail passes along the south (right) side of the field where, on my hike, white snakeroot was blooming along the edge of the woods and spotted jewelweed in wet places along the trail.

The author's fanny pack and hiking stick adorn a trail marker at Ramser Arboretum.

A trail post indicates another junction. This time, it's the entrance to the Valley Trail, a 1.1-mile trail that begins here and ends where it intersects with the Ridge Trail.

Follow the new trail as it goes to the right, into woods, heading south. Very soon it begins to lose elevation and arc to the left on the left hillside of a draw running toward Shadley Valley. The trail leaves the older woods and into fields of planted hardwoods. The trees higher on the hillside were planted in 1995, a year when the Ramser work crews put in five species of native Ohio oaks, white ash, sugar maple, tuliptree, and black walnut—quite a hardwood heritage. To the right, farther down the slope and out the valley, is where some of Ramser's last and biggest year's trees were planted. Thirty-nine thousand trees of 10 species were planted here and in the fields along Shadley Valley Creek that year.

The trail swings north on the hillside among the young trees, then makes a right turn and drops more toward the valley floor. Before it reaches the creek, it turns left to go north then west up a valley, still among young hardwoods. These red and white oak, white ash, tuliptree, and sugar maple trees were planted in 1994. Early records indicate that the original vegetation of the Ramser tract was likely mixed-mesophytic forest on the western side and mixed oak in here. Russ was doing a good job with his selection of nursery-grown trees in matching the mixture that once occurred here.

Soon the Valley Trail meets the Ridge Trail, which comes from high ground to the west. To continue hiking, make a right turn and follow the trail as it cuts across the entrance to another draw and begins a long climb up a re-forested ridge to the north-northwest. After gaining nearly 100 feet in elevation among the plantings of the early 1990s, it levels off and swing to the west. The hilltop to the north is above 1,260 feet but, fortunately, beyond the boundary of the arboretum. Heading west now, the Ridge Trail goes through older woods as it dips and rises to pass through a low saddle. Now onto the slope facing Jelloway Creek, it arrives at the Oak Trail and goes downhill toward the village with pasture over the fence to the north and the stand of first-planted Ramser oaks and ash on the left. Just before it reaches the end of the young hardwoods, the trail turns left to head for the old field and the parking lot.

The trails of Ramser Arboretum are open to cross-country skiing but not to bicycles or horses. New trails were recently established that afford especially good viewing of the dogwood trees that dot the hillside on the east side. They connect to the Ridge Trail and Owl and Oak Trails. Try them in late April or early May. Not all trails will have been just groomed or mowed when you arrive at Ramser Arboretum, so be prepared to adjust your route. The lay of the land is such and the trail markers good enough that you will have no trouble finding your way.

It will be fun to watch as this new facility grow and comes of age as Russ Ramser's dreams come to fruition. It's enough out of the way that it is unlikely you will encounter hordes of other hikers. Put it on your list of new places to check out. I think you will agree with me that we are fortunate that Russ Ramser passed this way and that his family is dedicated to carrying on. His daughter, Susan Ramser, serves as president of the board of trustees of the Ramser Arboretum. Her dad would be proud of her accomplishments.

48

Shallenberger State Nature Preserve

Total distance: 1.5 miles (2.4 km)

Hiking time: 1½ hours

Maximum elevation: 1,140 feet

Vertical rise: 270 feet

Maps: USGS 7½' Series Amanda; ODNR Shallenberger State Nature Preserve brochure

Southeastern Ohio's Hocking Hills region offers many parks with spectacular gorges, rock shelters, and vertical cliffs located amid hundreds of acres of hardwood forests. They all have their individual attributes, and most offer trails of far greater length than this 88-acre preserve. Yet I find it charming in its own special way. It's a spot not far from the home or highway where I can pull into the parking lot, be on the trail immediately without dodging Frisbees or fast-food wrappers, and, lost in my own thoughts, very quickly arrive at a place of natural beauty where I can look out over the land and push any problems that have been plaguing me completely out of my mind. The world of field, farmstead, and forest spreads out between me and the far western horizon.

Shallenberger State Nature Preserve exists today because one man, the late Jay M. Shallenberger, thought this special spot should be preserved for those who followed to enjoy as he did. When he died in 1971, he bequeathed it to the Fairfield County Commissioners who, two years later, turned it over to the new Division of Natural Areas and Preserves.

What makes it such a special place? Here three knobs capped with Black Hand sandstone stand out above the surrounding countryside. Two of these knobs, Allen and Ruble, are within the preserve. The third, privately owned Becks Knob, lies just north of the preserve, beyond Hunters Creek. More than 10,000 years ago, the Wisconsinan glacier, in some places as much as a mile thick, covered much of Ohio. Shallenberger

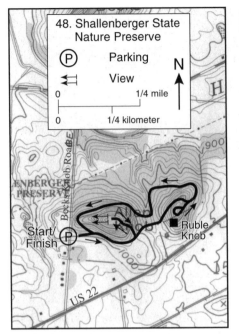

48. Shallenberger State Nature Preserve

(P) Parking

N

View

0   1/4 mile

0   1/4 kilometer

Cave . . . but high above the surrounding countryside.

Open to exploration by white settlers following the signing of the Treaty of Greeneville, this part of the country was settled by many Virgninans and even more folks from eastern Pennsylvania and Germany. In 1797 Ebenezer Zane opened the road known as Zane's Trace from Wheeling, Virginia (now West Virginia), to Limestone (now Maysville), Kentucky. It passed just to the south of the Shallenberger area. Zane's payment from Congress for cutting the wilderness road was three 1-mile-square tracts of the land. One of those was at the site where the trace crossed the Hockhocking (now Hocking) River, which would become Lancaster (originally New Lancaster).

County records show a Shallengberger (circa 1897) and a Shallenbarger (circa 1805) as being landowners, but not of this tract. The 1875 county atlas records the properties that comprise the preserve as belonging to an I. Allen and a G. Ruble, with structures shown on both properties. The area manager has not located any foundations. Likely the honeysuckle that grows in one area dates back to the time of a farmstead.

The top and north side of Allen Knob was quarried from the late 1830s to early 1840s. The sandstone was used to construct the noted stone-wall cemetery, a duodecadon dry masonry-walled enclosure located on nearby Stonewall Cemetery Road. A haul road is still visible down the back (north) side. Stone from the quarry is said to have been used for foundations and even entire structures in Lancaster.

Both knobs were grazed as late as the 1960s, and there was at one time an apple orchard on the north side of Allen Knob, so the original mixed-mesophytic forests of the slopes were cleared centuries ago. No

lies very near the southeastern limit of the ice sheet. Many geologists believe that the tops of the knobs remained free of ice. A reputable soil scientist reported finding traces of glacial soils on top of Allen Knob, but speculation is that this may have been from the earlier Illinoian ice sheet.

There is no doubt that the bases of the knobs were buried under end moraine—an accumulation of rock, gravel, and sand debris that had been frozen in the glacial ice and deposited there when the front of the ice sheet melted. You can see the glacial gravel in the small creek between the knobs, and granite glacial erratics can is found on the western slopes. This preserve is truly on the edge of the Glaciated Allegheny Plateau.

But when you climb the trail to Allen Knob, you will be face to face with the wind- and weather-pockmarked Black Hand sandstone, the same as seen in Blackhand Gorge, Conkle'e Hollow, and Old Man's

The large-flowered trillium, Ohio's official wildflower, greets hikers on woodland trails throughout the state each May. Note the wild geranium in the lower left corner.

endangered or threatened plant or animal species are known from the area. What grows on the top of Allen Knob today is considered a chestnut oak–mountain laurel–mixed-mesophytic forest.

How to Get There

Reach Shallenberger Preserve by traveling west from Lancaster on US 22 and turning north onto Beck Road. There is a small parking lot on the east side of Beck Road less than 0.25 mile after the turn.

As this book goes to press, a US 35 bypass is under construction to the west of Lancaster. It will come closer than I would like to see to the preserve, but will eventually provide access from the north without needing to deal with the Lancaster business district.

The Trail

There is no sign pointing to the trail. Reach it by entering the opening in the woods beyond the small mowed area at the far end of the lot. This is a natural-surface trail, in places sandy from erosion above. There is dedication plaque on a glacial erractic flush with the surface of the ground just as you enter the woods.

Fifty feet up the wooded trail is a bulletin board where you can obtain a brochure with a map. A short distance and rise away, the trail reaches a marker indicating that the pathway goes to the left or straight ahead, the direction I recommend. Soon you will see a Black Hand sandstone outcropping on the slope to the left, most of it covered with moss and lichen. These are the first of many slump blocks you will see along the trail. The single-file-type trail winds its way uphill, at one point passing a giant of a triple-trunked tuliptree. Beyond that is a 2-foot-diameter hackberry alongside the trail. Soon there is another trail juncture, this one with the Allen Knob Trail, which goes to the left.

This trail, supported with planks on the downhill side, rises steeply up the east side of the knob. An ice storm in March 1988 took down a number of large trees on this slope. With lichen-covered sandstone to the left, the trail soon reaches a set of five wooden steps that lead to a short staircase with handrails. The staircase curves to the left around the rock and, after 23 steps, brings you to an earthen trail. After a couple more railroad tie steps and a turn in the trail, you are atop Allen Knob. Though the map doesn't indicate one, there is loop trail around the top from which you can see the till plain to the west. The pit in the middle of the flat top is said to have been a grave site. The area is rimmed with mountain laurel bushes that must be exquisite in early June. Chunks of sandstone rubble seem to lend support to the report of quarry activity here long ago. As a hiker concerned about all things natural, you will want to be careful to avoid wearing away lichen on the rocks or stepping on plants.

After an exploration of Allen Knob, find your way back to the trail marker that identifies the route down. This is a good trail on which to have a spike-tipped hiking stick to serve as a third leg. Back at the trail junction at the bottom of the climb, turn left to continue your hike. The trail heads downhill, past a nice double-trunked sugar maple and two large tuliptrees. Soon the trail reaches a junction with what is identified on the master plan for the area as the Honeysuckle Trail. It goes to the left along the left bank of the small stream that the main trail will soon cross.

Continue straight ahead down a steep but sandy sloope where there is a handrail to hold on to. A 12-foot bridge carries you across the creek. Travel is uphill from here past young maple trees, the seeds probably having come from the 4-foot-diameter old open-grown maple on the hillside off to the side of the trail. Beyond, multiflora rose have intruded into the woods, and grapevines hang from a number of trees. An opening in the canopy indicates a blowdown at some time in the recent past. Soon Ruble Knob comes into view on the right with 25-foot cliffs on its side. The hillside below the cliff is dotted with sandstone rubble, the result of both human and natural weathering activity.

Among tall tuliptrees and sugar maple trees grow many spring wildflowers. At an intersection, a spur trail provides access to the knob. About a third of the way up the steep trail there is a papaw patch in the understory. On the summit is a loop trail that, when followed in a clockwise fashion, will allow you to explore among the chestnut oak and mountain laurel and more-than-ample greenbrier. The only way off Ruble Knob is the way you came up.

Back at the trail junction, go straight ahead on the Honeysuckle Trail. As it goes downhill, the trail turns to the left. There are some 4-foot-diameter trees on this north-facing slope. After passing a large stand of honeysuckle, multiflora rose, and sassafras, the trail crosses the creek not very far from the earlier crossing. Beyond the bridge, the trail rises to soon reach a marker. The trail to the left goes up the small creek past the Allen Knob access trail to the parking lot.

Choose the trail to the right and follow it as it winds around the north-facing slope. You can see the Black Hand sandstone of Allen Knob through the woods. This is also where you can see the old haul road used to bring sandstone building blocks from the quarry on Allen Knob.

The trail continues around the hill, gaining then losing elevation. As it nears Beck Road, it turns south. Here for the first time glacial erratics are visible near the trail in the woods. There is a great expanse of

Japanese honeysuckle here as you pass through trees young enough to have grown up since the state acquired the property. With a hillside full of large sandstone slump blocks to the left and right, the trail winds its way downhill toward the trail marker, where a turn to the right will return you to the parking lot.

49

Silver Creek Metro Park

Total distance: 2–3.25 miles (3.2–5.2 km)

Hiking time: 2–3 hours

Maximum elevation: 1,150 feet

Vertical rise: 30 feet

Maps: USGS 7½' Series Doylestown; AMPD Silver Creek Metro Park brochure

Silver Creek Metro Park came as a real surprise to me. I had driven within a few hundred yards of it dozens of times on my way via the back roads from Westerville to Akron. Even when I went hunting for it, it was well hidden from public view.

The 616-acre park on the outskirts of Norton on the very edge of Summit County was acquired and opened in 1966. It is difficult to tell today, but coal mines dating from the 19th century underlie much of the park. Located in the Glaciated Allegheny Plateau area of northwestern Ohio, its relatively thin till lies over lower-Mississippian sandstone and coals. Coal was being mined from valley walls elsewhere in Summit County as early as 1810. In 1888, with the Industrial Revolution well under way, 230 miners removed 112,034 tons of coal from beneath the surface of Summit County for use in industry, railroads, and home heating. Water from a spring in an old mine near Wall Street in the northwestern corner of the park still helps supply Silver Creek Lake. A railroad spur once ran to the mines of the area, the old grade of which can still be seen just west of the creek along Eastern Road.

Another face from the past can be seen in the Harter family farmstead that stands along Eastern Avenue, a reminder of the longtime Harter Dairy operation on the land. Part of the barn dates back to the Civil War. The lowing of cattle is no longer heard, but near the barn a stand of young pines speaks of a more recent past. Between 1967 and 1983 Girl Scouts planted 40,000 tree

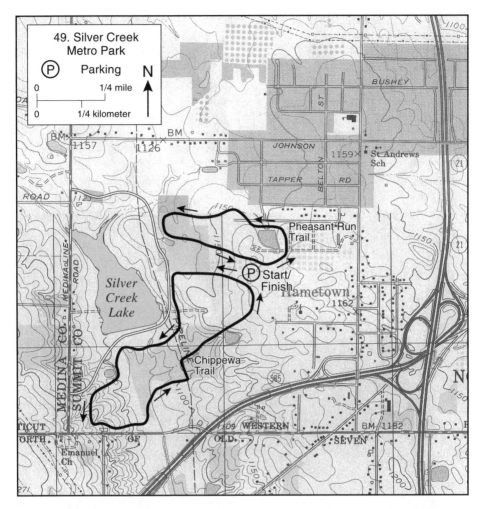

49. Silver Creek Metro Park

(P) Parking   N

0   1/4 mile

0   1/4 kilometer

seedlings at various sites in the park, providing the start for future forests. The oak–maple forests that had thrived on this hilly land for millennia before the arrival of white settlers at the beginning of the 19th century were cut in that century, much of the oak going for use in the mines and as railroad ties.

How to Get There

To spend a day at Silver Creek Reservation, travel south from I-76 on SR 21, then west on SR 585 to Eastern Avenue. Turn right onto Eastern Avenue and travel west to Medina Line Road. Turn right (north) to the entrance of the park on the right side of the road.

The Trails

The Pheasant Run Area parking lot is a good place to begin hiking Silver Creek Metro Park. You can access both the 1.25-mile Pheasant Run Trail and the 2-mile Chippewa Trail from there. For your convenience, there are rest rooms and picnic facilities close to the parking lot.

The connection to the Chippewa Trail is located at the southwest corner of the lot. I suggest that you travel in a clockwise manner, turning left onto the main loop. The trail passes through old field, crossing the main park road and heading downhill toward the area below Silver Creek Lake. In summertime this is a good place to see butterflies when the sky is bright. After about 0.25 mile of walking, you will enter a beech–maple–red oak woodland and, upon reaching a cleared pipeline right-of-way, turn left to travel straight south for a short way.

The trail then turns right to cut across the corner of more tall timber, then through old field and thicket to a wet woods and marshy area along Silver Creek. This area is of special interest. The iron-rich water flowing from the old mine shafts picks up nutrients and, more importantly, oxygen as it flows along. Iron-loving bacteria found in the water use oxygen to precipitate out a reddish brown iron-oxide powder that covers the bottom of the stream in this area. The orange cast of the stream seems to matter little to the many fish, frogs, and other animals that inhabit the stream here. After crossing the two channels of the creek, the trail heads south and climbs toward the Harter farmstead and dairy barns, passing a plantation of Girl Scout–planted pines as it does so. The familiar granite boulders that tell of the area's glacial past are in evidence along the trails of the park.

Leaving the farmstead, the trail heads downhill across a wooded ravine, then up through thicket and young trees, then downhill toward a small pond at the Big Oak parking lot, passing through mature woodland on the way. You are now at the Chippewa Trailhead where, like the other trailhead, there are toilets and a picnic area.

At the northwest corner of the Big Oak parking lot, the Chippewa Trail heads northeast through meadow toward the mowed area below the earthen dam. The trail stays along the edge of the woods below the dam; as it turns left and climbs, it travels more along the line where the mowed grass meets the meadow. Heading straight north now, the trail crosses the park road, entering thicket as it does so.

Once it's inside the large woods, it makes a sweeping right turn to travel due east. Just as it reaches the end of the woods, the trail turns right, and you find yourself back at the spur to the left that goes to the parking lot.

The Pheasant Run Picnic Area was added to the park in 1997–98. The entrance to the loop trail is to the right of the shelter. I turned to the right and traveled this trail in a counterclockwise manner, for no particular reason. Since much of this trail passes though former meadow being allowed to undergo succession, I carried my single-lens reflex camera with a 100-millimeter macro lens in search of butterflies that I could capture on film. The land is fairly flat, though it has enough contour to allow construction of one small pond. The reforestation work of the Girl Scouts is in evidence on this fairly straightforward hiking trail. Both trails are, of course, open for Nordic skiing when there is adequate snow.

Silver Creek Reservation features a bathing beach on the northwest side of the lake and a boathouse at the west end of the dam. On the west side of the lake there is a 2.5-mile equestrian trail partly on park property.

50

Tinkers Creek
State Nature Preserve

Total distance: 2.5 miles (4 km)

Hiking time: 1½ hours

Maximum elevation: 1,010 feet

Vertical rise: 10 feet

*Maps: USGS 7½' Series Twinsburg;
ODNR Tinkers Creek State Nature Preserve
and Tinkers Creek State Park brochures*

"Who's creek?" I thought, as I looked at the map of my destination for the next day. Somewhere in the back of my head a bell was ringing. "Wasn't there a nursery rhyme about a tinker?" I mused. My massive old third-edition *Oxford Universal Dictionary* said "1. A craftsman (usu. itinerant) who mends pots, kettles, and other metal household utensils. b. In Scotland and north of Ireland, a gypsy *[sic]*. Also applied to beggars, traders, and performers generally 1561." I couldn't imagine such a person taking up residence in the wetland area that my map showed along the western edge of Portage County, let alone being prominent enough to have the stream named for his trade.

A call to the preserve manager got a laugh and an "I don't know, but I have two Tinkers Creeks in the areas I manage and I don't know of any others in the state." With that, my research came to an end as we concluded that a family by the name of Tinker must have resided in the "whereabouts" near the creek that now bears the name.

Tinkers Creek is an interesting stream that originates in the Wisconsinan-glacier-created kame and esker country of western Portage County and flows south then northwest to join the Cuyahoga River, draining about 96 square miles in the process. Near its headwaters are some of the finest wetlands in Ohio. After leaving the wet headwaters area, it tumbles over the Sharon conglomerate, crosses the corner of Summit County, and passes through a strik-

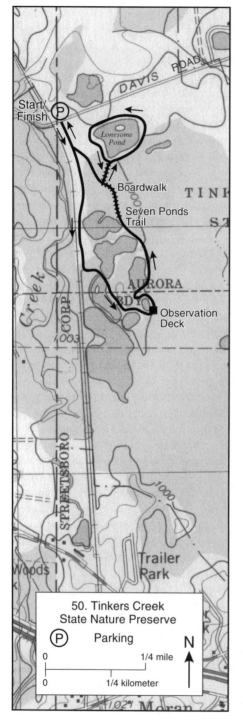

50. Tinkers Creek
State Nature Preserve

(P) Parking   N

0   1/4 mile
|----------|----------|
0   1/4 kilometer

ingly beautiful gorge lined with Berea sandstone cliffs.

Tinkers Creek State Nature Preserve is only one of several wetland preserves in the headwaters areas. Fens, wetlands created by alkaline-charged water rising to the surface, are common in the area. Herrick and Gott Fens, both known for their unusual flora, are just upstream in the Tinkers Creek wetland system. The land where Tinkers Creek Park and Preserve is today in all likelihood was the same kind of fen wetland at the time of settlement and would probably still be so had the Wheeling & Lake Erie Railroad not been built between it and the creek a century and a half ago. The railroad fill dammed the valley and raised the water level, changing the area from a fen to marshland.

Even though a part of the Connecticut Western Reserve lands, and thus open to settlement early in the state's history, the Tinkers Creek headwaters area remained untamed. Too wet to build homes on and unsuitable for farming even if it could be drained—and for that matter unsuitable do anything else with—the Tinkers Creek wetland system remained wild into the middle of the 20th century. From the late 1940s though the mid-1960s, a group of sportsmen owned the land where the preserve is located, using it as a hunting and fishing retreat, calling it the Seven Ponds Hunting Club. During the same period, on the land where the state park is (where a 10-acre lake was made) there was a private recreation park called the Colonial Spring Garden.

In 1966 the Ohio Department of Natural Resources purchased 1,140 acres of land in the area. For a time they considered operating it as a state wildlife area. Until 1977 they stocked trout in some of the lakes and held annual "trout derbies." There were, however, deed restrictions on the property that prevented shooting, so it could not be used for waterfowl hunting and the fishing opportunities were limited to panfish. So in 1973, 369 acres in the area of the old private recreation park were dedicated as Tinkers Creek State Park; in 1974, 786 acres were turned over to the fledgling Division of Natural Areas and Preserves to become Tinkers Creek State Nature Preserve.

The railroad along the western boundary of the property, originally the Wheeling & Lake Erie Railroad, went through Nickleplate, and the Norfolk & Western operation before abandonment as an active line in 1980. In 1991 a short-line operation reopened the line using the original name; it is still is used to move material to and from local industrial sites in this part of the state.

Populations of native wildlife thrive in the area, sometimes too much so for the local road department, which for years has had to deal with the flooding of Old Mill Road by beaver engineering. The put-and-take trout operation has been stopped. There is a good population of wild turkeys in the area. A small great blue heron rookery exists northeast of the observation deck, and since the late 1990s a pair of bald eagles have nested in a restricted area north of Old Mill Road. In spring it is a great place to look for warblers and other neotropical migrants resting and feeding during their passage to nesting areas farther north. Needless to say, as a wetland it has high populations of mosquitoes at certain periods of the year. It's a good place for butterflies in summer—one of the areas where turtlehead grows and the beautiful Baltimore checkerspot butterfly can be seen in June.

How to Get There

Tinkers Creek State Nature Preserve is located in Streetsboro township on the western edge of Portage County. From Cleveland, take I-480 to the Frost Road exit (one exit before it intersects with I-80, the Ohio Turnpike). Turn east onto Frost Road (TR 197) and immediately turn north onto Aurora-Hudson Road. Follow this road 3 miles, passing the Tinkers Creek State Park entrance, to Old Mill Road. Turn left and go 2 miles to the preserve parking lot on the north (right) side of the road, just before the railroad crossing. From the west, travel I-80, the Ohio Turnpike, to exit 13. Turn north onto I-480, turn east at the next exit, then turn north onto Aurora-Hudson as above.

The Trail

Begin your visit to Tinkers Creek by walking the trails of the nature preserve. From the preserve lot on Old Mill Road 1.5 miles west of Aurora-Hudson Road, cross the road to begin walking south. This sometimes gravel, sometimes cinder trail was laid down many years ago to provide access to a small lodge that the hunt club had here. There are now sections of Trex boardwalk that carry you over soft spots.

At a bulletin board a short distance from the road you can pick up a brochure with a trail map. The hunt club owners also planted pines along the trail, totally out of keeping with the natural wetland environment. Otherwise, the young woodland is, as you would expect, comprised of typical swamp forest species—trees that have shallow root systems and can survive with their roots close to the groundwater.

Several hundred feet into the preserve, a sign identifies the Seven Ponds Trail as going both to the left and straight ahead. This is a loop trail around the core of the preserve, so you can follow it either way and arrive back at this point. Farther south, a spur trail leads to an overlook area; to the northeast there is a loop trail that leaves and returns to the Seven Ponds Trail after circumnavigating one of the larger ponds.

I suggest continuing straight ahead. A hundred or so feet to the right you can see the roadbed and tracks of the Wheeling & Lake Erie. I am not sure why, but the railroad track is not on the map. The trail goes in and out of woods. Keep your eyes open for young trees that have been cut off a foot or so above the ground by beavers; then look for the beaver house along the edge of the land or out in the marsh. A hundred years ago beavers had been totally extirpated from Ohio but now they have, on their own, recolonized virtually the entire state. Women no longer sport beaver coats, stoles, and mufflers, and beaver fur isn't in large demand for men's fedoras.

As I dodged the "skeeters" on my September walk, blooming New England aster and swamp lousewort greeted me. Even more exciting was finding turtlehead, the larval food plant of the Baltimore butterfly. I wrote myself a note reminding me to return here some June during the Baltimore's flight period, to try for a photograph of this orange-and-black beauty on its food plant. The adult will use its tarsi to carefully locate turtlehead on which to lay its eggs so that when the larvae hatch, the obligate food plant will be at hand.

Not far beyond there is a side trail to the right that takes you to the farthest southward point that you can reach on the trail system. Near this intersection, I came upon a third-instar monarch butterfly larva munching away on the leaves of a common milkweed plant. It would be several more days before this "caterpillar" pupated—that is, changed to a chrysalis. It would then take 10 days to two weeks or more, depending somewhat upon the weather, before an adult monarch emerged from the chrysalis. By then it would be early October. This butterfly probably woudn't immediately seek a mate as earlier-season "hatches" do but, rather, begin the long flight to the traditional roosting sites in the oyamel fir trees at 10,000 feet on the slopes of the mountains in Michoacán province in central Mexico. Flying 50 to 90 miles a day, nectaring on the composites (daisylike plants) of late summer through the Great Plains, it wouldn't reach its wintering ground until December. Without compass or modern GPS instruments, it and millions of other monarchs would then gather for two or three months of torpor, hanging on to the fir trees and occasionally taking nectar from local flowering plants and water from streams or fog, before arousing in March to mate and begin the journey north. Depending upon its sex, its life would end far short of Ohio, somewhere in the southern tier of states; subsequent generations would bring its kind back to Tinkers Creek this time a year later. The directions for this incredible phenomenon are encoded somewhere in the DNA of the delicate creature I was staring at through the lens of my SLR. What miracles are the life stories of all us earthlings.

Bur marigold or tickseed sunflower, more beautiful than its name would imply, was turning its golden disk and ray flowers skyward here, and the lavender of one of the native thistles added to the glory of the fall afternoon. Follow the South Point Trail through the woods and around the ponds to eventually reach an elevated area along the trail where there is a nice grove of native hardwoods. Not surprisingly, there is a large granite glacial erratic here, reminding us that we are on land once covered by at least many yards of flowing glacial ice, carrying with it pieces of the Canadian Shield. In Iowa I recently saw several erratic in fields that were as large as the haystacks of the Ohio Amish farmers.

In September you expect to see goldenrod in fields across the state, but in this woods I was reminded that there are delicate woodland goldenrods with paler flowers that bloom in clusters along the stem rather as a plume all at the end of the stem. Through the trees from this point, you get an idea how large this wetland is. As the trail reaches its end, there are beech trees, not unexpected on higher land in northeastern Ohio. The dominant upland vegetation from here to Conneaut is beech–maple forest. There are also more out-of-place planted pines here. In September, when I did my reconnoitering, white snakeroot, the plant that when ingested by cows carries to humans the alkaloid that causes deadly milk sickness, is still in bloom in the woods. And much to my pleasant surprise, there was a stand of cucumber tree, a magnolia chiefly native to Appalachia. E. Lucy Braun in her *Woody Plants of Ohio* says, "In Ohio [cucumber tree is] more frequent in the northern part of the Allegheny Plateau. Generally occurring singly or in small groups; logging operations have greatly reduced its numbers." That fits the picture exactly, reminding us that we are indeed in the Glaciated Allegheny Plateau. Now turn around and head back up the trail.

At the trail junction, go right to continue the Seven Ponds Trail. The small-flowered, mauve-colored asters of late summer lie alongside the trail. The trail drops slightly downhill toward a pond with an overlook. Buttonbush grows in the water in front of the pond, and along the trail bottle gentian blooms in September. Again, from the platform you gain a good idea of the great expanse of this marsh. A huge beaver house is visible in the marsh.

Leaving the platform, turn right and in 20 feet you will reach an 80-foot-long boardwalk. Along here, the trail follows the top of a dike between open water in a pond to the

left and the marsh on the right. There is a bit of a moat of open water between dike and marsh. A tall tuliptree and many cottonwoods grow along here. As the trail swings left, thicket comes between the trail and the marsh. Round the end of a lake on the right and mount another section of boardwalk. Then the trail leaves these ponds behind as it enters a white pine woods, where it is again on planks. Still on boardwalk, the trail reaches a junction where there is an octagonal bench. A sign points the way to the Lonesome Pond and Seven Ponds Trails.

Still on the boardwalk, head north on the Lonesome Pond Trail among the white pines and hardwoods. The wooden surface ceases as the trail arrives at Lonesome Pond. Turn right onto the grass trail to walk around the pond. The pond is on the left; a creek flows very slowly along the right side between the trail and the open marsh. Soon the creek leaves the trail's edge and the trail enters a shrub tunnel, still following the pond's edge. The land falls off a bit to the right, and you realize that you are back near civilization when you hear the Old Mill Road traffic. The dike includes a nice glacial erratic. The woods to the right are now at a higher elevation than the trail and feature a nice stand of red maple with a few swamp white oak. The trail passes a nice red oak tree and, 100 feet later, arrives back at the boardwalk. A right turn carries you back to the octagonal bench for a short rest.

Heading now to the right, the boardwalk includes some dedicated planks honoring donors and VIPs. After 60 feet, the boardwalk ends and the trail is on gravel. Among the maples, oaks, and pines, head for the trail that connects to the parking lot. A right turn carries you past the bulletin board to the road crossing and parking lot.

For more walking in the Tinkers Creek area, drive east on Old Mill Road and south on Aurora-Hudson Road to the state park entrance. There are about 3 miles of labeled trails in the park. Three-quarters of a mile of that is a simple walk on the dike completely around the lake. About in the middle of the trail on the north side of the lake, the Pond Run Trail leaves the Lake-View Trail, heading in a winding route north then west to eventually travel around the far side of another pond and end at a parking lot near the north picnic area. Before it reaches the parking lot, a third route, the Gentian Trail, makes a 0.5-mile connection with another trail, the 1-mile Whitehall Loop. In winter the park entrance road is closed to the north parking lot, so it is necessary to park in the lots closest to the road and hike back to the trails. Rest rooms, picnic facilities, and a swimming beach are available at the park. Bank fishing is permitted on the lake, and the trails are open to cross-country skiing when snow is on the ground.

Index

Note: Page numbers in italics indicate photos.

A

Abbott, James W., 134
Abbott's Pond, 134, 137
Abbott's Pond Trail, 136–37
Acorn Trail, 41
Adena State Memorial, *226*, 227
All People's Trail, 112–14
Allen Knob, 249–53
Allen Knob Trail, 251–52
Alley Trail, 201–2
Ambos, Emil (statue), 99
American chestnut trees, 52
American columbo, 122, *123*
American elm trees, 53–54
Amphibians, 88–89, 115, 133, 152, 170, 219, 230, 241
Aphrodite butterfly, *36*
Artesian spring, 113
Augusta-Anne Olsen State Nature Preserve, 178–80

B

Bald eagles, 188, 259
Bald Knob, 226
Baltimore butterfly, 260
Bancroft, George Dallas, 99
Barkcamp State Park, 23–26
Basinger, Jack, 85–86
Battelle, Gordon, 99
Beach Ridge Trail, 174
Beaches, 188, 256
Bears, 56, 219
Beaver Dam Trail, 240–43
Beavers, 122, 241–42, 260
Becks Knob, 249–50
Bedrock, 52, 56, 60–61, 65–66, 72, 84, 101, 193, 213–14, 224
  See also glacial activity

Beech Ridge Trail, 150, 152, 175
Beechnut Trail, 29
Beechwoods Trail, 91
Bell flower, *206*
Bellaire, Zanesville & Cincinnati railroad, 23–24
Belmont County, 23
Belmont Lake, 23, 24–26
Berea sandstone, 213–14
Bicycling, 176, 214–15
Big Creek, 217–18
Big Meadows Path, 103
Big Pond Trail, 220
Big Trail Loop, 220
Big Tree Trail, 184
Big Woods Trail, 183, 220–21
Birch trees, 122
Bird Trail, 185
Birding, 29, 41, 53, 56, 64, 72–73, 74, 87, 89–90, 92, 98, 108, 123, 130–31, 134, 160, 185–86, 187, 190, 230, 241, 242, 259
Black bears, 56, 219
Black River, 181
Black walnut trees, 37, 76
Blackberry Island, 127, 128
Blackhand Trail, 203
Blendon Woods Metro Park, 72–77
Blount, George, 96
Blue Rock State Forest, 29
Blue Rock State Park, 27–29
Bluebirds, 108, 154, 197
Boardwalk Trail, 185, 186, 187–88
Boating, 29, 38, 117, 119
Bobcats, 56
Bobolink Grassland Trail, 164
Braun, E. Lucy, 228
Bread Pan Run, 63
Bridge, rock, 43, 46
Bridle trails, 29, 176, 224, 256

Brookside Trail, 76–77
Buck Run Trail, 203
Buckeye Furnace State Memorial, 42
Buckeye Trail, 52, 129, 215, 219–20, 221
Bur oak trees, 242
Bush honeysuckle, 173–74
Bush, Samuel, 99
Butterflies, 19, 35, *36*, 57, *63*, 64, 88, 94, 133, 137, 165, 173, 179, 197, 259, 260
Butterfly boxes, 81–82
Buzzard's Roost Lake, 164

C

Camp Lazarus, 159
Camping, 38, 57, 119, 124, 226, 240
Canoeing, 29, 38, 117
Cardinal flower, 137, 232
Cascade Valley, 217–18
Caves, 66, 209
Cedar trees, 62, 168–69, 195
Charles and Stella Gosling Nature Education Center, 201–2
Charles F. Alley Park, 200–3
Charles Mill Park, 204–6
Cherokee Trail, 106, 108–9
Chillicothe, 223–24
Chinese catalpa tree, 99
Chippewa Trail, 255–56
Chorus frogs, 88–89, 115, 133
Civil War, 32–33, 95, 97
Civilian Conservation Corps, 207
Clem's Pond, 124
Coal industry, 23
Cohen, Bill, 15
Columbus Lowland, 162
Comma butterfly, 88
Conkles Hollow, 46
Conrad, Joseph, 230
Cooper Stadium, 95
Copperbelly water snake, 122
Copperhead snake, 56, 62
Covered Bridge Trail, 165
Crane Creek Shooting Club, 187
Creighton, William, 222
Cross-country skiing, 190, 235, 237, 247, 262

Cucumber trees, 261
Cutler Lake, 28–29
Cuyahoga River, 212–13, 238
Cuyahoga Trail, 214–16
Cuyahoga Valley National Park, 207–11

D

Dalton, Isaac, 100
Dams, 51, 124, 143, 167, 206, 239–40
Darby Plain, 78
Daugherty, Harry M., 82
David, C. K., 39
Day Hike Trail, 55, 57–58
Deep Lock Quarry Metro Park, 212–16
Deer, 69, 195, 225, 235, 242
Deer Creek Lake, 80
Deer Creek State Park, 78–83
Deer Trail, 29
Defiance Moraine, 148
Devil's Backbone, 130
Dobbin, John, 85
Donaldson Family Trail, 204–6
Donaldson, Jack, 204
Dripping Rock Trail, 102–4
Durrell, Richard, 63
Dutch elm disease, 53–54, 132
Dysart Woods Preserve, 26

E

Eagles, bald, 188, 259
Earthquakes, 243
Ecological regions, 19
Edge of Appalachia Preserve, 58, 60–64
Edge of Appalachia Trail, 63
Edward F. Hutchins Nature Preserve, 102
Elm trees, 53–54, 132
End moraine, 105, 250
Equestrian trails, 29, 176, 224, 256
Equipment, 18
Erie Trail, 235–37
European beech tree, 97

F

Fen wetlands, 258
Fern Hollow Trail, 147
Fern Ridge Trail, 140–41
Fighting McCooks, 32–33
Fish Creek, 182–83
Fishing, 38, 121, 262
Five Oaks Trail, 163–64, 165–66
Flint, 41
Floods, 143
Forested Dune Trail, 192
Forked Run State Park, 30–33
Fort Amanda, 113
Fort Defiance, 110
Fowler, Chester and Hettie, 85
Fowler Woods State Nature Preserve,
  84–87
French Creek Reservation, 181–84
Frogs, 88–89, 115, 133, 152, 170, 219,
  230
Furnas Trail, 67–68

G

Gahanna Woods Park and State Nature
  Preserve, 88–91
Garlic mustard, 68
Gentian Trail, 262
Germantown Reserve, 176
Ghost Hedge Nature Trail, 175–76
Ghost Tree, 83
Ghost Tree Swamp Trail, 82–83
Gifford State Forest, 34–37
Ginkgo trees, 95
Girdled Road Reservation, 217–21
Glacial activity, 80, 86, 90, 105, 200–1,
  205, 212, 224, 244, 249–50
Glacial erratics, 182, 196, 242, 260
Goodale, Lincoln, 96
Goodale, Nathan, 96
Goslin, Charles, 201–2
Graber Woods, 228
Grant, Hiram Ulysses Simpson, 167
Great Black Swamp, 110
Great blue heron, 259
Great Seal State Park, 222–27

Green Lawn Cemetery and Arboretum,
  92–100
Greeneville Treaty, 106, 110, 117, 250
Grouse Ridge Trail, 53–54
Guelph formation, 193

H

Hackberry tree, 100, 197
Handicapped-accessible facilities, 47, 86,
  112, 131
Happy Days Camp, 207
Happy Days Visitor Center, 209, 210
Harding Cabin, 82, 83
Harding, Warren, 82
Harmony Trail, 146
Harrison Lake State Park, 124
Harter Dairy, 254
Haskell Trail, 209
Hawk Trail, 26
Hawkview Trail, 81–82
Hawthorn Trail, 26
Hayden, Peter, 99
Heart-leaf plantain, 133
Heidlebaugh Creek, 112
Heron Run Trail, 174–75, 176
Hickory Ridge Trail, 76
Hickory Trail, 114
Highbanks Metro Park, 101–4
Highbanks Park Mound II, 104
Hikes
  arrangement of, 19
  equipment for, 18
  overview, 6–9
  weather for, 19
Hikes at a Glance, 6–9
Hocking Canal, 44–45
Hocking River, 43
Hocking River Valley, 200–1
Hogback Pond, 124
Hollow Rock Nature Trail, 28–29
Honey Suckle Trail, 32
Honeysuckle Trail, 252–53
Hopewell Culture National Historic Park,
  227
Horse trails, 29
Hosak's Cave Trail, 48

Howard L. Collier Area, 148–52
Hubbard, W. B., 96, 100
Hummingbirds, 63, 94
Hunting, 26, 34, 121, 170, 186, 187, 195
Huntington, P. W., 97
Huron Trail, 237

I

Icy Box Cave, 209
Indian Lake State Park, 105–9
Indian paintbrush, 64
Indian Stone Trail, 36–37
Industry, 19th century, 38–39
Irwin Prairie State Nature Preserve, 192

J

Jelloway, Tom, 244–45
Jerry's Pond, 124
Johnson, Andrew C., 230
Johnson, Clela, 228, 230
Johnson, Orange, 96
Johnson Woods State Nature Preserve,
    228–32

K

Karst, 66
Kelley, Alfred, 97
Kendall, Hayward, 208
Kendrick, Raymond and Florence, 111
Kendrick Woods Metropark, 110–14
Kennedy farm, 49–50
Kenton, Simon, 117
Kettle lakes, 233
Kiser family, 117
Kiser Lake State Park/Wetlands State
    Nature Preserve, 115–19
Knob Trail, 63
Kokomo Wetland Trail, 164

L

Lake Alma State Park, 38–42
Lake Erie, 186–87
Lake La Su An State Wildlife Area, 120–24

Lake LaVere dam, 124
Lake Loramie State Park, 125–29
Lakeside Trail, 140, 141–42
Lakeview Trail (Barkcamp State Park),
    25–26
Lakeview Trail (Forked Run State Park),
    31–32
Lakeview Trail (Lake Loramie), 127–29
Lawrence, William, 131
Lawrence Woods State Nature Preserve,
    130–33
Ledges Trail, 209–11
Lincoln, Nancy Hanks, 67
Little Pond National Recreation Trail, 146
Lobelia, 236
Lockington Reservoir, 129
Lonesome Pond Trail, 261
Loop Trail, 74, 76
Loramie Creek, 125, 127
Loramie, Pierre, 125, 127

M

Magee Marsh State Wildlife Area, 185–88
Maple Grove Trail, 140
Marie J. Desonier State Nature Preserve, 32
Marietta, 223
McCook, Daniel, 32–33
McCook, John, 33
Meadow Trail Loop, 203
Meadowlark Trail, 174, 175, 176
Meigs, Return Jonathan, 30
Metro parks
    Blendon Woods Metro Park, 72–77
    Deep Lock Quarry Metro Park, 212–16
    Highbanks Metro Park, 101–4
    Kendrick Woods Metropark, 110–14
    Secor Metropark, 189–92
    Silver Creek Metro Park, 254–56
    Slate Run Metro Park, 162–66
Miami & Erie Canal, 106, 125, 127, 129
Migratory Bird Center, 188
Milk sickness, 67, 261
Milkweed Meadow Trail, 146
Mining, 23, 27, 38–39, 254
Mohican River, 206
Monarch butterflies, 35, 173, *196, 220, 260*

Morgan, John Hunt, 32
Morris Woods State Nature Preserve, 134–37
Moseley, Edwin Lincoln, 67
Mosquito Creek, 115, 117
Mosquitoes, 108, 112, 128, 168, 240
Mount Airy Forest, 65–69
Mount Airy Reservoir, 65, *68*
Mount Gilead State Park, 138–42
Mount Ives Trail, 225, 226
Mountain biking, 146, 224
Mourning cloak butterfly, 88
Multiflora rose, 49, 159
Mushers Trail, 237
Muskingum River, 27, 51
Muskrat Trail, 203

N

Native Americans, 23, 27, 44, 67, 103–4, 106, 145, 153, 157, 205, 222–23, 238, 241
Nature Center Trail, 182–84
Nature Discovery Center, 190
Nature preserves
    Augusta-Anne Olsen State Nature Preserve, 178–80
    Fowler Woods State Nature Preserve, 84–87
    Gahanna Woods, 88–91
    Johnson Woods State Nature Preserve, 228–32
    Kiser Lake Wetlands Nature Preserve, 115–19
    Lawrence Woods State Nature Preserve, 130–33
    Morris Woods State Nature Preserve, 134–37
    Rockbridge State Nature Preserve, 43–46
    Sears Woods State Nature Preserve, 153–56
    Seymour Woods State Nature Preserve, 157–61
    Shallenberger State Nature Preserve, 249–53

Tinkers Creek State Nature Preserve, 257–62
Nature Writing (Petersen), 18

O

Oak Openings, 189–90
Oak Openings Park, 192
Oak Trail, 203, 246, 247
Oak trees, 113, 242–43
O'Bryant, Michael, 222
Ohio & Erie Canal, 212–14
Ohio Almanac (O'Bryant), 222
Ohio Travel and Tourism office, 19
Oil industry, 111
Old Field Trail, 179
Old Town, 27
Olentangy River, 158
Olsen, William and Gussie, 178
Opossum Run, 34
Orchard Mound, 104
Oriental bittersweet, 205
Oriental spruce tree, 97
Ottawa National Wildlife Refuge, 188
Overlook Trail, 76, 103–4
Owl Trail, 246
Owls, 123, 160, 176

P

Packard, Frank, 99
Paint Creek Lake, 143, 145
Paint Creek State Park, 143–47
Pearl crescent butterfly, *63*
Perkins, Simeon, 217
Petersen, David, 18
Pets, 162, 165
Pew Island Trail, 106–8
Pheasant Run Trail, 255–56
Picnic areas, 76, 164, 184, 211, 226, 256, 262
Picnic Loop, 225
Pileated woodpeckers, *75, 77*
Pin oak trees, 242–43
Pinchot, Gifford, 240
Pine Tree Trail, 119
Piney Woods Trail, 140

Pioneer Loop, 219
Pipevine swallowtail butterflies, 64
Piqua Historical Area, 129
Plant life, 34, 49, 62, 63, 64, 69, 90, 130, 132, 159, 195
    See also specific types
Poison ivy, 77, 197
Pond Run Trail, 262
Ponderosa Trail, 68–69
Poor Man's Railroad, 23–24
Poplar Trail, 203
Possum Hollow Trail, 119
Prairie Trail, 191
Prairie warbler, 64
"Prayer of the Woods," 174
Prickly ash, 195
Pumpkin ash, 86
Punderson Lake, 233–34
Punderson, Lemuel, 234
Punderson State Park, 233–37
Pymatuning State Park, 238–43
Pymatuning Swamp, 238–39

Q

Quaker Oats, 214
Quarry Trail, 68–69

R

Ragweed, 108
Railroads, 23–24, 201, 259
Ramser Arboretum, 244–48
Ramser, Russell E., Jr., 245, 248
Red cedar trees, 62, 168–69, 195
Red Fox Trail, 168–70
Red Oak Trail, 69, 118
Redbud trees, 53
Reed, Eddie, 150
Rhino Tree, *132*
Rickenbaker, Eddie, 97
Ridge Trail, 80–81, 203, 247
Ripple Rock Trail, 76
Ritchie Ledges, 207–8
River Trail, 179
Riverview Trail, 31–32
Rock formations, 43–44, 46, 66, 193

Rockbridge, 43–44, 46
Rockbridge State Nature Preserve, 43–46
Rolling Hills Trail, 81
Roosevelt, Teddy, 97
Ruble Knob, 249–50, 252
Ruffed Grouse Trail, 29

S

Salt Fork State Park, 47–50
Sams Creek, 138, 139
Sams Creek Trail, 141
Sandhill crane, 123
Sandstone, 36, 43, 49, 72, 213–14
Sandusky State Scenic River, 148–52, 155
Sassafras Trail, 179
Sassafras tree, 164, 179–80
Schoolhouse, one-room, 54
Schumacher, Ferdinand, 214
Scioto River, 130
Sears Woods State Nature Preserve, 153–56
Secor Metropark, 189–92
Selby, William Gifford, 34
Sells, Peter, 100
Seneca Dam, 51
Seneca Lake Park, 51–54
Settlement, land, 84–85, 106, 110–11, 135, 145, 153, 158–59, 171, 181, 217, 238–39, 250
Seven Ponds Trail, 259–61
Seymour Woods State Nature Preserve, 157–61
Shagbark Trail, 165
Shale, 27–28, 72, 101, 163–64
Shallenberger, Jay M., 249
Shallenberger State Nature Preserve, 249–53
Shawnee Backpack Trail, 55
Shawnee Ridge Trail, 225, 226
Shawnee State Forest, 55–58
Shenango River, 238
Shepherst, Max, 191
Shivener homestead, 64
Shivener prairie, 63–64
Short-eared owls, 123
Silver Creek Metro Park, 254–56

Six-Mile Creek, 110, 113
Slate Run Living Historical Farm, 162, 166
Slate Run Metro Park, 162–66
Smith, Ovid, 95
Snakes, 56, 62, 122
South Loop Trail, 114
South Point Trail, 260–61
Southwoods Trail, 170
Spanish-American War, 97
Spring Run Trail, 225
Spring Trail, 179
St. Johns Moraine, 130
Starling, Lyne, 95–96
State forests
    Gifford State Forest, 34–37
    Shawnee State Forest, 55–58
State parks
    Barkcamp State Park, 23–26
    Blue Rock State Park, 27–29
    Forked Run State Park, 30–33
    Great Seal State Park, 222–27
    Indian Lake State Park, 105–9
    Kiser Lake State Park, 115–19
    Lake Alma State Park, 38–42
    Lake Loramie State Park, 125–29
    Mount Gilead State Park, 138–42
    Paint Creek State Park, 143–47
    Punderson State Park, 233–37
    Pymatuning State Park, 238–43
    Salt Fork State Park, 47–50
    Stonelick State Park, 167–70
    Sycamore State Park, 171–76
Stone House Loop Trail, 48, 49–50
Stonelick Creek, 167
Stonelick State Park, 167–70
Stump Lake, 235–36
Sugar Creek Trail, 184
Sugar Maple Trail, 164, 165
Sugarloaf Mountain Amphitheater, 226–27
Sugarloaf Mountain Trail, 225
Sullivant, Lucas, 96
Sullivant, William Starling, 96
Sullivantia, 63
Sumac, 196–97
Swamp Forest Trail, 192
Sweet gum trees, 36
Swimming, 119, 256, 262
Switzer, John, 53

Sycamore State Park, 171–76
Sycamore trees, 176, 224

T

Thomas, Edward S., 98–99
Thompson, Peggy, 100
Thurber, James, 98
Timber industry, 23
Timber rattlesnake, 56
Tinkers Creek State Nature Preserve,
    257–62
Toads, 115
Tree frogs, 152
Trillium, 152, 166, *169, 192, 251*
Trillium Trail, 190–92, 203
Tuliptrees, 87
Turtle Trail, 29
Turtlehead, 260
Twin Bridge Trail, 67

U

Underground Railroad, 167

V

Valley Trail, 247
Vermilion River, 178, 179, *180*
Visitors bureaus, 19
Vultures Roost Trail, 203

W

Walden Waterfowl Refuge, 73
Waldschmidt, Henry, 98
Walking Trail, 186, 188
Wayne, Anthony "Mad," 110
Wayne National Forest, 19
Weather, 19
Western Reserve, 217
Wetland Spur Trail, 104
White Ash Ravine, 68
White cedar trees, 62
White oak trees, 113
White snakeroot, 67, 261
White Star Park, 193–97

Whitehall Loop, 262
Wilderness Trail, 60–64
Wildflowers, 56, 63, 64, 84, 86, 112, 168,
  174, 230, 232, 261
Wildlife, 41, 53, 56, 69, 73, 78, 88–90,
  155, 170, 173, 190, 195, 219, 235,
  240–41, 259
Wilds, The, 29
Wolf Creek, 171, 175
Wolf Creek Rail Trail, 176
Wood ducks, 91, 122
Wood frog, 170, 219

Woodchuck Trail, 25, 26, 81
Woodchucks, 81
Woodland Pond Trail, 192
Woodland Trail, 136–37
Woodlands Ponds Trail, 91
Woodpeckers, 75, 77
World War II, 15, 94
Worthington, Thomas, 222, 227

Z

Zaleski flint, 41

Let Backcountry Guides Take You There

Our experienced backcountry authors will lead you to the finest trails, parks, and back roads in the following areas:

50 Hikes Series

50 Hikes in the Adirondacks
50 Hikes in Connecticut
50 Hikes in Central Florida
50 Hikes in the Lower Hudson Valley
50 Hikes in Kentucky
50 Hikes in the Maine Mountains
50 Hikes in Coastal and Southern Maine
50 Hikes in Massachusetts
50 Hikes in Maryland
50 Hikes in Michigan
50 Hikes in the White Mountains
50 More Hikes in New Hampshire
50 Hikes in New Jersey
50 Hikes in Central New York
50 Hikes in Western New York
50 Hikes in the Mountains of North Carolina
50 More Hikes in Ohio
50 Hikes in Ohio
50 Hikes in Eastern Pennsylvania
50 Hikes in Central Pennsylvania
50 Hikes in Western Pennsylvania
50 Hikes in the Tennessee Mountains
50 Hikes in Vermont
50 Hikes in Northern Virginia
50 Hikes in Southern Virginia

Walks and Rambles Series

Walks and Rambles on Cape Cod and the Islands
Walks and Rambles on the Delmarva Peninsula
Walks and Rambles in the Western Hudson Valley
Walks and Rambles on Long Island
Walks and Rambles in Ohio's Western Reserve
Walks and Rambles in Rhode Island
Walks and Rambles in and around St. Louis

25 Bicycle Tours Series

25 Bicycle Tours in the Adirondacks
25 Bicycle Tours on Delmarva
25 Bicycle Tours in Savannah and the Carolina Low Country
25 Bicycle Tours in Maine
25 Bicycle Tours in Maryland
25 Bicycle Tours in the Twin Cities and Southeastern Minnesota
30 Bicycle Tours in New Jersey
30 Bicycle Tours in the Finger Lakes Region
25 Bicycle Tours in the Hudson Valley
25 Bicycle Tours in Maryland
25 Bicycle Tours in Ohio's Western Reserve
25 Bicycle Tours in the Texas Hill Country and West Texas
25 Bicycle Tours in Vermont
25 Bicycle Tours in and around Washington, D.C.
30 Bicycle Tours in Wisconsin
25 Mountain Bike Tours in the Adirondacks
25 Mountain Bike Tours in the Hudson Valley
25 Mountain Bike Tours in Massachusetts
25 Mountain Bike Tours in New Jersey
Backroad Bicycling in Connecticut
Backroad Bicycling on Cape Cod, Martha's Vineyard, and Nantucket
Backroad Bicycling in Eastern Pennsylvania
The Mountain Biker's Guide to Ski Resorts

Bicycling America's National Parks Series

Bicycling America's National Parks: Arizona & New Mexico
Bicycling America's National Parks: California
Bicycling America's National Parks: Oregon & Washington
Bicycling America's National Parks: Utah & Colorado

We offer many more books on hiking, fly-fishing, travel, nature, and other subjects. Our books are available at bookstores and outdoor stores everywhere. For more information or a free catalog, please call 1-800-245-4151 or write to us at The Countryman Press, P.O. Box 748, Woodstock, Vermont 05091. You can find us on the Internet at www.countrymanpress.com.